TANGLED
HIERARCHIES

JOSEPH B. SHEDD

SAMUEL B. BACHARACH

TANGLED HIERARCHIES

*Teachers as
Professionals
and the
Management
of Schools*

Jossey-Bass Publishers
San Francisco • Oxford • 1991

TANGLED HIERARCHIES
Teachers as Professionals and the Management of Schools
   by Joseph B. Shedd and Samuel B. Bacharach

Copyright © 1991 by: Jossey-Bass Inc., Publishers
                      350 Sansome Street
                      San Francisco, California 94104

                              &

                      Jossey-Bass Limited
                      Headington Hill Hall
                      Oxford OX3 0BW

Library of Congress Cataloging-in-Publication Data

Shedd, Joseph B.
    Tangled hierarchies : teachers as professionals and the management
of schools / Joseph B. Shedd and Samuel B. Bacharach
       p.   cm.—(The Jossey-Bass education series)
    Includes bibliographical references (p.) and index.
    ISBN 1-55542-342-6
    1. School management and organization—United States. 2. School
supervision—United States.   3. Teacher participation in
administration—United States.   4. Teachers—United States—Social
conditions.   5. Teachers—Salaries, etc.—United States.
6. Teachers' unions—United States.   I. Bacharach, Samuel B.
II. Title. III. Series.
LB2805.S579   1991
371.2'00973—dc20   90-26937
                                                           CIP

Manufactured in the United States of America

The paper in this book meets the guidelines for
permanence and durability of the Committee on
Production Guidelines for Book Longevity of the
Council on Library Resources.

Portions of Chapter Seven appeared in "Power and Empowerment:
The Constraining Myths and Emerging Structures of Teacher Unionism
in an Age of Reform," *Journal of Education Policy,* winter 1989,
published by Taylor and Francis Ltd.

JACKET DESIGN BY WILLI BAUM

FIRST EDITION

Code 9145

The Jossey-Bass
Education Series

For
Daniel, Elizabeth, Hanna, and Jonathan

CONTENTS

Preface   xi

The Authors   xix

1. Introduction: Professionals in Bureaucracies   1

2. The Work of Teachers   13

3. Autonomy and Control   42

4. Restructuring the Job of Teaching   70

5. Compensating Teachers   103

6. Structuring Participation   129

7. The Changing Role of Unions   165

8. Conclusion: Restructuring Relationships in Schools   190

x   **Contents**

Appendix   197

References   201

Index   225

 # PREFACE

Sometimes the greatest barrier to organizational change is inertia, caused by a combination of sterile but predictable structures and powerful and entrenched interests. In this context, change often comes about as a response to external market, political, and/or cultural pressures. Frequently, it takes a dramatic external event to force the members of an organization to begin the process of self-reflection—a process that often begins as a series of reactive and defensive actions. Only after the dust settles will the organization go about the serious task of examining the inertia, contradictions, and flaws inherent in its institutionalized assumptions.

Such has been the case with the education enterprise in this country. With the publication of *A Nation at Risk* (National Commission on Excellence in Education, 1983), all sectors of the education establishment began to struggle with the future of education in America. Since then, the public has demanded dramatic improvements in our systems of education. Constituencies at the federal, state, and local levels have all demanded greater "results" (stated in terms of their particular goals, of course), often for the same amount of—or even less—money spent on our school systems. After the first wave of reform tightened up the bureaucratic control mechanisms by cracking down on teachers and blaming their unions, it became clear to many policymakers that improving the performance of teachers would require the active participation of those very teachers. Out of that recognition came the second wave of reform, with its emphasis on decentralization, school site management, and participative decision making, as identified in *Education Reform: Making Sense of It All* (Bacharach, 1990).

With many different and often contradictory arguments for specific reforms, it was tempting for us to throw up our hands in frustration and say that the pluralist process inevitably would work things out. The interest groups with the most resources would succeed in restructuring schools (or leaving them largely intact) around their particular values. However, in conducting numerous studies of teaching, schools, and school districts over the past dozen years, we noticed an underlying pattern to the cacophony of cries for different reforms. *Tangled Hierarchies* is about this pattern.

Purpose of the Book

Starting from a detailed study of the actual work of teachers within schools, this book is an attempt to demonstrate that school organizations can be improved in ways that respond simultaneously to many of the internal and external pressures schools confront. In doing so, we examine the relationships between individual teachers and the organizations that employ them, as well as the emerging pressures to redefine those relationships. Underlying these relationships is a division of labor that assigns individual teachers considerable discretion in decisions whose effects are confined to their individual classrooms but affords them little voice in the larger decisions made outside those classrooms. It is, we argue, this division of labor that needs to be restructured in order to allow closer coordination of classroom decision making and greater teacher participation in organizational decisions that affect their classrooms.

Because of these simultaneous needs, we believe that America's systems of public education require more discretion *and* more control, more flexibility *and* more direction, more room for professional judgment *and* more ways of ensuring accountability. Systems and organizations that produce compromises between these competing sets of needs are no longer sufficient. But neither are strategies that explicitly subordinate one set of needs to the other.

In making our case, we have brought together arguments from scholars of organizational behavior, education, industrial relations, and contemporary theories of management. Our hope is that teachers, administrators, school board members, education researchers, politicians, policymakers, and perhaps even parents might find this book a useful synthesis of the stronger arguments put forth in many apparently incompatible (and vehemently argued) viewpoints. The failure to question some underlying assumptions is what may be causing gridlock in our very political education reform process. It would be too much to hope that our vision would become a new consensus. Nevertheless, we hope that this book causes a ferment in the organizations we call schools. If new battle lines are drawn, then perhaps the old compromises will be replaced with new ones that are better suited to the demands of the twenty-first century.

Overview of the Contents

Looking at schools from the perspective of organizational behavior, we noticed that there is a convergence of many different pressures on school districts. Chapter One discusses the external pressures that are forcing schools to meet simultaneous goals of equity and excellence, quality and quantity, and providing students with both basic and higher-order skills. These goals have historically been considered to be incompatible. Internal pressures are at work too, from management and from the demands of the job of teaching. These pressures and conflicting goals require a basic reassessment of how American schools are structured.

Chapter Two demonstrates the depth and breadth of teacher responsibilities. The chapter starts with a detailed analysis of the actual work that teachers perform, based on data generated from teachers themselves, and presents evidence that teaching is a much more complex, demanding, and professional occupation than most observers (indeed, most teachers) recognize or are prepared to acknowledge. These data also provide striking evidence that teachers perform many management functions *within* the classroom but are mostly excluded from the same type of management decision making *outside* the classroom.

In an attempt to understand why this is so, Chapter Three looks at the relationship between teachers and other members of the system. It does so from the perspective of teachers and also from that of administrators, suggesting that there are fundamental needs for both teacher discretion and administrative coordination. The problem is that most people think these two needs are opposed to one another, which has resulted in "visions" of schools designed to either take sides or compromise between the needs of the two.

Just as teachers are demanding a share of decision-making power outside of their classrooms, administrators are realizing that educating "whole" students in more than piecemeal fashion will require new systems to coordinate the work of teachers across classrooms. They are also facing pressures to cut costs and eliminate repetition by centralizing and coordinating resources and activities. The traditional compromise of the administrators controlling whatever was done outside the classroom while leaving the teacher autonomous (some would say abandoned) inside the classroom will not continue to work under these pressures. The result is a hodgepodge of tacit deals among organization members, resulting in tangled hierarchies (Hofstadter, 1979).

Chapter Four suggests a possible way to untangle these hierarchies by deemphasizing formal structures and emphasizing the development of more informal relationships instead. The chapter returns to the basic work being done in schools: teaching. Starting from the premise that excellent schools require excellent and motivated teachers, this chapter demonstrates how the structure of the job of teacher can either interfere with or enhance the motivation and development of individual teachers. Drawing on the established general literature about the nature of motivating jobs, we argue that teachers should be encouraged and supported in their efforts to constantly develop their repertoire of skills. The key to this self-development process is breaking down the cellular structure of schools. The walls between teachers (not necessarily the physical walls between classrooms, but the sense of isolation felt by teachers in their separate rooms) need to be breached with new norms and forms of collegiality, so that teachers can learn from each other.

New organizational practices need to be invented to achieve this end. Job ladders represent one popular system for delineating different levels of professional responsibility and growth. Among these flaws is the problem of developing an affordable system of evaluating teachers that all perceive as fair but that is not self-defeating.

Chapter Five discusses appropriate principles to consider when compensating teachers. This is important because many efforts at changing schools as organizations have concentrated on how to control the teachers by using alternative systems of compensation (for example, merit pay and career ladders). The chapter addresses in detail the impact of such systems on individual teacher motivation, with reference to the vast literature on human motivation. Although merit pay systems, like steroids, may provide a temporary "shot in the arm" of extrinsic motivation, there is evidence that they may do long-term damage to the more important sources of intrinsic motivation.

Instead of looking for ways of motivating teachers individually, we believe that it is more fruitful to look at the potential energy (synergy) inherent in teachers' collective efforts to improve their own organizations. Chapter Six focuses on the emerging pressures to involve teachers in fundamentally different ways in the organizational decisions that affect their work. Chapters Six and Seven trace the implications of these various pressures: first for teachers' collective involvement in policymaking (Chapter Six), then for the unions that represent them (Chapter Seven). Chapter Seven suggests that both teachers and administrators are beginning to question the model of industrial unionism that they were handed in the sixties and that was never suited to the unique conditions of their experience.

Chapter Eight sums up conclusions on the changing relationships between and among educators. It emphasizes the *variety* of problems they must deal with and discusses trends and possibilities for the future.

xvi   **Preface**

Acknowledgments

This book is part of a series of collaborative efforts between the authors and their colleagues over a decade. After conducting numerous studies and publishing twenty or so articles, the authors decided that the time had come to bring their thoughts about restructuring school organizations together in one book. Although this book has our names on the cover, and thus we acknowledge equal contributions and equal liability, others should share in whatever credit is given for the ideas.

We have received generous support from a number of organizations, including the National Institute of Education, the Spencer Foundation, and the New York State School of Industrial and Labor Relations at Cornell University. Nevertheless, our early supporters were individuals. Thomas James, while serving as head of the Spencer Foundation, encouraged our early efforts in examining school structure and collective bargaining. At Cornell University, the school's research director, Ron Ehrenberg, and former dean Robert Dougherty supported our early work.

Most important among our teachers were the practitioners we worked with, including Thomas Corcoran, William Glass, Peter Kachris, Frank Masters, Jeffrey Graber, and Kay Lybeck. As an active consultant and chief education adviser to Governor James Florio of New Jersey, Tom Corcoran taught us much about the practical politics of public policy in education, as well as about the micropolitics of organizational change. William Glass, director of professional development for the Bridgeport (Connecticut) public schools, taught us about the relationships between staff development and teacher evaluation. As a superintendent of schools in Auburn, New York, and as superintendent of the Niagara-Oneida County Board of Cooperative Educational Services, Peter Kachris gave us insights into school management that come only with experience. As research director of the National Education Association, Frank Masters provided extraordinary intellectual vision and research support, giving us opportunities to go where few academics had gone before. Jeffrey Graber, then state coordinator of New Jersey's Cooperative Relationships Project, helped us to learn the lessons of cooperative school improvement. Kay Lybeck and her colleagues in the Tucson Education Association taught us how extraordinarily complex the job of teaching really is.

Our colleagues and close friends at Organizational Analysis and Practice, Inc. in Ithaca, New York, deserve more than thanks. This book would not have been possible without their courage and insight. Their courage is reflected in the fact that for eight years now, with a modest budget and often too little recognition, they have been at the cutting edge of efforts to restructure schools. While others were talking about restructuring schools and theorizing about reconstructing evaluation systems, Scott Bauer, Rose Mala-nowski, and Steve Mitchell were actually working with districts throughout the country in efforts to create change within schools. Their commitment to education is measured by nights and miles on the road, in hotel rooms and rental cars. Although they are academics by training, each of these individuals has shown a commitment to social action and applied research—the type of commitment that is truly the hope of education reform. There is not an idea in this book to which they did not contribute. We thank them as colleagues and we appreciate them as friends.

Sharon Conley of the University of Arizona participated in most of our work on career development and was instrumental in our efforts to synthesize our research into coherent papers. David Lipsky, dean of the New York State School of Industrial and Labor Relations at Cornell University, has been an exceptional colleague and has helped us rethink, reformulate, and refocus what we all too often thought was clear. His intellect and friendship have made this work better. Bryan Mundell has always had an uncanny ability to tell us where our logic was faulty, our arguments were skimpy, and our prose was overbearing. His patience and intellect made him an exciting new colleague who helped bring this project to completion. We thank our families and friends who supported us and helped us maintain our sanity during the past several years, especially Susan, Daniel, Elizabeth, Bill and Marthamae, David and Sandy, Bill and Janet, Harry, Candy, and Martin and Shula.

In closing, we are reminded of a colleague in a department of organizational behavior. When hearing that we, as students of organizational behavior and industrial relations, were going to study schools, school districts, teachers, and administrators, he asked us (as he was about to leave to continue his consulting at IBM) when we would get around to studying "real" organizations. This book is dedicated to those who believe that schools are as "real" as IBM and equally if not more important. Above all, it is dedicated to those who work in that real world and are struggling to make it better for those they serve.

March 1990   Joseph B. Shedd
                                                Syracuse, New York

                                                Samuel B. Bacharach
                                                Ithaca, New York

THE AUTHORS

Joseph B. Shedd is assistant professor of educational administration at Syracuse University and a senior consultant with Organizational Analysis and Practice, Inc., a management research and consulting firm based in Ithaca, New York. He received his B.A. degree (1970) from the University of North Carolina in political science and his master's and Ph.D. degrees (1972, 1989) from Cornell University in industrial and labor relations, with concentrations in public-sector collective bargaining, labor law, and organizational behavior.

Shedd's research and publications include studies of collective bargaining in public education, teacher compensation, evaluation and career development, and the management of professional work environments. He is coauthor of *Paying for Better Teaching: Merit Pay and Its Alternatives* (1984, with S. B. Bacharach and D. B. Lipsky). Other studies have been published in *Educational Administration Quarterly, Teachers College Record,* and the *Journal of Personal Evaluation in Education.*

In addition to his research and writing, Shedd served as senior consultant (1986–1990) to the Cooperative Relationships Project, a New Jersey State Education Department program that helped school boards, administrators, and teacher unions establish cooperative decision-making structures in nine pilot school districts.

Samuel B. Bacharach is professor of organizational behavior in the New York State School of Industrial and Labor Relations at Cornell University and graduate professor of educational administration in Cornell's Department of Education. He received his B.S. degree (1968) from New York University in economics and his Ph.D. degree (1974) from the University of Wisconsin in sociology.

For the last eight years, Bacharach's primary research has focused on the study of professionals in the public sector. His earlier research concentrated on an examination of schools and school districts. He is editor of two series, *Research in the Sociology of Organizations* and *Advances in Research and Theories of School Management and Educational Policy*. In addition, he is editor of two volumes, *Organizational Behavior in Schools and School Districts* (1981) and *Educational Reform: Making Sense of It All* (1990), and he has contributed to numerous other edited books. He is coauthor of *Power and Politics in Organizations: The Social Psychology of Conflict, Coalitions, and Bargaining* (1980, with E. Lawler) and of *Bargaining: Power, Tactics, and Outcomes* (1981, with E. Lawler). His articles have appeared in such journals as *The Academy of Management Journal, The Academy of Management Review, Industrial and Labor Relations Review, Educational Administration Quarterly, Teachers College Record,* and *Educational Evaluation and Policy Analysis.*

Bacharach is founder and chairman of the board of Organizational Analysis and Practice, Inc., an education consulting firm with which he has done research throughout the country.

TANGLED
HIERARCHIES

INTRODUCTION:
PROFESSIONALS
IN BUREAUCRACIES

After nearly a decade of education reform and higher taxes to pay for it, the public will soon wonder why Johnny still can't read. After studying the results of research on teaching, motivation, and effective schools, asking teachers about their work and work environment, and analyzing the results of several decades of union organizing in the schools, the authors conclude that different aspects of the current reform agenda are working at cross-purposes.

What has been identified as a second wave of reform (Bacharach, 1990) has coalesced around three propositions: Teachers are not (but ought to be) treated as professionals; schools are (and ought not to be) top-heavy bureaucracies; and no significant improvements can occur in America's systems of public education unless schools are fundamentally restructured.

The authors of this volume agree with the general tenor of these propositions, but we maintain that there is no consensus among reformers about what a professional does, what a bureaucracy is, or what kinds of structures might be *re*structured. In fact, they argue, many of the reforms currently being considered would *de*professionalize teaching, produce *more* bureaucracy, and reinforce the very structures that are most in need of change.

1

Teachers as Professionals

People have debated for years whether or not teaching is a profession. But the question is misleading. Most scholars have dismissed the notion that professional status is a simple dichotomy (X is a professional; Y is not). Instead, they propose the use of the concept "professionalization," defined as "the dynamic process whereby many occupations can be observed to change certain crucial characteristics in the direction of a profession." Adopting this notion from Vollmer and Mills and building on the work of Caplow and Wilensky, Hall (1975) suggests three groups of characteristics by which a given occupation's degree of professionalism can be measured:

1. *Structural* criteria: The degree to which there is a formalized code of ethics and a prescribed and lengthy training process in certified training institutes or the like.
2. *Attitudinal* attributes of members: The degree to which the members believe in service to the public, self-regulation, autonomy, and similar professional values.
3. *Societal* recognition: The degree to which society in general views the occupation as a profession.

If these are to be our criteria of professionalism, then the status of teaching is clearly ambiguous. Teachers undergo specialized training and certification processes, although these processes are not as elaborate as those of most established professions. Teachers promote values like public service and autonomy (at least in the classroom), but collectively they have no means of regulating individual adherence to these or any other standards. Respect for their efforts has increased recently, but their reputation still suffers from overexposure. More people spend more of their lives in close association with teachers than with any practitioners of any other occupation save their own, and good teachers all too often make their job look easy.

Despite this, we question whether Hall's criteria are either necessary or sufficient indicia of professionalization. They are heavily influenced by images of professionals derived from self-employment or entrepreneurial settings. Because of this, it is virtually impossible for anyone *employed by an organization* to meet them. The effect of these images is to consign anyone employed by an organization to the status of semiprofessional. A second limitation is that the above criteria say virtually nothing about what professionals do. They do not, for example, speak about the kinds of analyses required of professionals, or about their application of general principles and standard routines to unique, unpredictable situations, or even about their management of relationships with clients, individually or in groups. The more we focus on what professionals actually do, the more we are likely to afford teachers the respect that we give to members of the traditional professions.

Professionalism, in this sense, is a function of how individuals are treated within the organizations in which they work. Professionalism is not a function of credentials or public status but rather a state of mind that is sustained and enhanced by the way people are managed. In hierarchical organizations, the professionalization of all but those at the highest level depends on the attitudes of those with managerial responsibilities. More specifically, the professionalization of employees depends on the assumptions that managers make about the knowledge, skills, work processes, and resources line employees use in their jobs. As W. I. Thomas maintains (Thomas and Thomas, 1928, p. 81), "If man defines the social situation as real, it is real in its consequences." The professionalization (or *de*professionalization) of teaching is thus a reality socially constructed in the interaction of managers and their subordinates.

How should professionals be managed? Or is the question itself a contradiction in terms? Are people necessarily and correspondingly less professional to the extent that their work is managed by others? The answers to these questions depend as much on our concepts of management as they do on the meanings we ascribe to professionalism. But how are teachers who work in organizations called schools really managed?

The most prevalent form of school organization was designed to imitate nineteenth-century mass-production factories. As such, it was set up to treat teachers like assembly-line workers producing standardized products. More recently, labor laws and contracts patterned after industrial union models gave management exclusive rights to decision making in return for fair treatment and wages for all teachers. But the logic of tight central control that these models embody has usually (but not always) been qualified by managers' deference to what goes on *within* the classroom.

For individual teachers, the conditions within the classroom are more complex than screwing one piece of metal to another. The students they work with, over, and for are increasingly multicultural, multiethnic, multimotivated, and face a host of problems outside the classroom that inhibit their ability to learn *individually*, much less work *together* productively. Instead of one correct configuration for unit A to be attached to unit B, there are many successful output configurations: Students can grow up to be good citizens, hardworking volunteers, sportsmanlike athletes, Nobel Prize-winning scientists, Pulitzer Prize-winning novelists, teachers, or perhaps ecological superheros who save the ozone layer for all of us. There is wide variation in the inputs and outputs to and from the teacher's classroom (Bacharach and Conley, 1988).

The turn-of-the-century architects of America's systems of public education were not unaware of diversity. They consciously sought to *overcome* what variation they could, to *ignore* what they could not overcome, and to *control* as much of the attendant uncertainty as possible, from as high an administrative level as possible. It was their mission to homogenize American society, and they chose an organizational model that was plausibly suited to their purpose (Tyack and Hansot, 1982).

It was only later, when reformers began to suggest that school systems should adapt to the needs and abilities of different students, that the question of who should be responsible for the adapting arose. Organizations that must provide different services to different customers or clients cannot provide their employees with the detailed instructions that characterized supervisory relationships in the old mass-production factories. They must provide general policies and procedures and rely on their employees to fill in the gaps.

The tension between individual discretion and organizational control that emerges in these types of organizations gives birth to new kinds of structures that are designed to balance both sets of needs. Rational rules replace arbitrary supervision. There is a name for the structures that sit at the middle of this continuum: *They are called bureaucracies.* Bureaucracies are not the quintessential bastions of top-down control that many educational reformers paint them to be. They are the natural result when administrative superiors are compelled to rely on the discretion of subordinates to apply general principles to unique and unpredictable situations, and when superiors resort to general rules and procedures (rather than specific instructions and direct supervision) to control the performance of their subordinates. Bureaucracies are the quintessential *compromises* between competing pressures for autonomy and control.

That, we argue, is the fundamental problem. The problems now besetting America's systems of public education require more discretion *and* more control, more flexibility *and* more direction, more room for professional judgment *and* more ways of ensuring accountability. Systems that produce compromises between these competing sets of needs are no longer sufficient, but neither are strategies that explicitly subordinate one set of needs to the other.

Gale Winds

Few people can fail to notice the powerful pressures for reform in American education today (Bacharach, 1990). The public and politicians recognize the urgent need to produce competitive workers who can think for themselves with higher-order reasoning and problem-solving skills. They insist on improvement in both the quality and quantity of education; in excellence and equity; in basic skills, social skills, and thinking skills. Teacher unions are beginning to realize that the array of industrial-sector structures, principles, laws, and procedures that they were handed when they first won bargaining rights in the 1960s was never more than half-suited to the unique conditions and work of teaching in public schools. Teachers are realizing that what is needed is real involvement in the decisions that affect them collectively, not just autonomy within their individual classrooms.

Perhaps most importantly for the future of learning in our schools, teachers are beginning to realize that they, like their students, must learn how to share with each other the resources and techniques they have nurtured and developed in their individual classrooms, in an ongoing process of professional growth. Just as scientific and industrial innovations have occurred from cross-fertilization of ideas between different specialists, teaching innovations are likely to result from a new ethic of leadership and perpetual learning shared among all members of the complex organizations we call schools.

Yet this new ethic of leadership and learning must be cultivated in the appropriate organizational soil. Private organizations are working to rid themselves of the inflexible and noncompetitive features of the mass-production, assembly-line industrial model of management. At the same time, states, schools, and even some teacher unions are standardizing textbooks, exams, and procedures and dividing responsibility for the learning process into smaller and smaller segments. Teachers are isolated in their individual classrooms, structurally discouraged from exchanging knowledge either of the students they share or the teaching techniques they have discovered, and encouraged to leave all decisions affecting more than their own specific classrooms to "management."

If students are acculturated in such educational "factories" with strict and inviolable hierarchical distinctions, they will hardly learn to become active, participatory, and courageous learners themselves. Rather, they will passively accept direction and control of their work environment from their administrative superiors just as many teachers do today, negotiating only for more pay and benefits instead of attempting to improve the quality of teaching and learning.

If students are to become truly successful at whatever they choose to make themselves, they will have to learn how to actively seek out general knowledge and apply it to their own individual problems. If we are to regain our status as an economically dynamic and competitive society, Johnny must learn more than just how to read and write; he must learn how to *think*.

It is the premise of this book that students will not learn these skills if their immediate role models (the adults they spend the largest portion of their day with) are themselves isolated in classrooms with watered-down, homogeneous, generic, "teacher-proof" curricula to teach. Students will not learn how to share knowledge, how to teach each other (and get inspiration and a sense of accomplishment from doing so), or how to make their lives voyages of discovery if their teachers have no time built into their workday for such collegial sharing themselves. If teachers have no influence with administrators who fear that their bureaucratic turf is being invaded, the workers and managers of tomorrow will never develop norms of participation within their organizations. If teachers are rewarded for getting out of teaching and into administration (or receive bonuses or promotions for their nonteaching activities), everyone will get the message that teaching and learning are neither organizationally nor societally valued.

Rather than framing the relationships between administrators and teachers in terms of demands that are assumed to be basically incompatible (and which therefore can only be resolved by conflict or compromise), this book starts with a different premise. We claim that American teachers and administrators are in the midst of reconceptualizing their relationships with one another. They are searching for a perspective that allows teachers to work and develop as professionals without compromising the legitimate needs for overall direction and structural coordination that traditionally have been served by boards of education and administrators. By examining the work of teachers, the relationships between teachers and other adults in school systems, the job of teaching, systems of compensation, structures of participation, and issues of bargaining, this book makes an argument that avoids casting the interests of teachers and administrators as mutually exclusive. Only by moving beyond this ideological impasse can our efforts to restructure schools have any hope of success.

To break the impasse, this book analyzes the nature of the relationships between individual professionals and the organizations that employ them and examines the pressures that are emerging to redefine those relationships. At the heart of the relationships, we argue, is a division of labor that assigns individual teachers considerable discretion over decisions confined to their individual classrooms but affords them little voice over decisions made outside those classrooms. It is this division of labor that needs to be restructured—to allow closer coordination of classroom decision making and more teacher participation in organizational decisions that affect their classrooms.

This book develops this argument from the inside out. The remainder of this chapter reviews the traditional arguments that have been used to justify teacher involvement in school and district decision making, arguments, we note, that are beginning to give way to new ones, grounded in the nature of teaching itself.

Traditional Arguments

Four sets of arguments have traditionally been advanced in support of employee participation or involvement in organizational decision making. Each has several variations, but in general the arguments run as follows:

1. *Involvement is an ethical/moral right.* Employees have a right to a voice in decisions that affect their livelihoods and personal health. Autocratic approaches to management ignore basic human needs, such as autonomy, respect, and a sense of achievement. They are also inconsistent with the democratic principle that authority is derived from the consent of the governed (Nightingale, 1982; Sashkin, 1984).

2. *Involvement enhances employee morale and job satisfaction.* Involvement in decision making improves morale and job satisfaction, it is said, because it gives employees more sense of control over their work lives, enhances their sense of the importance of their efforts, and reduces their sense of isolation. It also is supposed to contribute to morale and satisfaction because employees are more likely to accept less-than-ideal policies or conditions over which they have had some influence. It does so indirectly, as well, by providing employees with opportunities to secure changes in conditions that have negative effects on their morale and satisfaction (Stogdill, 1974; Sashkin, 1984).

3. *Involvement enhances employee motivation, organizational commitment, and acceptance of change.* It does so (it is argued) by giving employees more opportunities to satisfy their personal needs for control, accomplishment, meaningfulness, and collegiality in the course of satisfying the needs of the organization: It brings individual and organizational goals into alignment with

each other, provides employees with a sense of "ownership" over new policies or initiatives, and increases their trust in the employer. Involvement also enhances motivation, commitment, and acceptance of change by increasing employees' understanding of decisions and increasing the feedback they receive as they first make or influence decisions, then implement and monitor them (Nadler, 1986; Locke and Latham, 1984; Hackman and Lawler, 1971).

4. *Involvement enhances cooperation and reduces conflict between individual employees and their supervisors and between labor and management generally.* It does so in part by reducing the *causes* of conflict and in part by enhancing employees' confidence in the *process* by which managerial decisions are made. All of the effects listed under the previous three arguments potentially contribute to these two results. In addition, participation provides employees with a legitimate cooperative alternative for voicing problems and expressing dissatisfaction, thereby reducing the possibility that they will feel forced to choose between leaving the organization, keeping quiet, or knocking someone over the head to gain attention to their problems (Kochan, Katz, and Mower, 1985; Hirschman, 1970).

The evidence to support these arguments varies. The first (ethical) argument is based partly on assertions about employees' psychological needs and the impact of hierarchical authority structures on employee health, but otherwise it rests on value judgments that are beyond the reach of empirical evidence. One either agrees with the argument or one does not. The other arguments have been tested, with various research approaches and degrees of rigor, producing some general conclusions.

There is solid evidence that employee involvement in decision making can have *all* of the benefits cited in the arguments listed above (Sashkin, 1984; Susman, 1979; Likert, 1967). There is equally strong evidence that involving employees in decision making does not, in and of itself, guarantee any of those benefits. Rather, the benefits of involvement seem to depend upon a variety of contextual and intervening factors (Locke and Schweiger, 1979; Lowin, 1968).

Although none of the potential benefits of involvement are guaranteed, certain benefits do seem to be easier to come by than others. There is general agreement among researchers that, of all the possible benefits listed above, involvement or participation is most often associated with higher levels of job satisfaction, improved employee morale, and other outcomes that are often closely linked to satisfaction and morale, such as reduced absenteeism and turnover (Locke and Schweiger, 1979).

As important as these findings may be, they all share the implicit assumption that it is teachers who benefit directly from being involved in decision making and their employers benefit only in a derivative way, by having a happy or (what may be more to the point) compliant workforce. What usually prompts attention to these arguments, we think, is not the conviction that these effects have any direct impact on individual or organizational performance; the conviction that "happy workers are more productive workers" has never held much credibility with managers or found much support from researchers. Rather, what prompts that attention is the conviction that such factors *do* affect workers' willingness to obey management orders. To the extent that a measure of employee involvement—or the semblance of involvement—might make employees more willing to accept directions from management, managers have often been willing to "give it a try." But the concept of involvement actually runs *counter* to the basic principles of hierarchical control.

Implicit in the traditional arguments for involving employees in decision making, then, is the assumption that it is employees who want involvement in decision making and that involvement is something management *gives* to its employees— perhaps out of good will, perhaps to buy something else, but certainly not because it needs their advice.

One does not have to press this line of reasoning too far to notice how shallow a commitment to involvement it implies. If managers do not really want their employees' advice, then their efforts to solicit it are likely to be halfhearted or limited, and if that is the case, their employees' perceptions of their own influence—on which most of the purported benefits of participation are supposed to rest—are likely to be correspondingly low (Locke and Schweiger, 1979; Filley, House, and Kerr, 1976; Lowin, 1968).

Indeed, research suggests that where employees have the formal authority to make decisions but their actual discretion is tightly circumscribed by organizational norms, carefully controlled agendas, limited resources, or similar factors, the purported benefits of participation are likely to be elusive. Similarly, where employees are offered opportunities to have input into decisions made at higher levels of the organization but view such opportunities as mere formalities or attempts to create the illusion of influence, the effects of such participation are likely to be ephemeral. Indeed, such strategies often backfire and generate *more* dissatisfaction, *less* commitment, and higher levels of organizational conflict (Duke, Showers, and Imber, 1980).

Rather than thinking of participation as something that administrators "give" to teachers, either to make them feel better about their jobs or else to buy more work from them, the remainder of this book takes a very different approach. It argues that participation will have to be at the very heart of efforts to reform the entire system of education.

Schools are organizations, and the way they are structured has important consequences. The structure of most American school systems is archaic and unsuitable for the needs of the twenty-first century. If American schools are to improve significantly, they will have to be *restructured* so as to release new energies from the efforts of all members of the system.

If there is a common thread running through this book, it is that systems for managing the relationships between individuals and organizations need not be inherently antagonistic to teachers' claims to professional status. Indeed, when we focus on what professionals *do*, there is every reason to believe that teaching is among the most difficult, demanding, and (potentially) highly skilled professions. By the same token, the organizations that represent teachers and those that employ them, rather than being antithetical to their professional status, are potential vehicles for promoting the professional standards, collegiality, accountability, and overwhelming sense of responsibility for the welfare of clients that represent elusive ideals in many other less tightly knit professions.

America's educators are in the midst of redefining what it means to be a professional. In the process, they are redefining what it means for boards and administrators to manage professionals and unions to represent them.

If we want today's students to know how to "think in action" to fill the professional jobs of tomorrow (Schon, 1983), our schools should encourage the development of professional norms and skills throughout the school. This includes but is not limited to topics covered in this book: governance structures, management philosophy and practices, teacher participation in curricular issues, career development systems, and compensation systems. "What our children see in the world depends upon what we show them" (Rose K. Goldsen, subtitle of an Ithaca radio show in the 1970s).

2

THE WORK OF TEACHERS

Everyone's an expert on education. Everyone's been in school and everyone thinks they know what does and doesn't work. . . . All the people we interviewed thought they knew what teaching is like. I tell people, "You're an expert on studenting, not teaching. You know what it's like to be one of twenty-five students facing a teacher. You don't know what it's like to be a teacher facing twenty-five students."

Tucson teacher
written comment[1]

Most people are sure they know what teaching is like. Most people are exposed to teachers as students and parents. Indeed, most people have more contact with more teachers over their lifetimes than with any occupation except their own. But few people have the opportunity to view teaching from the front of a classroom. This chapter presents a description of teaching from such a perspective.

The information presented in this chapter is drawn from a study of teaching that was prepared for the Tucson (Arizona) Education Association (TEA) in 1985 (Shedd and Malanowski, 1985). What is more important, the authors of the study derived the concepts used here to describe the job of teaching from lengthy discussions with Tucson teachers. The immediate purpose of the study was to help the TEA develop a reasonably parsimonious way of communicating to members of the general public what it is that teachers do. The point was to describe teaching *as teachers experience it,* to establish the case for *listening* to them in debates over how they are compensated and how their efforts are organized.

In order to serve that purpose, it became necessary to develop a vocabulary that would allow teachers to talk with each other

13

about their work. As the study progressed, and as the teachers participating in the study listened to what the others had to say, it became increasingly clear that teachers often hold their profession—and themselves—in as low esteem as the general public holds them. Their own images of teaching, no less than the images held by their students' parents, were particularized reflections of their childhood memories of some teachers' seemingly effortless success and of others' seeming incompetence or indifference.

Beneath the surface of all but a few teachers' descriptions of their efforts lay doubts about their own competence. What was *supposed* to be a relatively easy job manifestly was not. It was not until relatively late in our study that the teachers we were working with began to see that it was their suppositions (and not their skills) that needed to be questioned.

By drawing heavily on survey data and interviews with teachers and by retracing the steps by which a coherent description of teaching began to emerge, we sought to provide others with an opportunity to view what is unquestionably one of society's most important and influential occupations from the standpoint of those who work in that occupation.

The Responsibilities of Teachers

At the outset of their study, a committee of Tucson teachers identified thirty-seven sets of responsibilities, each defined as types of activities, that committee members believed are typically performed by classroom teachers. The authors were first engaged to survey all the teachers in the district to find out how many teachers actually performed those responsibilities and how often.

Responses to the survey confirmed that most teachers (more than half) perform all but nine of these responsibilities on at least a weekly basis. Most teachers, in fact, perform most of these responsibilities on a daily basis.[2]

The vast majority of teachers (over 80 percent) reported that they perform eleven responsibilities either daily or more often (the daily and weekly percentages are indicated in parentheses):

- Observing and directing student behavior to keep students "on task" and to identify and avoid potential discipline problems (96/99)
- Recording and reporting classroom attendance (94/95)
- Observing class, group, and individual behavior and progress in order to identify when plans might need to be changed (93/99)
- Communicating expectations to students concerning instructional goals and objectives, quality and amount of work, and behavior and discipline (91/99)
- Actually adjusting class, group, or individual plans while class is still in session (that is, making "midstream" changes) (91/98)
- Leading class discussions and demonstrations (89/97)
- Administering in-class discipline and/or referring students to others for discipline (89/96)
- Assigning in-class work and homework to individuals, groups, and whole classes (87/96)
- Lecturing to a class as a whole for purposes of instruction (85/94)
- Instructing or reviewing work with individual students for purposes of instruction, while other students work independently or in groups (84/96)
- Instructing groups of students, using a variety of techniques, while other students work independently or in groups (82/94)

A somewhat smaller proportion of teachers (but still a majority) perform five additional responsibilities daily or more often:

- Reviewing tests, homework, and other student assignments for purposes of identifying progress, problems, and special needs (76/96)
- Monitoring and supervising student behavior outside of the classroom, for example, in hallways, cafeterias, or on the playground (66/78)
- Planning, developing, and scheduling whole class and group lessons, activities, and assignments (65/97)
- Planning activities and assignments for individual students, adjusting them to fit plans for the class and groups (60/90)
- Discussing work with colleagues, for purposes of discussing

subject matter, student needs, and each other's instructional
plans and teaching techniques (52/90)

With the exception of monitoring and supervising out-of-
classroom behavior (a responsibility performed more frequently by
elementary and junior high school teachers than by high school
teachers), virtually all teachers, at all school levels, report that they
perform each and every one of the preceding sixteen responsibilities
at least weekly.

Nine other responsibilities are performed weekly or more
often by at least 50 percent of the teachers responding to the survey:

- Recording and reporting grades (42/64)
- Placing and adjusting placement of individual students at ap-
  propriate curriculum levels (34/69)
- Developing course outlines and special instructional materials
  not already available (29/72)
- Counseling with individual students (24/64)
- Responding orally or in writing to special requests for informa-
  tion from administrators or other school officials (22/61)
- Consulting with specialists and colleagues to identify and an-
  alyze the special needs of individual students (19/68)
- Developing tests (16/66)
- Attending faculty meetings (5/64)
- Planning and arranging for special resources for classroom in-
  struction (10/52)

The first point that deserves attention about this list of responsibilities is the sheer number of responsibilities that all or most
teachers perform on a regular basis: sixteen are performed daily or
more often and another nine at least weekly. But in fact, these figures tend to *understate* the volume and intensity of Tucson teachers'
performance responsibilities in several different ways.

First, the sixteen daily and nine weekly responsibilities listed
above are based on aggregate percentages (more than 50 percent
falling in one or the other category). Large numbers of teachers
report that they perform many of the responsibilities listed as

"daily" on an hourly basis, and many report that they perform what we have labeled "weekly" responsibilities on a daily basis.

Second, large numbers of teachers (but less than a majority) indicated that they frequently perform several duties not listed above on a weekly, daily, or even hourly basis, including directing the work of student teachers, scheduling and conducting meetings with parents, arranging with other school or district personnel for special support or placements for students with special needs, and ordering instructional materials and supplies for regular classroom use. In fact, of the thirty-seven responsibilities listed on the teacher survey, only five are performed on a weekly or more frequent basis by fewer than 20 percent of all teachers.[3]

The above list also understates the volume and intensity of teachers' responsibilities by collapsing into short statements responsibilities that take many different forms, and sometimes in the process misrepresenting the real character of those responsibilities. By far the largest number of observations submitted by teachers in response to the survey's open-ended invitation to comment further on their jobs (152 of 429 comments) addressed the variety of ways in which teachers counsel students; provide them with "nurturing"; serve as surrogate parents, psychologists, and social workers; and otherwise address the needs and special problems of individual students. Respondents properly noted that by collapsing all such activities under the single category of "counseling individual students" the survey data understated what, for many teachers, is one of their most important, most difficult, and most time-consuming responsibilities.

Significant but smaller numbers of respondents offered similar comments about how the survey understated the nature of teachers' relationships with parents, their dealings with the community, the burden of their administrative paperwork, and the variety of special assignments they frequently take on. Since survey respondents were not asked about these activities, or were not asked about them in much detail, there is no way of documenting here just how many teachers perform them or how often they do so. But again, these comments indicate that our list of sixteen daily and nine additional weekly activities represents a *conservative* statement of the volume and intensity of a teacher's responsibilities.

Differences Among Teachers

How accurate is it to speak of teaching as a single job and teachers as members of a single occupation? To provide at least a partial answer to that question, we examined the differences in how teachers at different school levels responded to the survey items. If there were substantial differences among teachers, we reasoned, they would be most likely to emerge in comparisons across organizational levels. Indeed, in other surveys, teachers at different organizational levels responded differently to questions about work activities, conditions, and consequences (for example, Bacharach and Bamberger, 1990).

The survey responses of teachers were analyzed by school level. Separate percentages were computed for elementary school teachers, junior high/middle school teachers, senior high school teachers, and teachers who identified themselves as "other teachers," most of whom were resource or special education teachers with responsibility for children with special handicaps or needs but also with ongoing responsibility for particular classrooms. Of the thirty-seven responsibilities listed on our survey, there were nontrivial (that is, more than a few percentage points) differences among teachers at different school levels on fifteen of those items, in terms of the proportions of teachers performing particular responsibilities daily or more often.

Considering that elementary school teachers typically have ongoing responsibility for a single group of students, it is not surprising that they report that they use a wider variety of teaching techniques on any given day. As a group, they lecture, instruct small groups, *and* provide individual instruction more frequently than other groups of teachers, whose individual members are somewhat more likely to report that they rely on one or another of those techniques on any given day. There are virtually *no* differences between elementary school and other teachers, however, in the proportions leading daily class discussions or in the proportions who lecture, instruct small groups, or instruct individuals on a weekly or more frequent basis.

Elementary school teachers are also somewhat more likely than junior and senior high school teachers to plan assignments or activities for individual students and to adjust placement of individual students at different curriculum levels; they are somewhat less likely to have to record and report grades and to respond to administrators' requests for information; and they are much more likely to report that they collect money from students.

Junior high school teachers are more likely than all other groups to report responsibility for monitoring students outside the classroom and are more likely than either elementary or senior high teachers to spend time each day consulting specialists and colleagues about the needs of individual students. On a weekly basis, they are somewhat more likely than either of those groups to hold meetings with parents. As a group, they fall between elementary school teachers and senior high school teachers in the frequency with which they adjust placements of students at different curriculum levels and respond to administrative requests for information.

Of all four groups, senior high school teachers are the most likely to report that they spend time daily and weekly responding to administrative requests for information. They are less likely to spend time planning assignments for individuals, developing special instructional materials, disciplining students, adjusting the curriculum placement of individual students, meeting with parents, and monitoring student behavior outside the classroom.

Given their responsibility for students with special needs, it is not surprising that those who identified themselves as "other teachers" are more likely than the other three groups to spend time each day planning assignments or activities for individual students, adjusting placements of students, consulting specialists and colleagues about the needs of particular students, getting special help for individual students, and meeting with parents. Nor is it surprising that they would be less likely than those in other groups to spend time developing tests. It should be noted, however, that these comparisons are all based on daily percentages. On a weekly basis, the percentages of these teachers reporting that they perform the above responsibilities (except for getting special help for students and developing tests) are much closer to those for other groups.

These statements of differences, standing alone, might be interpreted to mean that it would be more appropriate to speak of "the job of elementary school teacher," "the job of junior high school teacher," and so on, or even "the job of kindergarten teacher," "the job of high school science teacher," and so on. In one sense, it is entirely appropriate that such distinctions be emphasized. One of the basic reasons why "the job of teaching" cannot be reduced to a standardized set of procedures—and be closely supervised—is that the *specific* problems and situations that teachers face tend to vary widely and unpredictably.

Consider, for example, the following three illustrations offered by teachers in response to our survey question about how well the survey items "captured" their job as teacher.

> What other teachers besides kindergarten teachers work from 7:30 A.M. to 6 P.M. either training volunteers *or* preparing materials? *Everything* in a kindergarten class is *made by* the teacher for *double* the number of students. I have 55 students NOW! Kindergarten teachers reset the class for the afternoon *during* their lunch time. Everyday, I have 10 minutes for lunch before it is time to train the P.M. volunteers for work in centers.

A science teacher commented: "For science [lab classes] we have a desperate need for competent help in the management and maintenance of lab materials—many lab opportunities are missed because there simply is not time to do all the preparation and hunt up the equipment!" And a special education teacher remarked:

> The questionnaire "captures" the nature of my responsibilities as a teacher in general, but not as a special education teacher. The responsibilities go well beyond anything covered in teaching manuals or district job descriptions. We deal with health crises and behavior problems on a daily basis. Our students require constant supervision as they are often not capable of functioning safely. Many students require feeding, toileting, assistance in dressing, grooming, and the tasks of daily life easily taken for granted by their "normal" peers. Specifically:

1. Dealing with children who exhibit extremely self-abusive and/or violent behaviors.
2. Monitoring health needs and intervening when crisis situations occur.
3. Supervising large groups of students who lack the mental maturity to utilize safety procedures at work and play.
4. Develop behavior programs to facilitate appropriate behaviors.
5. Attend to grooming and hygiene needs of individual students (change diapers, bathe students, wash hair, etc.)
6. Counsel parents who often have difficulty dealing with the needs of handicapped children.

Each of these teachers deals with special situations and problems that the others do not have to confront. Each needs special skills and special kinds of equipment and supplies. But the specific details still follow the same general patterns. Each is responsible for performing a variety of generally comparable responsibilities; each uses a variety of different (but comparable) resources and confronts resource problems that are much the same. Each is largely responsible for seeing that all those responsibilities are performed and all those problems are resolved *on his or her own*, which is particularly important for our purposes.

Two general features of our data on differences among school levels help illustrate these points. First, all of the above contrasts were established by examining each responsibility separately. When the relative positions of different responsibilities are compared across all responsibilities, there are very few differences among these four groups. That is, while the members of one group might perform one responsibility more or less often than the members of other groups—and may perform that general responsibility in ways that are unique to a particular school level—the members of all groups tend to perform the same general responsibilities in roughly the same order of frequency.

Second, there are virtually no differences among these groups in the proportions reporting that they

- Lead daily class discussions
- Observe and direct students to keep them "on task"
- Observe student behavior to identify the need to change plans
- Make "midclass" adjustments to plans
- Assign work to students
- Record student attendance
- Review student work
- Counsel students
- Direct and supervise student teachers
- Evaluate and counsel student teachers
- Plan and arrange for special resources for instructional purposes
- Perform several other duties that all teachers perform infrequently

The same kinds of conclusions are reached when the four groups are compared in terms of resources used. Although there are nontrivial differences in the frequency with which different groups make use of some resources, the same resources tend to be heavily, moderately, or infrequently used by all groups.[4]

These observations allow us to recognize the many common-alities that the jobs of all teachers share and at the same time to appreciate that there are real differences in the specific situations that different teachers face at different levels of a school system. In fact, every teacher's job, in terms of specific responsibilities and resources, can be said to be unique. But the specific differences, while sometimes more apparent *because* they are so specific, do not negate the conclusion that teachers are all members of the same occupation.

Searching for Metaphors

When we first outlined our plans to analyze the Tucson sur-vey data, we broke teachers' responsibilities into five categories: instruction, instructional planning, classroom management, diag-nosis and counseling, and administration. The point was to identify groups of responsibilities that could be readily compared to those of other occupations familiar to the public. By drawing a variety of parallels—to trainers, personnel specialists, planners, data analysts, accountants, counselors, and persons in a variety of supervisory and managerial jobs—it would be possible to convey some of the rich texture of a teacher's responsibilities. Or so we thought.

We realized we had miscalculated after we began reviewing survey responses, analyzing written responses to open-ended questions, analyzing the comments of participants in our follow-up discussion, and comparing teachers' responses to those of employees in various other jobs (whom teachers working on the project had interviewed). The taxonomy of teaching responsibilities we had planned on using to analyze teaching and compare it to other jobs did, indeed, allow us to identify particular responsibilities that teachers shared with other occupations, but it did not capture what was most distinctive about teaching.

We found that teachers' *instructional* responsibilities were roughly similar to those performed by industrial trainers, employment consultants, public information officers, personnel officers, television news directors, and a handful of supervisors in professional organizations. Their *work planning* and *group planning* duties were comparable to those of news directors, many managers, supervisors, and a few professionals. Their *diagnostic and counseling* responsibilities paralleled those of employment consultants and trainers in some respects and those of budget analysts, accounting managers, and television news directors in others. We could compare their *administrative* duties to those of persons in a variety of different jobs.

These comparisons were useful starting points for analyzing the responsibilities of teachers, but what they illustrated most vividly was how different teaching was from most of the other jobs we studied. Teachers seemed to perform more discrete responsibilities, to perform more kinds of responsibilities, and to perform each more often than almost anyone else we interviewed. One job, however, seemed to match teaching in both nature and intensity of duties: Television news directors (those who directed evening news shows, not the anchors) were like teachers in many respects. News directors, like teachers, are responsible for selecting, analyzing, and synthesizing large quantities of information and deciding how that information can be most effectively communicated to a nonprofessional audience. They are responsible for assigning nonroutine duties (that is, duties that must be explained) to a large number of individuals (roughly twenty to thirty), some who work individually and some who work in groups. They supervise and orchestrate the subsequent performance of those duties, working under tight time constraints and adjusting quickly to unforeseen developments.

There are many differences in the specific responsibilities and circumstances of teachers and news directors, of course, but the two jobs were remarkably similar in volume, variety, and intensity of duties. How unique were they in these respects? Our original plans—to compare discrete sets of duties, rather than overall patterns—had prompted us to preselect a limited number of job categories (eleven) that we thought might illustrate particular parallels[5] and to interview only two or three persons in each of these jobs.[6] Our interview data were suggestive, therefore, but hardly conclusive. We obviously could not claim that the jobs we had selected were necessarily representative of jobs in general.

In order to provide some sense of where teaching might fit in a broader family of jobs, we analyzed what proved to be the most comprehensive and (considering its breadth) most detailed source of information on jobs in the Tucson area, the 1984 Pima County Employer Wage Survey, prepared by the Arizona Department of Economic Security. The survey covered the jobs of 10,174 persons, in seventy different job categories. In addition to wage information, the DES report includes paragraph-long descriptions of each of the seventy jobs surveyed. (Examples of these descriptions are provided in the appendix.) Using these descriptions and standard content analysis techniques, we identified twenty-two different general descriptors that served to distinguish the seventy jobs in the survey. We then scored each of the seventy jobs in terms of whether each of the descriptors applied or did not apply to that job. Using data from our teacher survey on duties that a majority of teachers perform weekly or more often, we scored teaching as well.

The twenty-two descriptors (and how we scored teaching on each of them)[7] were the following:

- Receives only *general* direction, rather than more direct supervision (yes)

- Experience required for "full" performance (yes)
- College degree required (yes)
- Special training required (yes)
- Special license required (yes)
- Trains others (yes)
- Supervises work of others (not professionals) (yes)
- Plans and schedules the work of others (yes)
- Diagnoses problems and determines needs (yes)
- Analyzes data (yes)
- Coordinates work with others (yes)
- Identified as "professional" (yes)
- Identified as "skilled" (yes)
- Files and records data (yes)
- Responsible for the overall operation of a large facility or department (no)
- Supervises professionals (no)
- Prepares reports (no)
- Orders materials (no)
- Operates equipment (no)
- Repairs equipment (no)
- Identified as "routine" (no)

After we scored teaching and each of the other jobs in the DES survey on these twenty-two items, we used two different approaches to identify those jobs that were closest to teaching. The first approach used an analysis technique called "searching for structure." The technique places survey responses in a "tree" format. The item that teachers have in common with the most survey respondents ("experience required") was placed at the base of the tree, together with the list of all jobs that have that feature in common. The item that teachers have in common with the largest number of those jobs ("skilled") was then identified, and the list of comparable jobs was reduced to reflect that item. Altogether, the procedure was repeated six times, at which point the list of comparable jobs was reduced to a single job.

After the fifth application of this technique, the list of jobs comparable to teaching had been reduced to the following:

- Buyer
- Personnel analyst
- Budget analyst
- Systems analyst
- Attorney (not self-employed)
- Civil engineer

Teachers, like all of the others on this list, need experience to perform their jobs, are skilled employees, are responsible for diagnosing problems and determining needed action, analyze and interpret data, and do not (as a regular function) operate equipment. (The paragraphs describing these six jobs are the ones provided as illustrations in the appendix.)

Of these six positions, the job that has the most features in common with teaching is that of the civil engineer, who supervises others, does not prepare reports as a regular function, and plans and schedules the work of others, in addition to the other features just noted.

The advantage of the "tree" approach is that it enables us to generate the most comparisons for the most jobs. It does not help us determine whether the items used to draw comparisons are necessarily the most important features, or whether there are groups of features that tend to characterize different types of jobs. To serve those purposes, we used statistical correlations to determine whether different types of features tend to "lump together," that is, whether the presence or absence of certain features tend to be associated with each other.

We identified two different groups of features. One group, labeled managerial/supervisory, consisted of the following items (again with notations of how teaching was coded):

- Works under *general* direction, as opposed to direct supervision (yes)
- Responsible for the overall operation of a large facility or department (no)
- Supervises professionals (no)
- Supervises others (nonprofessionals) (yes)
- Plans and schedules the work of others (yes)

Only three of the seventy jobs in the DES survey (accounting supervisor, purchasing director, and electronic data processing manager) have all five features, but jobs that have one feature tend to have each of the others, and jobs that do not have one feature tend not to have the others as well.

The other group of four features, labeled *professional/technical,* are the following:

- Identified as "professional" (yes)
- College degree required (yes)
- Diagnoses problems and determines needed action (yes)
- Analyzes and interprets data (yes)

Only four of the DES jobs include all four features (personnel analyst, budget analyst, attorney, and civil engineer), but, again, the presence or absence of those features tends to be associated.

The fact that the nine features listed above emerged as two different groups indicated that, in aggregate terms, the jobs on the DES survey tend to fall into either the managerial/supervisory or the professional/technical category (or into neither) *but not into both.* Since teaching has three of the five managerial/supervisory features and all of the professional/technical features, it was important to establish whether any other jobs in the survey did so as well.

For teaching and each of the seventy DES jobs, we assigned two overall scores, one indicating how many of the five managerial/supervisory features the job possessed and the other doing the same for the four professional/technical features. Figure 1 indicates the placement of all jobs possessing at least one of the nine features, using this scoring approach.

As the figure confirms, very few of the jobs covered by the DES survey combine professional or technical features and managerial or supervisory features. Although teaching is similar to several positions, in terms of professional/technical features, including the six we identified earlier with the tree approach, it is similar only to the job of civil engineer in the combination of both kinds of features.

Although much less detailed than the job comparisons we were able to make using interview data, the comparisons we made

Figure 1. Professional/Technical and Managerial/Supervisory Features of Selected Jobs.

Number of Professional/Technical Features	Number of Managerial/Supervisory Features					
	0	1	2	3	4	5
4	Personnel Analyst	Budget Analyst Attorney		Civil Engineer Teachers		Accounting Supvr.
3	Public Info. Off. Staff Nurse Buyer Pharmacist	Accountant Librarian Systems Analyst				
2	Respiratory Ther. Medical Technol.	Computer Progr. Training Coord.	Physical Ther.	Safety Officer	EDP System Program Mgr.	Purchasing Director
1	Refrig. Mechanic Accounting Clerk Auto Service Wrkr. Radiological Tech. Computer Operator Drafting Tech. Automotive Mech.	EDP Anal./Progr. Plumber Comm. Technol.			Physical Plant Manager	
0	(34 jobs)	Cook Food Serv. Supvr. Custodial Supvr.	Office Supvr. Stores Supvr.		Data Entry Supvr. Equip. Shop Supvr. Computer Op. Mgr.	EDP Manager

Source: Survey of TUSD teachers and Arizona Department of Economic Security, *1984 Pima County Employer Wage Survey.*

with the job survey data provide surer grounds for drawing conclusions about *patterns* of job features. Although similar to many different jobs, teaching is unlike most other jobs in that it combines features that are typically associated with different kinds of jobs. The two jobs that are closest to teaching—television news director and civil engineer—both involve a combination of professional/technical/analytical and managerial/supervisory responsibilities. Plenty of jobs included one or the other, but it is the combination that makes teaching and these two other jobs stand out. These categories and the idea of combining them served as the new starting points for our efforts to describe teaching.

Teachers as Decision Makers

The group of responsibilities that we labeled "professional/technical/analytical" illustrated one reason our original list of responsibilities was misleading: The list combined—but failed to distinguish between—two different sets of considerations. Some of the categories basically referred to the *processes* that teachers engage in when performing their jobs; other categories focused more on the *purposes* that teachers' actions are meant to serve, that is, on the kinds of goals or outcomes they are expected (or intend) to pursue. Together, the two dimensions illustrate the kinds of decision making in which teachers engage.

The process dimension was most readily apparent. The survey data reflected three general processes: *planning* (including identifying problems, needs, or objectives and deciding how to address them); *taking action* (carrying out a plan); and *evaluating* (assessing the effects of some action or set of actions, the extent of progress toward some goal or objective, and the nature of any obstacles that might have impeded such progress).

As soon as survey responses were analyzed in terms of these categories, two things became clear: first, teaching is an intensely active occupation; second, teachers are nevertheless responsible for planning and evaluating most of their own actions. Eleven of the sixteen responsibilities that a majority of teachers perform daily (and all of those they are most likely to perform hourly) are performed in the presence of students. Teachers even plan while they are, literally as well as figuratively, "on their feet." Monitoring student behavior and learning, changing overall instructional plans and individual assignments in light of classroom feedback, and making adjustments to avoid discipline problems are forms of assessment and planning that cannot be separated from "the act" of teaching.

Much of the activity that teachers (and by extension, their students) engage in, in other words, is *nonroutine*. It requires forethought and subsequent assessment. In fact, as one of the most well-known studies of teaching found, the typical classroom teacher makes over 200 substantive pedagogical decisions each class hour, or over three substantive decisions each minute that he or she is in contact with students (Jackson, 1968).

One of the things that makes it difficult to reduce these decisions to predictable routines is that teaching involves a variety of purposes as well as processes, purposes that are often ambiguous and sometimes conflicting (Metz, 1978; McPherson, 1972; Lortie, 1975; Lampert, 1985). But ambiguous or clear, conflicting or not, the sheer *variety* of purposes complicates teachers' relationships with students. Their relationships are not only those of instructor to trainees and mentor to scholars, but manager to subordinates, counselor to clients, craftsperson to material, entertainer to audience, and (sometimes) parent to child and jailer to prisoner, as well. Teachers work over, with, for, and "on" their students, sometimes as individuals and sometimes as a group.

For purposes of analysis, we collapsed these functions into three categories that seemed to encompass most of this variety. Teachers serve as

- *Instructors* (responsible for increasing the academic knowledge, skills, and achievement of students)
- *Counselors* (responsible for identifying and addressing the particular needs and problems of individual students)
- *Supervisors* (organizing and maintaining a physical and interpersonal environment conducive to instruction and counseling)

Again, they must perform most of these functions simultaneously, while classes are in session and students are physically present. In their survey responses, only one-quarter of Tucson's teachers reported that they "counsel individual students" on a daily basis (two-thirds indicated that they do so weekly). But many teachers objected that the wording of our survey item implied that counseling is *confined* to those occasions when a teacher sits down with an individual student and provides "counseling." Teaching, they pointed out, usually occurs in a group setting. Most of a teacher's explicit planning and acting must necessarily focus on his or her objectives for a group of students, generally concentrating on instructional purposes. But a lot of individual counseling occurs within the context of pursuing instructional objectives in that group setting.

One teacher noted in a written comment, "The survey noted counseling in terms of scheduling, coordinating, and conducting meetings with individual students . . . frankly, my job entails continuous, on-the-spot modeling and intensive counseling of students." Another, in a follow-up interview, explained why she could not afford to ignore the special needs of individual students, even if her overall plans were aimed at the group:

> [In most occupations, managers are] supposed to stay as far away from their subordinates' private lives as possible. We don't have that luxury. If a child spends all day shivering because her parents don't have enough money to buy her a sweater, or if she can't see the blackboard because of poor eyesight, or if she's worried sick about whether she's pregnant or not, she isn't going to learn much math. So you spend time sending notes home to parents to collect used sweaters, you keep after parents to get their child glasses, and you make time to talk with the girl who's worried about maybe being pregnant. We take on those roles because we're not going to get any teaching done unless we do.

These observations about the processes and purposes of teaching underscore the importance of an insight that more and more scholars, working from a variety of different perspectives, are using to describe the work of teaching, namely, that *teaching is fundamentally a process of decision making* (Bacharach and Conley, 1988), under circumstances of varying clarity or ambiguity as to means and ends. Mosston (1972, p. 18), for example, calls teaching a "chain of decision-making" and claims that that is the "one statement that is true and universal, and can therefore serve as the base for understanding and description [of the activities of teachers]." Mosston uses the decision-making rubric to analyze how teachers might share (delegate) responsibility for making different decisions with their students. Others have used it to analyze the intensity of the decision-making demands that classroom teaching imposes upon teachers or the effects of their having to make so many decisions in isolation from others (Jackson, 1968; Lortie, 1975).

Hunter (1985) bases her "clinical theory of supervision" on the premise that "the teacher is a decision maker" and argues that "research-based cause-effect relationships" can "tell teachers what to *consider* before deciding what to do" even though "no one can tell teachers what to do" (1985, p. 57). Sergiovanni (1985) takes vigorous exception to Hunter's "mindscape" but stresses the complexity of the decision making that "reflective practitioners" must engage in in the midst of constantly changing, unpredictable situations. Doyle (1985b), summarizing the work of several other scholars, notes that there is growing agreement that "teaching practice is not merely technical and rule driven, and teachers are not simply passive recipients who carry research-based practice to the classrooms. Rather, professional teachers are reflective, that is, they connect knowledge to situations through processes of observation, understanding, analysis, interpretation, and decision making" (p. 12).

These observations allow for the possibility that different teaching situations might let the teacher be more or less certain about the decisions he or she "ought" to make. They indicate, however, that the concept of decision making itself must be central to any description of teaching.

Teachers as Managers

As powerful as the decision maker descriptor is, it does not capture one feature of teaching that is inherent in the distinction between teachers as instructors, counselors, and supervisors. Teachers not only spend most of their time with other people—that is, with students—but they are responsible for organizing, planning, directing, supervising, and evaluating what those people do over extended periods of time.

Overlooked in most debates over whether teachers should be involved in the management of school systems is the fact that teachers are *already* involved in managing what goes on in most school systems in several fundamental respects. In functional terms, they perform virtually all of the functions normally associated with supervisory jobs and many of the functions associated with midlevel management positions:

- Teachers plan and schedule work activities for groups—and adjust the work plans of individuals to fit those group plans—on a daily basis. They develop personal, somewhat more formal work plans, and secure special resources needed to carry out those plans, on a weekly basis.
- Teachers assign work, communicate expectations, observe and take action to keep their "subordinates" on task, adjust group and individual work plans while "work" (that is, class) is in progress, and administer discipline (or refer students to others for discipline) on a daily basis.
- Most teachers review and keep records of their "subordinates'" individual and collective performance, as well as their adherence to organizational policies concerning attendance and conduct, on a daily basis. They are primarily responsible for identifying any special problems that impede their students' academic performance or social development and for seeing that such problems are addressed.

Most observers acknowledge that teachers perform certain management functions vis-à-vis students, but the term "management" is usually associated only with discipline and keeping students under control. The broader scope and intensity of teachers' management responsibilities are typically overlooked. Indeed, they are probably *more* intense than those of managers and supervisors in many other employment settings, in three important respects:

First, teachers must be more directive and take more action with respect to their subordinates than most other managers; second, most teachers have more kinds of relationships with their students than most managers have with their subordinates; and third, their direction of students is subject to little direction or review by their own superiors, either before or after the fact, despite the lack of an established, recognized body of knowledge on how to teach.

Teachers must generally exercise close supervision over their "subordinates," even though—and in part, perhaps, *because*—they do not have many of the advantages of those in more traditional management and supervisory jobs. Personnel authorities would scoff at the notion that a person could effectively manage (much less, closely supervise) the nonroutine work of twenty-five or thirty subordinates, yet teachers are routinely expected to function with such a "span of control." A teacher's students are less likely to have chosen to be where they are, are much less likely to have the option of leaving, are subject to fewer sanctions, and are offered fewer (extrinsic) rewards than the typical employee-subordinate.

Managers in other occupations rarely have to establish rules and procedures, communicate expectations, or build a cohesive work group out of an entirely new group of people all at once; teachers usually have to do so at least once a year, sometimes for several groups at once. In most occupations, employees who are already familiar with their managers' supervisory styles and with established work routines can help socialize newcomers to a work group. Even when a manager in a nonclassroom setting is new to a job, he or she generally inherits a group of subordinates with some sense of cohesion and knowledge of work processes.

Given all these considerations, it is hardly surprising that the group management responsibilities of teaching require such sustained and close attention, or that it is so difficult to draw distinctions between a teacher's personal work plans and his or her plans for a class and for individual students.

Integration

As we distinguished teachers' responsibilities by process (planning, acting, evaluating) and purpose (instruction, counseling, and supervision) and noted the managerial character of what teachers do, it became apparent to us that the essence of the job we were trying to describe does not lie in any one set of duties or even in any one way of characterizing them all. The heart of the job lies in each teacher's responsibility for *integrating* so many different perspectives. The volume and frequency of teachers' responsibilities, their intensely active orientation, their variety of relationships with students, and their relative isolation from administrators, peers, and known methods all serve to illustrate how much school systems rely upon individual teachers to tie together their various responsibilities.

Our first attempt to picture the multidimensionality of teaching was to contrast a "Responsibility Matrix" (see Table 1), which combined the roles that teachers must serve (instruction, counseling, and supervision) with the decision-making functions they typically perform in serving those roles (planning, acting, and evaluating). The matrix format proved helpful for illustrating the interrelationships between roles and functions. It proved even more useful in another way: Having divided teachers' responsibilities into neat, nonlinear categories, we were forced to confront the question of how teachers go about combining all those categories (Bacharach, Conley, and Shedd, 1987). As we did so, it became apparent that the question was among the most pressing (and often most troublesome) for teachers themselves, as many of their written comments on our original survey made clear. Several of our Tucson

Table 1. Teacher Responsibility Matrix.

Decision-Making Roles	Decision-Making Functions		
	Planning	*Acting*	*Evaluation*
Instruction	Instructional planning	Instructional implementation	Instructional evaluation
Counseling	Counseling planning	Counseling implementation	Counseling evaluation
Supervision	Supervisory planning	Supervisory implementation	Supervisory evaluation

respondents indicated that our lists of responsibilities had missed what is, in fact, the most distinctive feature of teaching:

> Teaching is more than the sum of its parts. Coordinating human and material resources as well as the resources of the learner is a task that cannot be broken down to be analyzed.

> The orchestration of teaching is unique. That's the big difference [between teaching and most other occupations.] We have to be masters of a three-ring circus.

> This survey really has little to do with the process of teaching. It deals with a lot of the whats and not many hows.

> The survey over-simplifies the time, acquisition of knowledge, continuous effort expended, and development of expertise, flexibility, "on feet" adjusting of plans and ideas, utilization of prior knowledge, reconstruings of content, and intensity of inter-personal contact with 160 students and the adult faculty and staff.

> The questionnaire states everything neatly. Nowhere does it indicate the level of stress and degree of frustration under which the above are carried out or attempted. Nor does it indicate student attitude, level of endeavor, amount of time spent dealing with behavior problems, lack of effective means to deal with disruptive students, etc. The questionnaire gives me the feeling that all of the duties and responsibilities are carried out in a nice businesslike fashion and problems identified and satisfactory provision made for their solution. [It] does not reflect reality in that the same problems return daily and little progress seems to be made in spite of one's best efforts.

Observers have generated a variety of models that purport to capture the overall character of this integrative process. Some scholars describe teaching in terms of the technical application of what is known about effective teaching to solve classroom problems (Gage, 1972; Slavin, 1984). Most of these scholars define effectiveness in terms of student acquisition of prescribed bodies of information or knowledge, generally measured by scores on some kind of standardized test, and in terms of their adherence to particular instructional practices that have been shown to have a statistically significant effect on such outcome measures.

Not surprisingly, these scholars have been criticized for ignoring teachers' counseling functions and for focusing only on those instructional and supervisory duties that make a direct contribution to a limited category of educational goals. (There is a heated debate whether the same "technical" rules apply when the purpose is the promotion of student creativity or acquisition of higher-order thinking skills.)

Nevertheless, these scholars have made an important contribution to our understanding of teacher decision making. The rules of thumb they have generated almost all focus on what might be called the horizontal integration of teachers' planning, execution, and assessment decisions. Rather than treating lesson planning as a set of isolated decisions, skillful teachers try to anticipate what might occur in the classroom and develop alternative strategies for keeping students focused and on task. Similarly, many of teachers' most important assessment decisions occur not as isolated evaluations of individual students or overall results but as efforts to monitor classroom events and identify when alternative strategies may be needed.

Other scholars tend to highlight the variety of purposes teachers are supposed to serve and the ways in which they provide for vertical integration of these different purposes. Teachers, they point out, are expected to promote equality and excellence, teach specific bodies of subject matter, promote acquisition of learning and social skills, respond to particular students' particular needs, foster independence and creativity, and maintain standards and discipline.

Some scholars characterize the teacher as one who makes

choices between dichotomous alternatives (Metz, 1978). Others cast the teacher as a victim, managing the conflicts generated by conflicting expectations and unpredictable situations but generally unable to do much more than "muddle through" (McPherson, 1972). Still others call the teacher a dilemma manager. The teacher, according to this perspective, may be unable to resolve the contradictory pressures that different goals impose, because the solution to one problem often generates its own problems and compromises other expectations. But he or she can often use the tension between different objectives to produce creative, if only temporary, "solutions." The point, according to this perspective, is to minimize the extent to which any one objective is compromised and to maximize possibilities for making at least some progress toward several objectives at once (Lampert, 1985).

One Tucson teacher illustrated the creative potential in this sort of integration when she told a story to explain the importance of teachers being able to adjust their plans in midstream.

> It's good when you have the self-confidence to switch gears quickly. One day several of the kids in my [junior high school] English class got into a fight. I could have tried to stick with my previous lesson plan, but then I would have had to treat the incident as a major discipline problem and I probably would have lost the class. So I switched gears and started talking about synonyms for the word "fight" and how different words had slightly different meanings, different feelings. We talked about which words best fit different students' feelings about the classroom fight. Sure, I didn't accomplish what I meant to accomplish in that session, but I did a good job. We had a good session on values clarification. And the next day I gave a quiz on synonyms and discovered that the concept had really sunk in.

This teacher was reevaluating her instructional plans and changing them while class was still in session. She was leading a class discussion that had, at least in part, an instructional purpose.

She was also evaluating the situation from the perspective of class-room supervisor: She would "lose" the class if she chose to treat the incident as an occasion for disciplinary action, so she had to generate and then act on a plan that would allow her to reassert personal control over the flow of classroom events. As supervisor and manager, she drew other students into the discussion, thereby avoiding sending the message that being disruptive is the way to receive attention. As counselor, she structured a situation that allowed her to address the needs and concerns of those who were involved in the fight, without neglecting the feelings of those who were not involved: She used the different feelings of different students to help *all* students appreciate the different values involved and to help *each* student clarify his or her own. She took advantage of a situation she did not create and could not have planned for.

In terms of our responsibility matrix, that teacher was planning, acting, and evaluating as instructor, counselor, and classroom supervisor all at once. Like most teachers, she was under constant pressure to find ways of integrating all of her different responsibilities. Rarely, could she or her colleagues afford the luxury of selecting "an" objective or "a" purpose for a particular class session and then planning, acting, and evaluating in the tidy "logical" order that textbooks on decision making might prescribe. She—and by extension, all teachers—must pursue several different objectives at once and find ways of adapting to situations without losing control of them.

Is it more accurate to characterize teachers as technicians, choice makers, victims, or managers of the dilemmas they face? To ask the question is to indicate how limiting each perspective is. Policymakers debate which purposes public schools ought to promote, but teachers are expected to pursue *all* of them. Within the context of these roles, teachers are sometimes required to make unfortunate but necessary choices between contradictory outcomes. Having made such choices (or having had such choices externally prescribed), their work sometimes involves the technical application of recognized strategies or techniques to clearly defined problems, to produce desired outcomes. It sometimes places teachers in hopeless dilemmas where the only choices are burnout or resignation (in either sense of the term—see Bacharach, Bauer, and Conley,

1986). But it often can afford teachers opportunities to creatively manage and occasionally resolve dilemmas as well.

The more responsibilities a person performs, and the more often he or she performs them, the less likely it is that anyone *but* that person can make what are ultimately the most critical decisions about that job: deciding how to allocate time among different responsibilities, deciding when to stop doing one thing and start doing another, deciding when something needs to be done in the first instance, deciding how to achieve many different objectives at once, and deciding what to do when two or more responsibilities appear to make inconsistent or even conflicting demands.

It is the variety of decision-making situations that teachers confront, the variety of criteria they are expected to use to guide their decision making, and the fact that they are responsible for managing groups of young people and not just their own actions that make the orchestration of all their more specific responsibilities so fundamental to the job of teaching. We will consider the kinds of conditions that might enable teachers to fulfill these specific and overarching responsibilities effectively, but first we must set their jobs in a broader context. Education, after all, does not occur in isolated classrooms. It occurs in schools.

Notes

1. Here and throughout, teacher comments identified as "written" were drawn from responses to open-ended questions on the survey of Tucson (Arizona) classroom teachers described in this chapter. Interview comments were drawn from a wide-ranging discussion with a selected group of Tucson teachers, also described in this chapter.

2. The teacher survey asked respondents whether they performed each responsibility (1) hourly or more often, (2) daily, (3) weekly, or (4) monthly or less often. The school level of the respondents answering the question heavily influenced distinctions between hourly and daily responses. That is, elementary school teachers, who typically have all-day responsibility for a particular class, were more likely to report that they had daily responsibility for many duties that junior and senior high

teachers (with several different classes) perform hourly. Since the emphasis here is on features that all or most teachers have in common, we will discuss duties performed hourly or daily as duties performed "daily or more often."

3. Those responsibilities (and the percentages of teachers performing them weekly or more often) are as follows: evaluating district or school plans, programs, and curricula for the purposes of communicating problems and personal recommendations for changes to appropriate officials (19 percent); attending professional meetings, conferences, or training workshops (12 percent); directing and supervising field trips and other out-of-class instructional activities (12 percent); and serving on or chairing committees to develop or revise plans, programs, curricula, or selection of textbooks (11 and 5 percent, respectively).

4. The only significant exceptions to this generalization are that "other teachers" tend to make much heavier use of paraprofessional aides and much less frequent use of published instructional materials than other teachers.

5. The job categories selected were teacher/trainer, employment consultant, public information officer, personnel specialist, manager (professional), manager (nonprofit organization), television news director, budget analyst, accountant, bookkeeper, and stock clerk.

6. Once incomplete interviews were discarded, we had only twenty-five to draw on.

7. On a handful of items, our scoring of teaching might be subject to debate, but as we point out later, only nine of these items proved to be useful in drawing overall comparisons. We are confident that the survey data fully justify the scores we assigned to teaching on those nine items.

3

AUTONOMY AND CONTROL

The work of teachers involves the simultaneous pursuit of many objectives, using uncertain techniques in unpredictable situations. So too does the work of schools. If observers view the relationships between individual teachers and the organizations that employ them from the teacher's point of view, they are apt to find persuasive evidence of teachers' need for flexibility and ready access to the time, information, and other resources that enable them to exercise their discretion effectively.

But if these same observers view the same conditions and relationships from the point of view of administrators or school boards, they are likely to find reasons to restrict teachers' flexibility and to control what they do. The pressures for controlling what teachers do received considerable attention in the early 1980s in the first wave of reform proposals (Bacharach, 1990), but they have been largely ignored in more recent years. The pressures are real, however, and lie just beneath the surface, ready to overwhelm the reformers who neglect them.

School systems are not like some service organizations, where one person provides one product or service to one particular customer or client at one point in time. No one teacher has complete responsibility for providing services to a school system's students. Students acquire an education over twelve or thirteen years of their lifetimes, as they move from classroom to classroom, grade to grade, and building to building. Research on school effectiveness confirms that there must be some coherence and consistency to a school system's educational program—the efforts of individual teachers and the flow of students through the system must be effectively *coordinated*—or else enormous amounts of resources will be wasted, enormous amounts of confusion will be generated, and the likelihood that the system can meet the needs of any of its many constituencies is relatively slim.

The tension between these two demands—discretion and coordination—not only permeates debates over how to reform public education but defines the relationships between teachers and administrators themselves. Failure to resolve this tension, or to produce anything more than a succession of ad hoc, watered-down compromises, leaves reformers, administrators, teachers, and their students tangled in hierarchies that serve no one's interests.

The Need for Discretion

There is no generally accepted yardstick for measuring how much discretion a person has in a job, much less some magic formula for determining how much he or she "ought" to have. Some observers define discretion in terms of formal delegation of authority; others focus on how much independent judgment people are allowed to exercise, with or without authorization.[1]

Most people perform some responsibilities that allow (and require) the exercise of judgment and other responsibilities that basically involve the execution of decisions made by others. Since even the most routine assembly-line job requires the exercise of some judgment over some matters, the distinction is one of both kind and degree. There are four features of teaching, however, that tend to require teachers to exercise more, rather than less, discretion over certain kinds of decisions.

First, *public school systems are accountable to many different constituencies,* each with different expectations and different ways of making them known. Even if a school system does a reasonably good job of defining goals and objectives and establishing priorities among them (a subject we will address in the next section), teachers invariably wind up having to wear several different "hats" at once (Metz, 1978; McPherson, 1972; Chubb and Moe, 1985; Bacharach and Conley, 1988). They therefore need the flexibility to set particular goals and objectives for their day-to-day activities, goals and objectives that serve several different purposes at once.

Second, *teachers are expected to serve as professionals attending to the needs of individual clients.* That role has assumed increasing importance over the past two decades, as more and more school districts have opted for instructional programs that allow individual students to progress at their own pace (Erickson, 1977). Since teachers are the only ones with direct and ongoing contact with students and those students' needs are varied, variable, and sometimes difficult to identify, teachers need flexibility to adapt ends and means that may have been set for large groups of students to the needs of individuals and smaller groups of students.

Third, *the situations teachers face are unpredictable,* largely because they involve intensive and extensive interaction with (and among) students, whose needs and abilities vary widely, are constantly changing, and are often difficult to identify (Lortie, 1975; Jackson, 1968; Bacharach and Conley, 1988). As a consequence, it is difficult to anticipate the resources that teachers will need, particularly for addressing the needs of individual students. Such situations, like those noted above, require flexibility in the selection of both ends and means; they also require flexibility to adjust previously identified ends and means to unforeseen developments and unforeseen resource limitations.

Fourth, *there is no well-established or generally accepted body of practical knowledge* concerning what steps or techniques teachers either should or could use in any given situation. That is partly because teachers must constantly be looking for ways of accomplishing many different purposes at once, partly because the interactive nature of teaching makes it difficult to predict all the possible effects of any given technique in advance, and partly because (until recently) there has been little research addressing the subject.[2] Teachers therefore need the flexibility to select teaching techniques that are most likely to be appropriate in particular situations.

Job design experts and organizational researchers recognize

these different conditions—multiple purposes, work techniques with uncertain consequences, unpredictable situations involving interaction with others, and direct contact with organizational clients or customers with particular needs—as ones that require organizations to give their employees room to exercise discretion and judgment in the planning, execution, and monitoring of their own work (Bacharach, Bamberger, and Mitchell, forthcoming).

Scholars have long recognized that certain kinds of technologies and work processes and certain kinds of raw materials may require an organization to give its employees discretion over how they conduct their work. The key question is how predictable or unpredictable the technologies and raw materials they work with are (Price, 1968; Perrow, 1972; Susman, 1979). Technologies or work processes that are understandable and analyzable can be reduced to a limited number of predictable routines. Such jobs require the exercise of less employee discretion than those that require employees to constantly invent new solutions, or combinations of solutions, to problems that arise in the course of their work. Similarly, raw materials that are of uniform quality and character and that therefore present few unpredictable problems allow organizations to centralize the planning, direction, and routinization of work in ways that are not possible for organizations that deal with raw materials that frequently vary in unpredictable ways. The latter kind of organization must rely more on the discretion and judgment of employees who deal directly with raw materials and who are skilled in recognizing and analyzing the unique potentialities and problems that different materials present.

Technology and raw materials are what might be called factors internal to an organization. Recent scholarship has added a new dimension to our understanding of factors requiring the exercise of discretion, by focusing on what might be termed external factors. Efforts to identify the characteristics of private-sector organizations that are particularly successful have looked at how organizations define the markets they serve and how they adapt their products or services to the needs of customers or clients in those markets (Ouchi, 1981; Peters and Waterman, 1982). Organizations that operate in volatile product markets and that must constantly adapt their products to the unique needs of different clients or customers must rely heavily on the initiative, information, and insights of those employees who have immediate contact with those clients or customers. Organizations that serve such markets must allow such "boundary spanners" more discretion than those organizations with a limited number of standard products that they mass produce for homogeneous markets.

Teachers, of course, are primarily responsible for "doing" the work of a school system and therefore are the employees with the most intimate knowledge of work process problems and the characteristics of "raw materials." They are also the employees with the closest, most sustained contact with the organization's primary clients (its students and their parents) and thus are in the best position to identify the needs that the organization ought to address. The argument for allowing teachers broad discretion is therefore doubly persuasive.

Unlike organizations that enjoy the benefits of product standardization and stable markets, school systems find it difficult to specify standard procedures for producing their "products." They cannot anticipate all (or even most) of the production problems their employees will face and spell out procedures for dealing with each of them. Rarely can their administrators be certain what resources will be needed at each step of the work process. Like other organizations that do not enjoy that predictability, school systems are under heavy pressure to rely upon their individual employees—their teachers—to either make or help make many, if not most, of the important day-to-day decisions affecting their work (Perrow, 1972; Hackman and Oldham, 1980).

The case for guaranteeing teachers flexibility is compelling—compelling, but not (it seems) incontrovertible.

The Case for Coordination

The need to allow teachers discretion and flexibility is only half the picture. The need for coordinating the movement of people and resources within a school system introduces a tension into the relationship between individual teachers and school systems that would go unnoticed if the work of individual teachers existed in a vacuum. Consider, from the point of view of those responsible for coordinating a school system, the conditions we cited earlier as sources of pressure to allow individual teachers flexibility:

1. Multiple constituencies with different goals
2. Pressure to adapt to different students' need and abilities
3. Unpredictable classroom situations
4. Uncertainty about which teaching strategies to use and when to use each of them

Public school systems must be responsive to a variety of interest groups, each with different expectations, different resources that a school system needs, and different ways of making their expectations known. Taxpayers and voters; federal, state, and local governments; court systems; the business community; particular interest groups; parents; and students themselves all have opportunities to make demands upon school systems and offer or withhold different forms of support.

Different outsiders' expectations are generally reflected in different kinds of school system goals, few of which can be dismissed altogether. Sometimes those goals are reflected in the expectation that certain students should receive a particular kind of service, implying, in effect, that a school system should produce a variety of different "products." Other goals pertain to all students, or "students in general," implying that each "product" should meet a variety of different specifications. Some goals treat students themselves as the school system's "clients"; at other times, employers or "society" are the relevant constituencies and students are cast in the roles of workers or raw materials.

This multiplicity of "consumer demands" could be readily handled if a school system were assured that it would have sufficient resources to meet them all. Private-sector organizations can turn away potential customers who are unwilling to meet their costs of producing the products they demand. They are able to do so because the process of meeting consumer demands and the process of securing needed resources occur in a single transaction in the exchange of a product or service for money.

In public education, however, there is almost always some separation between the times and processes that outsiders use to demand particular services of a school district and the times and processes that afford them influence over the financial resources it will receive.[3] The adequacy of most school systems' resources is a constant problem for school managers because of the separation of policymaking and resource acquisition in school districts. The overall level of demand for public school services generally exceeds the supply of services the system can offer, since those who make demands are not necessarily those who must pay for them.[4] One consequence is that new policies or programs are often enacted without adequate consideration of their costs and then are passed on to lower levels of the organization without allocation of the resources needed to effect them.

The same separation of processes generates an opposing set of pressures that can be equally troublesome for boards and administrators. The fact that many outsiders do not think of themselves as recipients of public school services at all but only as taxpayers required to foot the bill means that school managers are always under pressure (sometimes severe, sometimes mild) to make tax reduction and cost-cutting goals in their own right. The tendency for political factions to polarize around different demands—for particular services and for tax reduction—leaves school managers struggling to find "technical" solutions that bridge (or appear to bridge) the two.

The lack of an impersonal market mechanism to mediate these cross-pressures has yet another consequence. Outsiders can make demands on a school system without ever having to talk to those responsible for securing needed financial resources. Virtually everyone in a school system has contact with outsiders, is subject to outside influence, and is in a position to either make commitments that the system will have to meet or to generate outsider complaints that others in the organization must deal with. School systems are so permeable—so exposed to outside influence at every level—that managing, preventing, controlling, and/or dealing with the effects of that permeability almost always represents a basic theme in school administrators' dealings with each other, with outsiders, with board members, and with their teaching staffs (Bacharach and Mitchell, 1981).

Designing and regulating the flow of students and the distribution of resources through such a system would be a challenge even if school managers did not have to make allowances for students' different rates of progress, different choices of direction, and the difficulty of anticipating or identifying obstacles to their progress. The same factors that generate pressure to give teachers wide flexibility also generate pressure on boards and administrators to closely coordinate the efforts of teachers and other members of the system.

Conflicts and Compromises

How do organizations manage these different kinds of cross-pressures? According to Bacharach, Bamberger, and Conley (1990), much of the field of organizational behavior has focused on the tension between two different solutions to the management of variety and uncertainty, one administrative, the other professional (see also Sonnenstuhl and Trice, 1988). The *administrative solution* stresses the need to minimize the impact of uncertainty by controlling how the organization and its individual members respond to different kinds of demands. Deciding how the organization will respond to variety and uncertainty is, from this perspective, a function of managers, who use centralization, specialization, and various reporting mechanisms to maintain accountability and control (Shepherd, 1961; Kornhauser, 1962; Glaser, 1964; Wilensky, 1964; Scott, 1966; Bacharach, Bamberger, and Conley, 1990).

The *professional solution*, in contrast, stresses the organization's need to adapt to different pressures. It maintains that the management of uncertainty should be left to the discretion of trained employees; and it emphasizes the value of innovation, individual autonomy, decentralization, and minimum specialization (see Raelin, 1985; Miller, 1986; Bacharach, Bamberger, and Conley, 1990).

Many (but not all) researchers assume that one solution or the other will come to dominate how particular organizations are managed. Researchers who argue in favor of professional control of the work environment adhere to a "professional-dominant perspective." The appropriate way to address the conflict between professional and administrative values is to adopt a managerial strategy that consistently gives preference to professional over administrative concerns (Shepherd, 1961; Scott, 1966; Katz, 1969; Freidson, 1974). The organizations most widely studied from this perspective are hospitals. The management of a hospital as an organization is guided by norms dictated not by its day-to-day administrators but by its dominant professional group, namely, doctors (Katz, 1969; Freidson, 1974).

Researchers at the other extreme maintain an "administrator-dominant perspective" (Glaser, 1964; Clark, 1966; Benson, 1973; Sorensen and Sorensen, 1974; Organ and Greene, 1981; Guy, 1985; Gross and Etzioni, 1985; Lachman and Aranya, 1986). This group of researchers espouses a managerial strategy that accedes to administrative rather than professional preferences whenever the two come in conflict. Accounting firms have often been examined from this point of view. Studies by Sorensen and Sorensen (1974) and Lachman and Aranya (1986), in particular, point out that, over time, the professional orientation of beginning accountants gradually gives way to an organizational orientation dominated by administrative norms.

While most researchers maintain that there is an inherent tension between professional and administrative perspectives, not all of them believe that one perspective must necessarily predominate. Some adopt an "equilibrium perspective," maintaining that the tension between administrative and professional norms is properly resolved by a managerial strategy that aims for rational and equitable compromises. A stable order results, in which the professional becomes subject to systems of rational rules while the organization becomes more professionalized (Kornhauser, 1962; Wilensky, 1964; Gouldner and Ritti, 1967). Kornhauser's (1962) research on scientific professionals in industrial organizations suggests that compromise is indeed a viable management strategy, at least in some kinds of organizations.

It is this equilibrium perspective that prompts scholars to talk about a *continuum* of management strategies, ranging from administrative to professional domination of the work environment, rather than about two discrete and mutually exclusive approaches. The idea of continuum is important because it raises the possibility that those responsible for managing an organization might *create* responses to uncertain situations, rather than simply choose between two already available alternatives.

But using a single continuum to characterize how an organization might deal with uncertainty can also be misleading. Arranging strategies along a single continuum focuses on differences among approaches, diverting attention from what may be important similarities, even between approaches at opposite ends of the ostensible continuum. Using a single continuum also diverts attention from the different kinds of uncertainty an organization faces and how particular kinds of uncertainty might influence an organization's choice of strategies. Finally, using a single continuum implies that the "best" strategy open to an organization is one that represents a watered-down compromise among competing needs, that it is fruitless to search for a way of serving *all* of them more effectively.

All three of these objections to using the image of a continuum are important when the organization in question is a school system. In school systems, if not in all organizations, what appear to be contradictory pressures—for professional autonomy and administrative control—are actually reflections of the same set of environmental and work process pressures simultaneously working on different levels of the system. The more complex and unpredictable the demands on a school system, the more likely it is that the pressures for *both* teacher discretion *and* overall coordination will mount. The more goals a school system pursues and the more it has to make provision for the heterogeneity of its students' needs, abilities, and rates of progress, the more difficult it will be for administrators *or* individual teachers to anticipate the resource needs of different persons in the system and the more problematic its overall level of resources is likely to be. Compromise strategies that may have provided satisfactory levels of individual flexibility and system coordination in the past may not afford enough of either in the future.

What, then, is the alternative for scholars or practitioners? Any approach to school management, we argue, will reflect certain basic assumptions about the purposes of education, about students, about teaching, and about the resources needed to support a school system.[5] Each will focus attention on some particular issue, or combination of issues, that is thought to be particularly problematic. Each will imply that authority and responsibilities should be distributed among different persons in a school system in a particular way.

If a person happens to agree with an approach's assumptions, its emphasis, and its associated distribution of authority, then he or she is likely to perceive it as a *rational* or *technical* approach to the management of a school district. If a person disagrees with the assumptions, emphasis, or distribution of authority, then he or she is more likely to think of the approach in terms of the *ideological* values it reflects.

For the moment, it does not really matter whether a reader wants to hang a rational/technical or ideological label on the approaches discussed here. (The distinction will become more useful later, when we discuss the possibility that a strategic approach to school management might allow for combinations of different technical approaches.) Here, the important point is that there are different rational/technical/ideological approaches to the management of school districts, and each of them has a different logic that holds all of its different elements together.

The Factory Management Approach. Consider the following set of assumptions:

- The purpose of a public school system is to provide students with training in a common, basic set of academic skills.
- Teaching is a relatively straightforward process. The situations that teachers face can be anticipated, and appropriate behaviors for handling those situations can be specified in advance.
- Except for age differences, students are a relatively homogeneous group. Differences in their needs and abilities within age groups are minimal or irrelevant.

Notice that these three assumptions appear to dispose of three of the four issues we listed earlier as being likely problems in any school system (lack of coherent goals, uncertainty concerning the nature of the teaching process, and differences among students). What remains is the fourth issue: the inadequacy of resources needed to met public expectations.

If that issue is assumed to be the only real problem a school system confronts, the basic function of school managers would be to structure a school system that produces a given quantity and quality of output at the lowest possible cost. Given clear goals, a well-understood instructional process, and a relatively homogeneous group of students to be educated, their job would be to find and implement the least expensive way of combining teachers, groups of students, curricula, time schedules, classroom space, and other instructional resources. The role of teachers (and students) would be to follow instructions.

It is not an accident that this summary sounds like a factory approach to school management. The hierarchical organization of our mass-goods–production industries was originally premised on the assumptions that their overall goals and product outcomes were clearly defined (and measurable), that there was a clearly understood process for producing those outcomes, and that raw materials would not vary in any respect that would make the specification of production procedures or the attainment of desired outcomes problematic. In fact, the belief that school systems can and should be managed like factories gained popularity in the first two decades of this century and was heavily influenced by the popularity of the "scientific management" principles developed in private industry (Callahan, 1962).

It would be a mistake to dismiss this factory model—as many observers do—simply by attacking its assumptions. Clearly, the educational goals of a school system are likely to be less clear, the needs and abilities of its students more varied, and its teaching processes more problematic than the factory model implies. But the real purpose of assumptions in any organizational model is to spell out those conditions that must be controlled in order for the model to work as expected. The factory model frames school management in terms of the *efficient use of school district resources*. It defines other issues—goal clarity, differences among students, and uncertainty concerning the nature of the teaching process—in terms of their likely impact on efficiency, and it dictates that such issues be resolved in ways that promote, rather than detract from, that end.

The concept of efficiency implies providing a given level of service at the lowest possible cost. In theory, an organization can promote efficiency by improving the quality or quantity of output while holding costs constant. In practice, the issue almost always gets reduced to one of minimizing costs. In organizations like school systems, where the organization has little control over the number of students to be educated and where measures of quality vary, the issue of efficiency tends to be defined in terms of providing a *fixed and minimum level of service at the lowest possible cost.* Setting minimal "product specifications" is the easiest way to guarantee that all or most teachers and students can meet them. Doing so is the best way of holding failure rates down, so that the system won't appear to waste its resources (it won't have to discard raw materials) and won't prompt questions concerning the quality of the education it provides. Doing so is also a way of ensuring that people won't question whether a system does enough to address the needs of particular groups of students, or whether teaching itself really is a relatively routine process.

The logic of the factory management approach dictates that managers try to avoid issues that might raise doubts about the basic premises of their approach. It dictates, further, that when they cannot avoid such issues, they must interpret them in terms of their implications for a school system's efficiency.

The Bureaucratic Approach. Press the logic of a particular management approach too far—use it to generate solutions to problems it was not developed to address—and you are likely to wind up with a different kind of organization, demanding a different kind of management. The "scientific management" approach focuses attention on how managers can routinize the work of individual employees, make the most efficient use of time and raw materials, and thereby cheaply produce large quantities of standardized products. Yet one of the direct effects of efforts to apply "scientific management" principles to public education was the development of increasingly complex systems for *adapting to the different needs and abilities of individual students.*

The more school administrators and university researchers pressed the factory management analogy, the more they bumped up against a reality at odds with that approach: The "raw materials" that school systems have to work with (their students) come in all sizes, shapes, and textures, each with properties that react differently to different kinds of treatment. The notion that school systems could produce large quantities of identical products from such different materials, or that they could design a single production process without accounting for those differences, became increasingly suspect.

Proclaiming their intention to make the "most efficient use" of each *student's* resources, school systems began to develop elaborate (and expensive) guidance, testing, tracking, remediation, college preparation, and vocational education programs, as well as highly differentiated curricula for different groups of students: curricula designed to let individual students progress at their own pace and to create junior high schools to channel students from a common elementary school program into one of several differentiated high school programs (Tyack and Hansot, 1982).

Clearly, saving money was *not* the guiding principle of the bureaucracies that developed to administer such school systems. Rather, these new systems were based on a different set of assumptions:

- The purpose of a public school system is to provide students with whatever education and services they need in order to pursue further education or employment once they leave the system, given their individual abilities.
- The public can be expected to provide the money needed to support such educational services, provided a school system can make a rational case for them.
- If different students have different abilities and future career prospects, and different programs are needed to reflect those differences, it is necessary to identify those differences and therefore place particular students in appropriate programs, classes, or levels of a curriculum. Specialized expertise is needed to identify student differences and decide how such services should be designed and delivered, but the delivery processes themselves are well understood. Those processes can therefore be reduced to established diagnostic and delivery routines that all teachers can readily follow.

With the problems of goals, resources, and teaching processes thus "disposed of," and all defined in terms of how the system might be designed to reflect the heterogeneity of its students, a different conception emerges of how authority and responsibility ought to be distributed. Administrators and staff experts would be responsible for identifying and documenting the need for particular educational services, for determining their costs, and for translating service decisions (once board approval has been secured) into procedures for placement of students and delivery of services. Individual teachers would be responsible for adhering to established policies and procedures and making appropriate use of the resources they were given.

Like the factory management approach, this bureaucratic approach assumes that teachers' responsibilities will be defined in terms of *how* they are to carry out their work and *what* they are supposed to do. Pushed to an extreme, the logic of such an ideology could be used (and sometimes is used) to justify policies and procedures that are every bit as prescriptive as the individual instructions dictated by a factory management approach.

But the bureaucratic approach does not really presume that such tight specification is necessary, appropriate, or even possible (Bacharach and Mitchell, 1986). With its emphasis on tailoring whole programs to groups of students—and its deemphasis of cost considerations—the key question becomes how much specification is needed to guarantee that students are placed in appropriate channels and moved at appropriate speeds through the system as a whole. The notion that teachers might exercise some discretion and judgment *within* those limits is entirely consistent with a bureaucratic ideology.

In fact, in such bureaucratic systems, teachers make some of the most sensitive decisions, such as placement and movement of students along different curriculum paths. More generally, when school or district policies do not address specific classroom situations (always a possibility when they have been designed for application in the whole school or in the whole district), teachers are responsible for exercising discretion and judgment in deciding how to handle them. Such decisions should always be made, however, within the framework of school and district policies and programs.

The bureaucratic approach assumes that staff or outside curriculum experts know (or can determine) what students in any particular program ought to learn and that they will specify minimum achievement expectations for any program they develop. The expectation, however, is that each student will be allowed and helped to make as much progress as his or her individual abilities permit. Since different students will make different kinds and amounts of progress, the central issue, on which all others are likely to turn, will be *equitable distribution of educational opportunities*, not outcomes.

Because the district's professional employees are the only ones with sufficient expertise to make judgments about students' academic abilities and how best to address them, lay boards and outsiders are not in a position to judge the relative success or failure of their efforts in technical terms. Student performance on standardized tests, college admission rates, job placement rates, and dropout rates might be used as indicators of whether the system is properly serving its students' interests. In practice, however, programs for students with particular needs or abilities, and policies or procedures to guarantee that students in similar situations are treated equally, become ends in themselves. In a bureaucracy, definitions of "success" turn on whether the system can maintain its reputation for responsiveness, consistency, expertise, and competence, on whether their systems run smoothly without apparent disruptions, and on whether their policy recommendations win board approval.

The Craft Workshop Approach. Despite many differences, factory management and bureaucratic approaches both assume that it is relatively easy to measure the performance and progress of individual students, that teaching is a relatively well-understood process, and that it is therefore possible for school managers to tell teachers how they should measure progress and teach their students. Those assumptions may be more tenable in some districts than in others, but they are always subject to challenge.

Most teachers—and many administrators—maintain that it is not possible for those without direct and ongoing contact with students to specify *how* a teacher ought to teach in any given situation. Instead, they argue that school systems should define teachers' responsibilities in terms of expected outcomes and allow them what some organizational scholars call "operational autonomy"[6] to plan, adjust, execute, and evaluate their work with students according to their own judgment.

Those who characterize teaching as a craft typically acknowledge that students' needs and abilities vary (Bacharach and Conley, 1988). Indeed, they cite the variety of needs and abilities as one reason why no single pedagogical approach is likely to be effective under all circumstances. They cite the difficulty of identifying such differences ahead of time as one reason teachers must have the discretion to adjust their classroom approaches to the unique and unpredictable situations that arise in the course of instructing students and managing a classroom.

The more teaching is perceived as a craft, however, the more likely it is that students will be assumed to be sufficiently homogeneous to justify their placement in classes and curricula that are *not* tailored for those with particular needs or abilities (Bacharach and Conley, 1988). Heterogeneity of students' needs and abilities is a manageable problem, according to this line of thinking, provided teachers are allowed sufficient discretion to adjust their teaching to take those differences into account.

The key decision maker under such a system would be the individual teacher. Boards and administrators would specify the outcomes they expect individual teachers to achieve and then play essentially supportive roles, relieving teachers of custodial responsibilities, insulating them from parental and other outside interference, handling student discipline problems, and securing and distributing needed resources.

As in other craft settings, where workers themselves are presumed to know as much (if not more) about the work process as their employers, and where each situation is likely to be sufficiently unique to preclude routinization, system managers would coordinate the activities of teachers-as-craftspersons through the specification of expected outcomes and the allocation of resources. In theory, the goals expected of teachers would guarantee a rational division of responsibilities and a rigorous educational program for students who pass from one teacher's classroom to another's. In practice, the program's rigor is likely to vary, depending upon how homogeneous students really are and how adequate are the resources made available to each teacher. The more varied the one or inadequate the other, the less ambitious each teacher's assigned goals are likely to be. But resources and heterogeneity are not likely to pose too many serious problems, or else the craft metaphor would not have been adopted to begin with. Thus, the craft model is most often associated with the pursuit of some relatively coherent, singular (some would say narrow) notion of excellence, rather than with the pursuit of either efficiency or equity.

Tacit Deals and Tangled Hierarchies

Most school systems are not the tightly controlled organizations that many policymakers and managers would like them to be, but neither are they the collections of autonomous craftspersons that many teachers would prefer them to be. As organizations go, they are remarkably complex combinations of "loose" and "tight" elements (Bacharach and Mitchell, 1986). Individual teachers are isolated or insulated (depending upon one's point of view) from direct contact with administrators and each other, with what (at first glance) seems to be extraordinary freedom to decide what they and their students will do. Yet these teachers are also tightly constrained by curriculum policies, student assignments, and resource limitations that are all beyond their control.

The physical structures, staffing patterns, and time schedules of most school systems make it virtually impossible for building principals to provide close supervision of individual teachers, and the same features prevent teachers from communicating and coordinating their activities with each other (Lortie, 1975; Jackson, 1968). Teachers and administrators generally respect each other's "zones of influence," teachers deferring to administrators' decisions concerning matters outside or transcending classrooms and administrators deferring to teachers' professional autonomy within the classroom (Kunz and Hoy, 1976; Little, 1982a).

Although formal models of education have drawn parallels between schools and tightly knit bureaucracies or smoothly running factories (Callahan, 1962; Tyack and Hansot, 1982), most studies confirm that the working relationships among adults in most school systems are actually extraordinarily loose (or loosely coupled) Weick, 1976; Shedd and Malanowski, 1985; Bacharach and

Mitchell, 1986). As two researchers who have studied the failure of ambitious federal programs to reform whole school systems have noted: "A school district is not a single, centrally directed, coherent system that can, upon decision, change direction. It consists of many units and individuals with different needs, interests, and opinions. And the work of central administrators, principals, and teachers is only weakly interdependent—they by no means all pull together."[7]

One recent study of teachers' working conditions, conducted by the authors, reinforces this conclusion.[8] We found, for example, that many teachers and administrators talk with each other infrequently, and that when they do talk, they are most likely to discuss ad hoc problems (like student discipline and parental complaints) rather than goals and objectives, teaching approaches, curriculum policies, subject matter knowledge, or anything else related to the teacher's instructional efforts (Bacharach, Bauer, and Shedd, 1986).

If relationships between teachers and administrators are so loose, how is it that teachers and reform panels so frequently complain about "top-heavy" bureaucracy? One explanation may be that when school policymakers do address the need to coordinate their teachers' separate efforts and provide for a smooth flow of students through their systems, they almost invariably choose to issue general policies and procedures (applicable to all teachers in roughly comparable situations) to address the needs for coordination, rather than communicating specific instructions or assignments to particular teachers. Indeed, many teacher responsibilities are defined and communicated as *student* policies that teachers are expected to interpret and apply (for example, discipline codes and promotion requirements). These general policies and procedures (often issued by district rather than school officials) have the double effect of imposing constraints on teachers' day-to-day decision making and reducing their expectation of receiving substantive direction from real people (that is, their building administrators). This increases teachers' perceptions of an impersonal, unrealistic bureaucracy and isolation from immediate supervisors and peers (Lortie, 1975).

Focusing on how teachers' responsibilities are defined and communicated highlights similarities and differences among the factory management, bureaucratic, and craft workshop models we presented in the previous section and indicates where we might look for yet another model.

There are two basic ways in which a school system (or any organization) can define the responsibilities of its employees. They can define them in terms of the *specific tasks or procedures* people are expected to follow in performing their work (that is, in terms of *how* people are expected to perform). They can define them in terms of the *objectives or outcomes* employees or work groups are expected to achieve (that is, in terms of ends). When tasks or procedures are specified for teachers, the goals or objectives of their activities are implicit in whatever instructions they have been given. When responsibilities are defined in terms of objectives or outcomes, the implied message is that the teacher is expected to either know or figure out how to achieve them. Therefore, teachers tend to have more flexibility when their responsibilities are defined in terms of expected outcomes or objectives, rather than tasks or procedures.

Particular responsibilities might be communicated to individual employees in two different ways: They can be communicated *directly* to the individual as particular instructions or assignments, usually by his or her immediate supervisor, or they can be communicated *indirectly* through organizational policies or procedures that the individual—and others in his or her position—are expected to follow.

Responsibilities can be communicated directly by giving particular teachers special instructions or assignments or by giving them evaluative feedback that tells them what they will be expected to do or accomplish in the future. Responsibilities can be communicated indirectly through any number of general policies and procedures, such as those governing the following:

- Curriculum and textbook selection
- Student placement and ability grouping
- Securing special help for students with special needs
- Grading students and communicating grades to parents
- Student conduct and discipline

- Standardized testing (that is, how student progress will be measured)
- Requisitioning equipment and supplies
- School calendars and class schedules

Although either way of communicating responsibilities might be used to impose restrictions on a teacher's flexibility, indirect communication, through policies and procedures, tends to allow (and require) the exercise of more discretion and judgment than direct communication.

Although general policies and procedures are often designed to promote uniformity and coordination among teachers, they are often an indirect way of acknowledging that only a certain general level of uniformity or coordination can be expected. When more than one teacher is to follow policies or procedures, each is likely to have to exercise some judgment and discretion in deciding when and how to apply them. When policies and procedures refer specifically to what students are expected to do or accomplish, individual teachers have to infer many of their specific responsibilities from policies or procedures that may or may not have a clear application to the specific situations they face. In fact, making those inferences is itself a responsibility that most teachers are expected to perform.

Responsibilities must be both defined and communicated. Tasks or step-by-step instructions can be communicated either directly to individuals or indirectly through general policies or procedures that apply to more than one person. Expected outcomes or objectives can also be communicated either directly or indirectly. Either way of defining responsibilities, therefore, might be communicated either directly or indirectly, producing the four combinations illustrated in Table 2.

Most school districts confine their use of individual instructions to responsibilities performed outside the classroom (Lortie, 1975; Kunz and Hoy, 1976). School systems or individual administrators that do try to dictate step-by-step classroom instructions for individual teachers—through close monitoring of individual lesson plans or highly directive performance evaluations, for example—are those that most clearly reject the notion that teachers are and ought to be active decision makers.

Table 2. Ways of Defining and Communicating Responsibilities.

Ways of Defining Responsibilities	Communicating Responsibilities	
	Directly	Indirectly
Tasks/Procedures	Individual instructions	General policies and procedures
Objectives/ Outcomes	Individual outcomes	Organizational goals and objectives

Most districts, however, reserve their high-constraint policies for areas of teacher responsibility that are most likely to generate parental complaints. In many cases, even these formal policies communicate responsibilities only indirectly, by indicating what teachers are *not* permitted to do. Otherwise, most districts tend to use some combination of general procedures and individual objectives to define and communicate their teachers' classroom and instructional responsibilities (the upper right and lower left cells of Table 2).

The amount of flexibility that teachers are likely to enjoy under any of these arrangements will depend not only on how responsibilities are defined and communicated but also on whether or not system managers actually pay attention to what teachers do. Many school districts, for example, specify general procedures that teachers are expected to observe and then simply leave their teachers alone, providing supervision only when some problem arises that a teacher cannot deal with alone. In other districts, the same kinds of general procedures may justify constant supervision and second-guessing of decisions that teachers have made. In still other settings, what appear to be close supervisory techniques are only loosely employed. One Tucson respondent, for example, reported:

> In one school I was in, all teachers had to give the assistant principal their lesson plans for the following week on Fridays. If someone was going to give real feedback on the plans, teachers probably wouldn't mind; some of them would really appreciate it. But you know no one's going to spend their weekends

reading lesson plans. They just make you fill them out
to make you think you're being watched. One teacher,
every week, wrote in in the middle of each lesson plan,
"I'll buy you a steak dinner if you actually read this,"
and no one ever said anything to him.

Each of the three models that we have discussed so far fits one
of the cells of our matrix (Table 2). Fitting the three models into
the cells of Table 2 gives us Table 3. The principles of scientific
management that guided the organization of mass-production factories (at least in the first few decades of this century) required a
careful delineation of the tasks and procedures each worker was to
follow.[9] The use of impersonal general policies, procedures, and
routines to govern the decision making of individuals, and thereby
restrict the scope of individual supervisors' influence, is a classic
feature of bureaucracy (Weber, 1947). The specification of outcomes, rather than tasks, to communicate expectations to individual
craftspersons is a basic element in the relationship between contrac-
tor and craft worker.

Of these three models, school systems probably most often
resemble bureaucracies, simply because the bureaucratic model
comes closest to accommodating the twin needs (individual discretion and coordination of collective efforts) that are essential to the
operation of school systems (Bacharach and Conley, 1988). Given
the fixed salaries, laws protecting jobs, and impersonal rules that
structure relationships and afford employees some discretion in a
bureaucracy, it is probably much more accurate to characterize bu-

Table 3. Models of School Systems.

Ways of Defining Responsibilities	Communicating Responsibilities	
	Directly	*Indirectly*
Tasks/Procedures	Schools as factories, teachers as laborers (or foremen)	Schools as bureau-cracies, teachers as technicians
Objectives/ Outcomes	Schools as work-shops, teachers as craftspersons	Schools as learning workplaces, teachers as professionals

reaucracy as the midpoint between the extremes represented by the two other models, rather than as the oppressive (or inflexible) alternative that the term "bureaucracy" often implies. Those who denounce bureaucracy and demand a new balance between flexibility and control are often surprised to find themselves reinventing the bureaucratic forms that they thought they were overcoming.

Yet grounds for dissatisfaction certainly exist. Research on schools as organizations provides ample evidence of the apathy, passivity, minimal expectations, avoidance of responsibility, lack of innovation, and (what is most troublesome) impersonal treatment of students/clients that are typically associated with bureaucracies (Anderson, 1968; McNeil, 1986; Goodlad, 1983; Sizer, 1984). Research on school effectiveness leaves little reason to doubt that lack of certainty or coherent purpose causes serious weaknesses in many schools' educational programs (Rosenholtz, 1985; Purkey and Smith, 1983; Wynne, 1981).

It is not only understandable but appropriate, then, that many efforts to reform public education are designed to provide closer coordination of teachers' separate activities. But as Corcoran (1987) points out, until quite recently most school reformers have assumed that coordination necessarily requires the kinds of closely held controls popularized in the traditional bureaucratic and factory models of schools. Increased individual discretion, in turn, has been equated with being freed from such controls.

Must teachers and school officials resign themselves to constant tugs-of-war and periodic compromises between teachers' needs for discretion and administrators' needs for coordination? In one sense, the answer is probably yes: There is bound to be tension between the two sets of needs, if only because teachers and administrators each tend to perceive one set of needs more clearly than the other and must constantly remind each other of their different perspectives. In some cases, compromise is probably all that one can expect to result from such interactions.

If all that is expected from school systems is "satisfactory" performance, the persistence of competing models of the way that schools ought to be managed might actually provide room for higher levels of performance than we would otherwise have reason to expect. Believing that they *ought* to be treated as autonomous professionals, teachers probably exercise more initiative and are more responsive to the needs of their individual students than they would if they thoroughly accepted the bureaucratic logic of their administrative superiors. They are almost certainly willing to accept with relative equanimity the administrative constraints—and thus, the coordination—that they experience, in part because they see their willingness to do so as the price they must pay for otherwise being left to do what they think is appropriate.

Where paradigms differ, the tensions between them can often be eased by tacit, day-to-day bargains. In fact, the periodic recognition and temporary reduction of such tensions may serve as some of the most effective coupling mechanisms possible in an otherwise loosely coupled organization like a school system. In a sense, the ad hoc adjustments and minor skirmishes that characterize day-to-day life in many school systems take the place of more rational planning and priority-setting processes, which presuppose more goal consensus, more predictable situations, more control over resources, and more knowledge of cause-effect relationships than the typical school environment allows.

But there is a fourth cell to our matrix that we have yet to consider. This characterizes schools as organizations in which responsibilities are defined primarily in terms of objectives or outcomes, rather than as tasks and procedures, but in which organizational goals and objectives are the focus of attention. Might such a goal-oriented formula provide an alternative that avoids the weaknesses of other approaches? If so, why has it been so long overlooked?

The rest of this book addresses these questions and considers what kind of organization and people might fit within the fourth cell of our matrix. The model that emerges is similar in some respects to a bureaucracy and in other respects to a crafts workshop setting. (It even has some features in common with a factory!) But it is different from all three in one fundamental respect. It challenges what has probably been the most basic structural feature of American public education for most of this century—the division of labor that assigns individual teachers responsibility for decisions within the classroom and administrators responsibility for coordination among classrooms. To begin, let us go back to the classroom and the work of individual teachers. Because teachers are responsible for the basic work in schools, their jobs ought to be the basis of a new reform order. The next chapter considers how the job of teacher should be restructured so that it is consistent with the above challenge.

Notes

1. Elliot Jaques (1964) suggests that amount of discretion can be measured for any particular responsibility or job by determining the amount of time it takes for an employer to catch and correct any mistakes in an employee's performance (what he labels "the time-span of discretion"). His method is useful for sensitizing observers to the "real" or effective discretion allowed employees, as opposed to just the formal discretion reflected in explicit delegations of authority. It also indicates the importance of after-the-fact monitoring and feedback mechanisms.

2. Lortie (1975) emphasizes this point. For a discussion of why recent research on teaching effectiveness is not likely to provide a definitive knowledge base for the practice of teaching, see Shedd, Malanowski, and Conley (1985), especially pages 35–46.

3. There are a handful of exceptions to these generalizations, such as public budget or bond referenda and categorical grants from federal or state governments.

4. On the surface, this line of argument might seem to suggest that some "market mechanism" like tuition tax credits should be introduced into public school decision making. In fact, such a mechanism would *aggravate* the problem noted here. Pricing mechanisms can serve to balance supply and demand pressures only if the seller can turn away customers that are unwilling to pay the seller's price and restrict its sales to those who are willing to pay that price. *The seller must be just as free to reject customers as customers are to reject a seller.* Tuition tax credits would leave public school systems with those parents and children who have the least personal ability to pay and would undermine the incentive for more affluent groups to support public education.

5. The distinctions drawn in this section closely parallel those

drawn by Anglin (1979). Anglin argues that four types of school systems can be distinguished using two criteria: whether students are assumed to be homogeneous or heterogeneous, and whether the instructional process is assumed to be well or poorly understood. Our own analysis adds two further criteria and focuses on issues that his overlooks, but the four resulting categories are essentially the same.

6. For discussion of the concept of "operational autonomy," see Bailyn (1985). For discussions that contrast this approach with others in educational terms, see Anglin (1979) and Schlechty and Joslin (1984). For detailed and articulate statements of the need to treat teachers as autonomous professionals (not explicitly stated, however, in terms of the *management* of a school system), see Adler (1983) and Sizer and Koermer (1983).

7. Cowden and Cohen (1979), quoted by Ravitch (1983), pp. 260–261.

8. Survey reported in National Education Association (1988). The authors and their colleagues designed the survey in 1985, in association with Frank Masters, director of the National Education Association Research Division, to explore many of the environmental issues raised in our earlier work in Tucson. The basic premise of the survey was that teachers, like other professionals, have a personal stake in doing well in the classroom and are therefore likely to be most sensitive to those working conditions that enable or prevent them from performing effectively. In political terms, the purpose was to help the NEA redefine the concept of "working conditions" to bring it closer to the professional concerns of the NEA's members.

    The so-called CART survey was mailed to a nationwide, representative, and randomly selected sample of 2,530 NEA teacher members. A total of 1,789 completed surveys were returned, for a response rate of 71 percent. CART is believed to be the most comprehensive survey of teacher working conditions, based on the largest and most representative sample of American teachers, to date. If there is any bias in drawing a sample from NEA's 1.8 million name membership list, it is that the NEA is not heavily represented in the nation's largest urban school districts. Not surprisingly, a recent study of working conditions in seven metropolitan school systems suggests that the working conditions in such systems are significantly more onerous than those reflected in the CART data, but that the same kinds of conditions—those that affect teachers' ability to be effective—are important to all teachers. See Corcoran, Walker, and White (1988).

The CART data reported in this chapter are offered to illustrate points and develop hypotheses, rather than to prove points or confirm hypotheses.

9. For our purposes, the factory metaphor falls within the upper left cell, whether teachers are considered assembly-line workers (and their students raw materials) or foremen (and their students line employees). Frederick Taylor, who first formulated the principles of scientific management, assigned the planning of work to staff experts, not first-line supervisors. Indeed, spelling out the details of each worker's duties, after careful "scientific" analysis, was held to be a check on the arbitrary power of foremen.

4

RESTRUCTURING
THE JOB OF TEACHING

Recently there has been a lot of talk about the quality and motivation of teachers, but very little of that talk has involved detailed consideration of the actual work that teachers do on a day-to-day basis. Until we clearly understand (and achieve a consensus about) the job of teaching, simplistic arguments like "better pay for better teachers" miss the point. This chapter follows up on Chapter Two's discussion of the individual work of teachers by discussing the way that the job of teaching can be structured better.

How does the job of teaching affect a person's motivation and ability to teach? Do different ways of structuring the responsibilities of teachers make the job easy or difficult or even impossible to learn? How much does one teacher have to depend upon other people to do his or her job? Is it possible to provide individual teachers with the "space" they need to develop and exercise independent judgment and still hold them accountable for the decisions they make? These are the questions we will address in this chapter, as we consider how the job of the individual teacher reflects the tension between discretion and coordination.

Motivation and Jobs

There are many reasons to believe that the people one finds in any particular kind of job are likely to have needs or preferences that can be satisfied by that job (Bacharach and Mitchell, forthcoming). People tend to gravitate toward jobs that are likely to satisfy their needs (Dyer, Schwab, and Fossum, 1978; Holland, 1973). Organizations reinforce these tendencies by using their recruitment and screening procedures to seek out job candidates whose interests and needs seem to fit the jobs to be filled (Heneman, Schwab, Fossum, and Dyer, 1980). Workers who discover that their needs cannot be satisfied by particular jobs are more likely to leave those jobs. When they do, they leave behind those whose needs the job *is* able to satisfy (Chapman and Hutcheson, 1982).

Some studies suggest that people even change their perceptions of their own needs based on characteristics of their jobs. A job might "activate" certain needs. For example, if people have to work closely together and coordinate their activities, the need to maintain amicable social relationships might assume special importance: Work seems to go well (that is, is experienced as pleasurable) when such relationships are attended to and poorly when they are not. There is a substantial body of social-psychological research that points to the importance of such activation mechanisms in the workplace (McClelland, 1951; Kornhauser, 1965).

Some researchers suggest that what we refer to as "needs" may not be psychological characteristics of the individual at all, but instead they are concepts that individuals invent to provide positive explanations for doing things they probably would have to do anyway. Thus, in the previous example, employees might convince themselves that they have a "need" to maintain amicable social relationships, rather than believe that they do so to keep the boss happy. Salancik and Pfeffer (1977) argue that need-satisfaction models that assume that individuals react to their surroundings in terms of relatively fixed, unchanging needs "den[y] persons the creative capacity to cope with their environment, in part, by constructing meaning that makes the context more satisfying, and, in part, by redefining the situation and attending to selected aspects of the situation" (p. 440).

As diverse as these scenarios may seem, they all suggest that the sources of satisfaction and motivation in the workplace are not necessarily a function of different needs, randomly distributed among workers, nor a function of universal "satisfiers" and "dissatisfiers'' that all workers share in common.[1] Some kinds of jobs may actually *generate* the motivation to perform well. If that is so, then the question of how teachers (or any employees) are motivated cannot be separated from the question of what kinds of work they perform.

In a now classic study, Hackman and Lawler (1971) decided to test this line of reasoning, using an approach first suggested by Turner and Lawrence (1965). They studied employees of a phone company to determine the relationships between particular job characteristics and employee work attitudes and behavior. They hypothesized that if certain jobs are to provide intrinsic motivation, they have to (1) be sufficiently complex to require the worker to use a variety of skills, (2) provide feedback so that the worker can actually know whether he or she has been effective, (3) provide sufficient autonomy for the worker to feel personally responsible for the outcomes he or she produces, (4) provide a whole and identifiable piece of work (what they called a "task identity") so the worker can see a beginning and end to his or her efforts and can recognize the impact. In subsequent discussions, Hackman, Lawler, and their colleagues add a fifth factor, "task significance," to their model (Hackman and Oldham, 1980). This addition is valuable for some purposes, but we have not found it particularly useful for analyzing sources of variation in the teacher's work environment. Thus, we have chosen to use the original, simpler version of their model here.

Hackman and Lawler found support for all of these hypotheses. They discovered that workers whose jobs were high on these dimensions reported having higher intrinsic motivation—performing well was itself a source of satisfaction and performing poorly a source of dissatisfaction—while those whose jobs were low in these core dimensions tended to be indifferent about the quality of their own efforts. Hackman and Lawler also found that supervisors tended to give higher performance ratings to employees whose jobs were high on the core dimensions of autonomy and variety.[2]

Again, it is not clear whether or not these job characteristics motivate all workers to do well or are likely to influence only those who *want* variety, autonomy, and challenge in their work.[3] But given the selection, self-selection, and weeding-out mechanisms noted earlier, it probably doesn't matter for our purposes here. A number of subsequent studies have confirmed that jobs with Hackman and Lawler's four key dimensions do have inherent motivation potential, and that those who hold such jobs tend to be recognized as effective performers (Hackman and Oldham, 1980).

How does teaching fare when measured against Hackman and Lawler's four key factors? The data on teaching and the teaching environment presented in earlier chapters indicate that teaching potentially meets all four motivational job characteristics: the required use of a variety of skills, immediate feedback, felt responsibility for outcomes, and an identifiable whole piece of work. But none of these conditions holds consistently or completely in education. *How individual schools and districts structure their teachers' jobs can make a difference.*

The rest of this chapter uses Hackman and Lawler's framework to analyze the structure of teaching and how it affects teachers' performance.[4] The first section addresses skill variety and feedback, the second autonomous outcomes and "task identity," the third the integration of all four.

In discussing skill variety and feedback, we will focus on the individual teacher's job, without paying much attention to what other teachers, administrators, or staff persons do. The key question in this section is whether the motivation to do well automatically translates into a desire to *improve* one's skills and performance.

Autonomy and task identity, by contrast, prompt consideration of how each teacher's efforts fit together with those of others. The question that we will address in this section is a variation on one we posed in an earlier chapter: How can school systems strengthen their teachers' sense of autonomy and "task identity," and still coordinate their separate efforts?

The final section addresses the issue of teacher evaluation, to illustrate the tension between formative processes designed to help teachers improve their decision making and summative processes designed to hold teachers accountable for the decisions they make.

Variety and Feedback: Growth or Stagnation?

In Chapter Two, we noted that teachers are responsible for making decisions, managing groups of people, and integrating the

various cross-pressures that these two sets of responsibilities generate. What kinds of skills does such a job require? How do teachers
acquire them? *Do* they necessarily acquire them, or do some teachers
somehow get by without completely mastering the demands of their
job? If some teachers do get by, what factors either allow or compel
them to do so and how might such conditions be overcome?

Most efforts to answer the first question (what sorts of skills
teachers need) fall into one of two categories: discussions of the skills
or behaviors that have been identified by researchers as constituting
"effective teaching practices" and discussions that refer to the "art"
of teaching, "intuition," "knowing more than I can say," "tacit
knowing," "thinking on your feet," "keeping your wits about you,"
"developing a feel for a situation," or recognizing when something
does or does not "fit" or "feel right." The first perspective, standing
alone, implies that teaching is a relatively straightforward process of
applying well-established technical principles to particular situations; the second, by itself, implies that teaching is an intuitive,
potentially creative but essentially unanalyzable process.

One of the most important developments in the study of how
professionals make decisions is the discovery of relationships between such seemingly incompatible bodies of knowledge (Schon,
1983). Technically rational models that characterize professional
decision making as the "application of established knowledge and
techniques to recurrent events" are increasingly being recognized as
inadequate, even in such well-established professions as medicine
and law (Schon, 1983). But models that imply that professionals use
nothing but artistry, intuition, and seat-of-the-pants decision making are just as inaccurate. The skillful practitioner is now being
recognized as one who is capable of using established theories and
knowledge of demonstrated apparent cause-effect relationships as
tools for analyzing the unique situations presented in most real-life
settings. Put simply, there is a lot of science and technique in the
professional's craft (Gage, 1972).

This line of scholarship is breaking down some of the supposed distinctions between theoretical knowledge generated by research and practical knowledge gained from experience. Schon's
(1983) analyses of the decision-making processes employed by "reflective practitioners" indicate that both kinds of knowledge serve

some of the same purposes. Both provide advance signals that allow practitioners to anticipate the effects of different courses of action. They provide opportunities to reflect on which course or courses of action to choose, without having to conduct all of their mental experiments on real patients, clients—or students.

Perhaps the most obvious way in which these different kinds of technical knowledge can benefit the real-life practitioner is by providing *alternatives for action,* depending upon the specific situations encountered in practice. A person cannot be said to actually decide upon a course of action if he or she has only one approach to choose from. These alternatives might be provided by different theories, by repertoires of specific techniques, or by some combination of the two.

To the extent that alternative theories are available to the practitioner to explain different situations—or to analyze similar situations from the vantage point of different goals or objectives—practitioners who have ready access to such theories can employ them as devices for considering the possible consequences of alternative actions. With the exception of recent research on selected aspects of teaching practice, such as "signal systems" in classrooms (Kounin and Gump, 1984) and the relationships between "academic work" and "activity management" (Doyle and Carter, 1984), there is relatively little theory directly tailored to teaching practice. Nevertheless, more general theories drawn from fields like development psychology and social psychology do provide practitioners with possible alternative frames of reference for analyzing teaching and learning situations.

What teachers tend to rely upon more heavily, however, are repertoires of specific techniques that serve the same general function as theoretical propositions: They provide choices for the practitioner, not only to use but to structure his or her consideration of alternative courses of action (Nemser, 1983). The skillful practitioner is one who has such alternatives seemingly at his or her fingertips, enabling considered choices of action. Some of the so-called "effective teaching practices" represent characterizations of just these sorts of quasi-theories.

Adherence to a *single* model of what ought to be happening in the classroom can only serve to tell the teacher when something

may be going wrong; having *several* models at one's fingertips—
whether they be formal theories, lists of principles, or simply
alternative techniques—allows the teacher to engage in what Shulman and Carey (1984) call "pedogogical triangulation," planning
and evaluating while still implementing decisions, and thereby pac-
ing themselves and their students' activities most effectively.

Shulman and Carey (1984), Doyle (1985), Nemser (1983), and
even Hunter (1985) point out that if established knowledge of apparent cause-effect relationships is treated as a rigid body of "rules
to follow" in practice, it can limit creativity and discourage the
development of a teacher's own problem-solving abilities. The
teacher who has only a limited repertoire of practical techniques to
draw upon is likely to be just as ineffective as one who is dogmat-
ically wedded to a single theoretical model of how to teach. Both
are likely to have difficulty adapting to specific and unanticipated
classroom situations.

Knowledge, whether theoretical or practical, can be used
either *prescriptively* or *proscriptively*. That is, it can be used as a
guide map of what to do, or as a map of things or places to avoid.
Most formal theories and many attempts to document the practical
lessons of professional practice are presented prescriptively, that is,
as if they were cookbook-style guides to action. But established
knowledge about cause-effect relationships often proves more helpful when used proscriptively. That is, it is often more useful for
anticipating and (if possible) avoiding the adverse consequences of
possible courses of action. Planning activities that appear illogical
based on "pure" decision-making models are quite logical when
viewed from this perspective. Take, for example, the practice that
many teachers use of first considering possible learning activities
and then establishing goals for a class session based on the activities
considered (Mintz, 1979; McCutcheon, 1980; Clark and Yinger,
1979). Thinking may appear fuzzy and intuitive when decision
making is defined solely in terms of choosing the "right" course of
action to achieve a particular objective. The same thinking can be
quite sophisticated and skillful when defined in terms of evaluating
the appropriate *boundaries* to action (that is, choosing a course of
action that is most likely to avoid serious problems and promote as
many objectives as possible at once).

Most of the knowledge provided by research on effective teaching, we would argue, represents a catalogue of such proscriptive knowledge, providing (tentative) "don'ts" for teaching practice but very few "dos." This, we think, is the sense in which Hunter (1985) argues that her clinical theory of instruction provides a frame of reference for considering choices of action but cannot be employed to direct action. In the sense that Hunter's research provides teachers with a catalogue of *likely* (negative) consequences of different courses of action, it provides useful guideposts for practices that teachers ought to consider avoiding.

Research on so-called "effective teaching practices" has usually employed as its dependent variable some test of student mastery of certain basic skills or a preidentified body of information. The research, in other words, is most sensitive to teaching practices that might impede the attainment of a limited category of instructional objectives. That does not mean that those same practices might not represent obstacles to the attainment of other objectives—indeed, some of them are more immediately relevant to the maintenance of classroom discipline than they are to the achievement of instructional goals—but it cannot be assumed that they represent obstacles to all possible objectives.

What the research on such practices does provide is a catalogue of apparent tendencies, relating certain practices and certain outcomes. Its value, properly employed, is that it provides a set of shorthand tools—what might be called "intuitive knowledge," if it weren't written down—for anticipating the possible (negative) consequences of certain teaching behaviors.

It is in this sense that we can appreciate the creative reflection made possible by recognition of the dilemmas of teaching practice (Lampert, 1985). The teacher who appreciates that there is no "one best way" to teach in any given situation—and who can anticipate and evaluate the problems that different ways might entail—is prompted to search for innovative solutions that might steer clear of recognized obstacles and serve several purposes at once better than previously used solutions may have done. As one teacher in our Tucson study noted, "Teaching isn't just [a matter of] giving kids information or help. It's important that they learn how to find answers for themselves. That's one reason why it's good for us to

experiment and try new things, even if we fall on our faces sometimes. We're teaching them that learning is *searching* and sometimes searching means making mistakes."

Reflection, variety, anticipation, on-the-spot adaptation,
experimentation, and innovation, whether guided by some theory
or by what seem to be intuitive hunches, are not merely discrete
activities that might be expected of the skillful practitioner. They
are part and parcel of what it means to be a professional (Schon,
1983).

Where do these skills come from? How are they learned? No
other observation about teaching is better documented than the observation that most teachers learn how to teach by being teachers
(Waller, 1932; Lortie, 1975; Nemser, 1983). That may be a reflection
on the quality of training offered by schools of education, but it is
even more a reflection of how many of these skills involve interaction with students and coordination of more specific responsibilities. There is no practical way of developing these skills without
actually interacting with students and making "real" decisions.

Research indicates that most professionals develop their
decision-making skills sequentially, that is, in a particular rather
than haphazard order (Hall, 1976). First, and most obviously, professionals are likely to concentrate on developing a certain basic
level of competence that allows them to understand and carry out
their various individual duties. Beginning teachers invariably find
the practical demands of teaching more difficult than their previous
exposure and training had led them to expect (Lortie, 1975; Burden,
1980; Christensen, Burke, Fessler, and Hagstrom, 1983; Nemser,
1983). In what Burden (1980) calls the "survival stage" of a teacher's
career (typically, the first year of practice), the teacher generally
concentrates on establishing a basic set of practices that enables him
or her to fulfill responsibilities. They must develop some minimal
ability to perform each of their duties—design a class activity, get
a class started, handle a disruptive student, and so on—before they
can begin to integrate these different routines or adapt them to the
unique situations posed by particular activities, particular classes,
or particular disruptive students.

Only after the professional becomes comfortable handling
basic responsibilities is he or she able to direct attention to the

variety of different needs and levels of ability of students in his or
her class, in what Burden calls the "adjustment stage" of a teacher's
career. Building on preservice training and personal experience, the
teacher becomes more perceptive about the relationships between
planning, implementation, and evaluation and more conscious of
the trade-offs and potentially conflicting objectives that any teaching situation presents. As the teacher becomes more perceptive and
conscious of such factors, he or she develops alternative approaches
and a facility for adjusting midstream.

By the time the teacher reaches what Burden calls the "mature stage" of his or her career, teachers feel they have "a good
command of teaching activities and the environment. They [are]
more child-centered, [feel] confident and secure, and [are] willing to
try new teaching methods" (1980, p. 22). Fuller (1970), Fuller and
Brown (1975), Newman (1978), and Peterson (1978) trace career (and
skill) development patterns roughly analogous to those documented
by Burden (1980). When professionals reach this stage, they often
emerge as organizational innovators and leaders, that is, leaders
who can adapt and create new solutions to problems and share and
legitimize these innovative solutions with their colleagues throughout the organization (Peters and Waterman, 1982; Dalton, Thompson, and Price, 1977).

Researchers have found teachers at this stage eager to learn
new skills, open to new methods and ideas, and thriving on new
discoveries that might allow them to reach and benefit as many
individual students as possible (Burden, 1982; Unruh and Turner,
1970; Gregorc, 1973). But many teachers never reach the mature
stage. Glassberg and Oja (1981) and Lortie (1975) present evidence
that many teachers tend to stablize at a particular level of development and grow resistant to new ideas that conflict with what their
previous experience tells them will "work" in practice.

What explains the different choices that teachers seem to
make at these last two stages? Do some teachers simply lack motivation? Are those who continuously improve more committed to
reaching their students? There may be some truth to these suggestions, but our own work with teachers suggests a different kind of
explanation. Some people have likened the process of learning to
teach to one of sinking or swimming. For too many teachers, how-

ever, we have found that the process seems more like a choice between sinking and learning to tread water.

Teaching is such a demanding occupation, and learning to
teach is so difficult, that many people count it a substantial achievement merely to master a limited number of techniques that appear
to work reasonably well with their students. When teachers are
given the choice of continuing to use those techniques or abandoning them and possibly "losing" their students, it is hardly surprising that many continue to do what they think will allow them to
keep their heads above water.

The desire to master teaching situations, reach students, and
develop a sense of personal competence is *not* a guarantee that
teachers will continue to improve their skills throughout their careers. The same motivation can produce either rigidity and resistance to change or an orientation toward teaching that treats each
situation as an opportunity for learning, experimentation, and
growth.

What makes the difference? The research on school effectiveness and effective staff development practices in education, as well
as the general research on career development in other occupations,
makes it clear that the choice between these two orientations depends largely on the culture and organizational processes of a
school. As Nemser (1983), paraphrasing the findings of Hawkins
(1973), points out:

> Becoming a *learning* teacher is not only a matter of
> individual disposition, it also depends on how
> teachers are prepared and the conditions under which
> they carry out their work. . . . If education courses
> nourish the belief that theory and research can give
> teachers rules to follow, they undermine the teacher's
> own problem-solving capacity and convey a false se-
> curity about the authority of science. . . . Basically,
> beginners [are left to] work things out on their own.
> This leaves room for self expression. But it also nar-
> rows the range of alternatives that will be tried and
> increases the likelihood that the novice will misinter-
> pret successes and failures; this may help in the short

run, but may not be educative in the long run. Nor
need "what works" build and sustain a teacher's
capacity to learn from teaching and to keep asking
questions (Nemser, 1983, pp. 150, 155, 159).

Sometimes the dangers that Nemser cites are directly incorporated into a school district's formal policies and procedures. They
are reflected, for example, in the "remedial" approach that many
school districts take toward in-service training. Rather than designing staff development programs on the premise that even the most
effective teacher can benefit from opportunities to consider new
ways of improving his or her performance, many districts base their
in-service programs on the premise that teachers' skills are deficient
and that some outside (or central office) expert can repair the damage (Nemser, 1983; Christensen, Burke, Fessler, and Hagstrom,
1983).

Closely related to this is the tendency of many districts (and
states) to premise their evaluation systems and training programs
on the assumption that there is "one best way to teach" and that
teachers must be made to conform to whatever principles may have
been most recently generated by university researchers. Because one
of the first (and most reliable) lessons teachers learn from experience
is that practices that have proven effective in some situations may
be ineffective in others, such evaluation and training checklists triv-
ialize even the most useful research findings and prompt many
teachers to ignore them altogether.

We will have more to say about evaluation processes later in
this chapter. Before we do, we should note that the obstacles that
are placed in the paths of teachers who might want to develop their
skills are probably due more to omissions than commissions. Most
school districts give little consideration to how beginning teachers
go about acquiring their teaching skills. Indeed, many districts treat
their beginning teachers as if they are fully experienced from the
moment they are employed. They are assigned classrooms or classes
of their own, receive only slightly more supervision and training
than other teachers, and are often blamed for making mistakes that
any beginner could be expected to make.

Employers can assist their professionals' growth by placing

their beginning professionals in situations with reasonably high levels of predictability and gradually introducing them to more and more situations of uncertainty and unpredictability (Schon, 1983). Research on skill development in other technical occupations indicates that initial job challenge—providing individuals with challenging job assignments early on and affording them the opportunity to exercise independent initiative—is a clear predictor of career success. Studies at AT&T (Campbell, 1968) and General Electric (Peres, 1966), for instance, show that the more challenging a person's job is in her or his first year with the organization, the more effective and successful the employee is even five or seven years later (Hall, 1976). But challenges without *feedback* and *support* can be devastating. Hall notes the delicate task of balancing the novice's needs for challenge and feedback: "There is a fine line between the supervisor's controlling and directing his subordinate's work (and thereby interfering with individual initiative) and coaching him when the subordinate requests it. . . . Most supervisors either provide too much help or direction, and are perceived as over-controlling; or they provide too little, letting the person sink or swim" (Hall, 1976).

This research casts further light on the weakness of job ladders in professional settings. The general literature on career development indicates that employees should not have to wait until late in their careers to exercise independent judgment and initiative. Instead, opportunities for individual initiative and personal responsibility should be provided early in a person's career, thus ensuring a self-perpetuating cycle of success (Hall, 1976). Such cycles lead individuals to assume more initiative as they progress in their careers. Rather than segmenting higher-level activities like innovation and leadership in particular jobs, effective organizations provide carefully controlled opportunities for employees to develop and demonstrate initiative, independent judgment, and leadership from the very start.

If formal distinctions are to be made at all in teachers' careers, one of the first principles should be that the first few years of a teacher's career—the pretenure period, for states that provide for tenure—should be thought of primarily as a time of skill development: an *apprenticeship* period as much as a *probationary* period.

During these years, district and school administrators and a teacher's colleagues can provide ongoing feedback and advice to the candidate on his or her strengths and weaknesses and on ways in which he or she might perform more effectively. Teams of experienced teachers might serve as mentors for beginning teachers; special workshops can be instituted to allow beginning teachers to share their experiences and learn from each other.

Once the beginning teacher has completed such a period of apprenticeship and probation, the transition to tenure (and perhaps an accompanying salary increase) can represent a career development step (or the first of several steps, if suggestions later in this chapter are implemented as well). With clarification and rigorous application of criteria and standards for tenure, districts might even change the general public's perception of tenure—from that of tenure as merely conferring job security to a view of tenure as signifying basic competence and a significant transition in a person's career. The state of Alabama has adopted such an approach, developing new standards for the granting of tenure and providing for substantial salary increases upon its conferral ("Career Ladder Plan Subject of Controversy," 1985).

As intriguing as approaches like Alabama's may be, the most important lessons to be drawn from research on professional development do not concern the formal structures that employers might put in place but the obstacles to communication that they should remove. As Hackman, Lawler, and their colleagues note, feedback about one's performance is essential for those who must develop and maintain the ability to exercise discretion and solve unexpected problems (Hackman and Oldham, 1980). Yet physical structures, time schedules, assignment practices, and norms of noninterference severely restrict the amount of feedback or interaction that teachers have with administrators (or with each other).

One of the most remarkable features of our Tucson survey data concerns the isolation of individual teachers from administrators and from each other. Most teachers spend little time with people outside their immediate classrooms. Of the sixteen duties or activities listed on our survey that teachers normally perform daily or more often, only two typically involve any contact with adults. One of these two activities is a routine administrative procedure (recording and reporting attendance) and the other is typically hurried and informal (discussing work with colleagues).

Most of the remaining twenty responsibilities covered by our survey involve at least occasional contact with other adults, but of the nine performed at least weekly by at least half the teachers, only one necessarily requires a substantive discussion about work: consulting with specialists and colleagues to identify the special needs of individual students. The others are generally routine and administrative or else involve substantive work discussions with others on only a haphazard basis: recording and reporting grades; responding to administrative requests for information; adjusting student placements; developing course materials; counseling students; developing tests; attending faculty meetings; and planning and arranging for special resources for classroom instruction.

Despite this overall lack of communication with the other adults in the system, there is strong evidence that communication is critical to teacher job satisfaction and career commitment. Of several hundred questions about teachers' jobs and working conditions on the NEA's recent nationwide survey of teachers, the areas that were most closely linked to the respondents' job satisfaction and career commitment were those that involved relationships with supervisors: whether or not consultation with principals is an effective source of knowledge and skills; whether or not principals give helpful information and suggestions; and how often problems arise involving either the amount or quality of advice, feedback, or direct assistance from building administrators. Teachers who reported helpful relationships with their building principals were much more satisfied with teaching and had the fewest second thoughts about their choice of teaching as a career (Bacharach, Bauer, and Shedd, 1986; National Education Association, 1988).

Those teachers who participated in our group discussions in Tucson reported vast differences in the quality of assistance available from different principals and administrators and indicated that teachers' eagerness or reluctance to approach administrators for advice varies accordingly. One participant illustrated how different supervisory styles can encourage or discourage communication: "I could talk about problems with the principal I had last year, and I learned a lot from him. I could admit that I had really messed up on something and we could talk about how I might have handled the situation differently. But I'd never talk about problems with the principal I have this year. Within the hour, he would 'write me up' and stick negative comments in my personnel folder."

This teacher's experience is an exception in some respects and typical in others. According to the NEA's survey data, most building principals are not personally hostile or threatening to their teachers. Only a handful of teachers (less than 10 percent) indicated that their principals question their personal competence, criticize things they do, or criticize their ideas or plans. Nearly two-thirds indicated that their principals "frequently" or "almost always" show confidence in them, and over half said principals show appreciation for their work.

But while relationships with principals are generally pleasant, they are much less likely to be helpful. Over half (54 percent) indicated that they speak to a building administrator no more than a few times a week, and when they do speak, only one-third said their administrator frequently gives helpful information or suggestions or clarifies what is expected of them. Conversations with administrators only occasionally concern a teacher's own performance (15 percent), personal career plans (8 percent), or training needs (5 percent).[5] Nor do they concern instructional problems and techniques (20 percent), subject matter and course content (15 percent), or school goals, objectives, and priorities (16 percent) that might provide occasions for general feedback and reflection on a teacher's experience. The issues that teachers and administrators most often discuss are those that are most likely to be problem oriented and focused on particular students: student behavior (44 percent), student achievement (34 percent), and parent-teacher relationships (22 percent). Any work-oriented discussion is likely to provide some opportunity for feedback and advice, of course, but these are less likely to provide them than others.

It is hardly surprising, then, that of fourteen possible "sources of knowledge and skills," teachers rate consultation with building administrators among the *least* effective, ahead of only undergraduate education courses and in-service training provided by districts. Table 4 lists each of these knowledge and skill sources and indicates how many teachers held each to be "definitely effective."

Table 4. Effectiveness of Different Sources of Teaching
Knowledge and Skills.

Source	Percent Indicating "Definitely Effective"
Direct experience as a teacher	91.5
Consultation with other teachers	52.2
Your observation of other teachers	49.5
Study and research pursued on your own	46.1
Graduate courses in field of specialization	36.7
Consultation with grade-level or subject-level specialists	31.5
Undergraduate course in field of specialization	30.7
Professional conference and workshops (other than in-service training)	23.9
Professional journals	19.7
Graduate courses in education	19.0
Formal evaluation of your performance	16.0
Consultation with building-level administrators	14.9
Undergraduate education courses	13.0
In-service training provided by your school district	12.9

Source: National Education Association, *Conditions and Resources of Teaching,* Washington, D.C.: NEA Research Division, 1988.

Given the active decision making teachers must engage in, it is not surprising that they rate "direct experience" to be the most effective source of knowledge and skills. But the potential value of feedback and interaction with others is underscored by the fact that consultation with other teachers, and observation of other teachers, are rated the second and third most effective sources.

Members of our Tucson discussion groups stressed the variety of ways in which interaction with other teachers helps them improve their own teaching. Collegial discussions provide information about teaching approaches that may have proven effective for others, as well as information about special resources that might be available and opportunities to share different teaching materials. They also serve less concrete but equally important functions, such as providing opportunities to reflect on one's own interpretation of classroom situations and opportunities to share different interpretations, thereby developing the personal capacity to analyze situations from different perspectives. As two discussion group members noted: "Brainstorming with other teachers charges you. You feed on each other's ideas. You get excited about trying new things." "It helps you maintain some perspective when you can talk with an adult. That's no small thing when you consider that teachers usually spend almost all of every day talking with children." Despite the obvious value of collegial dialogue, nearly half of the teachers responding to our survey (48 percent) report that they do not discuss work with colleagues on even a daily basis. One out of ten report that such conversations are more likely to occur monthly or less often rather than weekly.

Several of our Tucson discussion group members pointed out that building administrators play a critical role in encouraging or discouraging communication among teachers. Some participants indicated that their principals go out of their way to encourage teachers to talk with each other and to rely on each other for help. Others indicated that their principals actively discourage any "talking behind their backs." Research indicates that principals in particularly effective schools invariably promote collaboration and close working relationships among their teachers (Little, 1982b; Wynne, 1981). Research on teachers' acquisition of skills indicates that the most effective teacher learning occurs informally among teachers in settings where building principals actively promote a "norm of collegiality" (Little, 1982a; Nemser, 1983).

The down side of these research findings is that these features have been identified as prominent characteristics of particularly effective school systems in part because they are so often absent in the average system. The knowledge and skills of individual teachers are almost certainly the most valuable—and, in many cases, the most underutilized—resources that any school system has available.

All of these comments indicate what a mixed blessing it is that so many teachers spend so much of their time working on their own, without much contact with or assistance from others. In part, teachers develop resourcefulness, adaptability, and a sense of personal initiative because they have to in order to survive in what one observer calls the "cellular" structure that is typical of most schools (Lortie, 1975). The teacher who responded to our invitation to comment on teaching resources by noting simply "I'm my own best resource" evidenced a pride and confidence that undoubtedly serve her—and her students—well.

But lack of contact with others can also deprive teachers of valuable information, and, more important, can deprive them of opportunities to step back from what Jackson (1968) calls the "overpowering torrent of classroom interactions" and gain some perspective on their own efforts. If those teachers who participated in our discussion group are typical of their colleagues, teachers who are proud of how much they have learned from personal experience are equally aware of how much they could learn from each other's experience and, as we have shown, from administrators who provide the time and support for such sharing to take place.

Autonomy and Identity: Connections and Constraints

To encourage work commitment and self-motivation, jobs must provide more than variety and feedback. They must provide employees with sufficient autonomy and a recognizable whole piece of work so that individuals feel personally responsible for outcomes and are able to identify the effects of their own contributions (Hackman and Oldham, 1980).

At first glance there seems to be little doubt that teachers enjoy a considerable degree of autonomy in their work, given the isolation that they experience. But first impressions can be deceptive. Teachers do make most day-to-day decisions without explicit direction or supervision, and often they have wide latitude to decide what material they will cover in their classes and how they will present it. But their decision making is constrained by a variety of factors that leaves them with less autonomy—and considerably less "task identity"—than people might suppose.

Roughly two-thirds of the teachers responding to the NEA's recent nationwide survey indicated that they are always, almost always, or often involved in deciding what to teach, what textbooks are available, and what textbooks they actually use, and three-quarters reported that they are involved that often in deciding how they will teach. Although teachers generally believe that they should be involved in these decisions even more than they are, the discrepancy between how often they think they should be involved and how often they actually are involved is smaller for these issues than for most, an issue that is discussed later.

As Hackman and Lawler would predict, having opportunities to participate in such decision making has a significant impact on teachers' job commitment. Those who do report that they have such opportunities are much more likely to reaffirm their commitment to being teachers; those who report less involvement are more likely to have second thoughts about their choice of teaching as a career (Rosenholtz, 1986).

Although teachers are responsible for making most of the day-to-day decisions about what they and their students will do, and generally without prior clearance or close supervision, their real autonomy is limited in a variety of ways. In many school systems, general policies, limited resources, and severe time constraints restrict the discretion that teachers are actually able to exercise.

Policy Constraints. Most teachers responding to the NEA's recent survey reported that they know what their responsibilities are, that they know what is expected of them, and that they and their fellow teachers have clear goals and objectives that guide their day-to-day efforts. Smaller numbers (but still more than half) denied that they have to work under vague directions or orders or that they often work under incompatible policies and guidelines. Three-fourths indicated that teachers in their schools have "a clear sense of priorities," indicating which goals or objectives should take precedence when two or more come in conflict.

But most teachers have some reservations about the clarity of school priorities: Only 23 percent reported that they and their colleagues "definitely" have clear priorities, whereas twice that number said the same about goals or objectives. The most telling sign of possible conflict or ambiguity, however, is the fact that two-thirds reported that there is not enough time during their regular workday to do everything expected of them.

The pattern of these survey responses is instructive. The problem in most school systems is not that *particular* job responsibilities are ambiguous or conflicting. The problem is that ambiguity and conflict tend to surface when teachers have to put all their different responsibilities together, without adequate resources and without common agreement on which responsibilities should take precedence over others.

Teachers, in turn, often blame themselves for their inability to accomplish everything that is expected of them, internalizing conflicts and ambiguity and experiencing high levels of stress and burnout (Bacharach, Bauer, and Conley, 1986). NEA survey data indicate that teachers who report high levels of role ambiguity[6] and role conflict[7] (relative to other teachers) are significantly more dissatisfied with their jobs and are more likely to report that they would not become teachers if they could "go back and start over." For example, 51 percent of those who indicated that they probably or certainly would not become teachers again said they "work under vague directions or orders," whereas only 31 percent of those who said they would become teachers again said they work under such conditions. Nearly the same percentages responded that way when asked whether or not they often receive instructions without the resources to carry them out and often work under incompatible policies and guidelines.

Conflicting time pressures, lack of priorities, and ambiguity and conflict in overall responsibilities are always dangers when employees' responsibilities are communicated through general policies and procedures. State and district officials who promulgate new policies are often in a poor position to anticipate how their policies might affect other policies, and they generally are not available, as are immediate supervisors, to answer questions or resolve inconsistencies.

These sorts of problems might be avoided, of course, if teachers were more heavily involved in making the policies they must subsequently implement. As we suggested earlier, teachers generally report that they are involved in decisions that are most likely to concern only their immediate classrooms, such as what, how, and with what texts they will teach. But the greatest discrepancies between desired and actual participation involve policies that affect many classrooms and other teachers: standardized testing policies (65 percent), student rights (56 percent), grading policies (55 percent), student discipline codes (51 percent), expenditure priorities (47 percent), facility planning (43 percent), procedures for communicating with parents (42 percent), procedures for removing students from class for special instruction or assistance (42 percent), and budget development (41 percent).[8]

Resource Constraints. One of the sharpest contrasts between teaching and other occupations is the extent to which teachers must rely upon their own resources in carrying out their jobs. Every job requires resources. Some job resources are intangible and personal to the individual, such as knowledge and skills gained from college training, personal experience, or training made available by an employer. Others are intangible and personal to others, such as expertise and effort of persons who can be called on for advice or direct assistance in carrying out particular responsibilities. Other resources, such as equipment and materials, are more concrete and can be stored either in some central location or with the individuals who will actually use them. Information is a resource that is important in virtually any job, but the kinds of information and the ways in which they are generated, stored, and retrieved vary widely from one job and employment setting to another (Mitchell, 1986).

Effective employee performance in any setting depends on a proper match between responsibilities and job resources. It is easier to maintain that principle, however, in settings where job responsibilities are specified for each individual and defined in terms of specific tasks or step-by-step procedures. The more responsibilities are defined in terms of goals and objectives and are communicated through general policies or procedures that apply to groups of employees, the more difficult it is for an organization to anticipate and monitor each employee's need for resources.

Significant numbers of teachers responding to the NEA's survey reported that the available quantity and quality of a variety of resources often cause problems for them in performing their jobs. Although they were somewhat more likely to cite quantity problems, as opposed to quality problems, roughly one-third reported that classroom, storage, and special activity space frequently pose both quantity and quality problems, and roughly one-sixth to one-quarter reported the same for advice and feedback from building administrators and direct assistance from administrators, staff specialists, teachers' aides, and custodial staff. Thirty-six percent said that the amount of money available to purchase supplies or equipment for special instructional purposes causes frequent problems for them in performing their jobs. Many reported that they often contribute large amounts of their own money to the purchase of special materials.

Our Tucson discussion groups offered a variety of different illustrations of how communication among teachers can provide valuable resources. Some talked about teachers directly assisting each other, while others talked of how much valuable information teachers can share with each other. One teacher, for example, stressed the value of the knowledge that previous teachers have accumulated about their current students: "[They can tell you] what sorts of problems different kids had and what sorts of approaches 'worked' with which kids." She called such knowledge a "decision-making resource."

Another teacher picked up on these comments, illustrating how lack of communication with other teachers deprived her of that resource and caused problems. A gym teacher who prides herself on being able to work well with "tough" kids, she reported that she had spent nearly an entire year "getting nowhere" with one student who was a constant discipline problem. Toward the end of the school year, she learned from some other teachers that the boy's father had left home when he was a child and the boy had always had problems with female authority figures. She commented:

> There was no reason why he or I had to be put in that position. He could have been placed in the other gym teacher's class—the other teacher is a male—and neither of us would have had to spend the year locking horns. He needed a male authority figure and didn't need another woman giving him directions. I should have known about that boy's background, and if the teachers in my school were encouraged to spend more time talking about their different students' problems, I would have known about his background.

The same teacher said that her current building principal encourages precisely that kind of communication, and she added: "It's one of the things that makes my school such a good one." She provided yet another, more concrete illustration of how communication among teachers can provide access to resources. Several teachers had commented on their own tendency to hoard resources, not only paper, pencils, and other general materials but more specialized equipment like projectors, typewriters, and other instructional tools. They acknowledged that keeping so many resources in each individual classroom was probably inefficient, from a school perspective, but they insisted that the systems for ordering, maintaining, and distributing supplies were too unreliable—and the likelihood of being second-guessed by file clerks too great—for them to be willing to give up their caches.

The high school gym teacher, as it happened, had a contrasting story of a cache that she was *willing* to relinquish. For several years she had been disappointed about the low level of knowledge and skills that her high school freshman students exhibited in most sports. Her own program was supposed to concentrate on building students' teamwork and sense of athletic strategy, but she had to devote much of her time to teaching basic skills instead. Disappointed, she decided to query the physical education teachers at the middle schools that sent students to her high school. Each of them reported the same problem: Inadequate supplies of sports equipment prevented them from giving their students the instruction in particular sports that the district's formal physical education curriculum said they were supposed to be offering. Our high school teacher recognized that her own school had more than enough equipment for its own needs. Rather than turning these supplies over to her middle school colleagues (she did not have enough to meet every school's needs), she got her colleagues to agree to coordinate their programs, so that one (for example) would be teaching volleyball while another would be teaching field hockey and yet another softball. Her own storeroom had enough equipment to meet this need and became a "lending library" for the feeder schools. Within two years, she reported, her freshmen were arriving with the skills they needed to begin her own program.

Time Constraints. The resource that most often causes problems for teachers, however, is time. More than half the teachers responding to the NEA's survey reported that they constantly or often experience problems because of lack of time for counseling individual students and for grading and reviewing student work.

Nearly half said the same for class planning and preparation, and approximately one-third reported not enough time for direct instruction.

These findings illustrate the kinds of compromises that teachers are forced to make when many of their responsibilities must be inferred from general policies and procedures. Insufficient time for counseling, grading, and preparation can have serious negative effects on the quality of a teacher's instruction and on student progress, especially since teachers must use time to create or track down other resources that they might need. These activities are likely to be treated as organizational afterthoughts to be performed in whatever time is left over after other, more explicit responsibilities have been attended to, unless a school district makes an explicit commitment to provide for and protect them.

The fact that many teachers devote large amounts of their own time to student (and parental) counseling, class planning, and grading is a mark of their motivation and commitment. But motivation and commitment can be effectively undermined if lack of organizational support appears to signal lack of concern for activities that teachers recognize as essential but that are not explicitly prescribed in policies or procedures.

It is not enough to decry the lack of time available for needed activities. School systems waste enormous quantities of time forcing their teachers to work through problems, reinvent solutions, search out information, and duplicate resources that have already been worked through, invented, discovered, or acquired many times before. Lack of money is only the most proximate cause of the problem. The real culprits are the work calendars, time schedules, staffing practices, and physical structures that prevent teachers from working with each other more closely. All the hierarchical features that were originally meant to *control* and *coordinate* what teachers do now serve to undermine that very coordination.

Evaluation: Accountability for Growth

Ask teachers privately if they "need improvement" and most will readily acknowledge that they do: If they are professionals, concerned about doing the best possible job, one would expect them to be looking for opportunities to improve. Indeed, it is the teachers who deny that they have any room for improvement who are probably most likely to need it. But include the phrase "needs improvement" on an evaluation form as the lowest or next-to-lowest standard on a rating scale (as many, perhaps most, districts do) and you have announced to your staff that it is a "bad thing" to need improvement, which is implicitly a criticism in an enterprise supposedly devoted to promoting continuous learning! Such phrases create a powerful incentive for teachers to deny that they need improvement. That an enterprise supposedly devoted to continuous learning would criticize its members for "needing improvement" indicates how easily different organizational processes can work at cross-purposes. As one Tucson teacher put it: "If evaluation were treated differently, we would think of it differently. Everyone wants to improve and would like feedback on how they could improve, but that isn't how evaluations are treated here. They're used to play 'gotcha!'" Nothing is more indicative of how school systems actually discourage their teachers' efforts to develop their skills.

School systems have rendered their evaluation systems nearly meaningless by their failure to reconcile the tension between the needs for teacher discretion and system control. If teachers are to be allowed broad discretion to decide how and what to teach, how can they be held accountable for the results they achieve? The answer is that this is the wrong question. *How* they are to be held accountable is not that difficult to determine. But *for what* are they to be held accountable?

Trying to hold individual teachers directly responsible for what their students achieve merely encourages timidity, risk aversion, scapegoating, and a reluctance to acknowledge and learn from mistakes. No hospital examining board would think of holding individual surgeons, much less an entire hospital, at fault just because a patient died on the operating table. (Indeed, there would be reasons to question a hospital's policies if the death rate on its operating tables were too low.) But they will always insist on asking why a patient died, and why a physician or team of physicians made the decisions they made. Professionals are not held accountable for results per se but for *their decisions.*

Lack of progress in a class or school or school system is like a death on an operating table. It should not be treated as grounds for concluding that someone has necessarily done something wrong but as a starting point for asking questions and for engaging in a professional dialogue about how decisions might have been made differently. Such dialogues can be threatening—they demand skills that most schools and schools of education don't cultivate—but they are the surest way of building a sense of professional accountability among educators.

One of the principal reasons for engaging in such dialogues, in teaching, as in any other professional setting, is to promote continuous growth in a person's knowledge and judgment. School systems should assume that *all* their teachers—and administrators, and other staff members—need improvement. They should expect their teachers to show evidence of their efforts to improve.

We recently helped the Bridgeport (Connecticut) public schools design and implement an evaluation system that reflects these principles. The criteria used by the Bridgeport evaluation system are not much different from those of other evaluation systems. They reflect Bridgeport's conception of the basic responsibilities that teachers perform (see Exhibit 1). If there is anything that distinguishes this list from other sets of evaluation criteria, it is that the task force of teachers and administrators that developed Bridgeport's system made a determined effort to frame criteria that focused on classroom teaching.

What really distinguishes Bridgeport's system is not its criteria but its standards for assessing *how* teachers perform on each set of criteria.[9] There are really two distinctive features about the standards that the district uses. The first has to do with how standards are framed, the second with how they are ordered. In framing its standards, the task force decided that adverbs and adjectives (such as "outstanding," "effective," "satisfactory," or "needs improvement") would be avoided for three basic reasons: They had no intrinsic meaning or value in themselves, they provoked disagreements that served no useful purpose, and they diverted attention from more substantive issues. Instead, the task force set about to develop a set of verbs that would define Bridgeport's expectations of its teachers. The first set of verb-statements defined the district's basic expectations. Each teacher, the task force maintained, should

Exhibit 1. Illustrative Evaluation Criteria.

Criteria Group: PLANNING

A: Identifies and sequences instructional goals, objectives, procedures, and learning activities.
B: Plans learning activities to address individual differences among students.
C: Identifies and secures resources to support instruction.
D: Encourages, secures, and maintains the involvement of parents and other community members in support of instruction.

Criteria Group: MANAGEMENT OF CLASSROOM ENVIRONMENT

E: Establishes and maintains standards for behavior that foster student self-discipline and positive relationships among students.
F: Develops and maintains classroom routines that facilitate instruction and minimize disruption of learning.
G: Organizes classroom space, equipment, materials, and appearance to support instruction, encourage student interest, and maintain order.

Criteria Group: INSTRUCTION

H: Uses different teaching styles, instructional methods, materials, and media, depending upon the learning situation.
I: Presents instructional activities in a logical sequence that is developmentally appropriate; paces activities to achieve objectives and maximize students' time on task.
J: Uses a balance of individual, small group, and large group instructional arrangements.
K: Communicates directions and explanations to students, both individually and in groups, concerning objectives, activities, assignments, and the quality and amount of work expected.
L: Communicates with students, both individually and collectively, about their needs and progress.
M: Provides opportunities for students to develop independence, self-confidence, and high expectations for themselves as learners.

Criteria Group: ASSESSMENT

N: Identifies students' entry-level knowledge and skills.
O: Monitors and evaluates students' progress in relation to objectives.
P: Identifies student problems or needs that require special attention, and provides (or arranges for) necessary attention.
Q: Uses information on student progress, problems, and needs to assess instructional objectives and the effectiveness of instruction.
R: Develops and/or selects methods of assessing student progress, problems, and needs; develops and maintains systems for keeping group and individual records of such information.
S: Involves parents in the assessment of their children's progress, problems, and needs.

Source: Bridgeport (Connecticut) Public Schools, "Appraisal of Professional Performance (Classroom Assignments)," 1989.

Perform each responsibility listed in the criteria group, without the need for close supervision

Demonstrate a sound knowledge of subject(s) to be taught

Demonstrate a sound knowledge of human development, group behavior, and pedagogy as they relate to the teaching/learning process

Address the needs of individual students

Observe district/school policies

Avoid patterns of personal behavior that are likely to undermine learning and/or students' development of self [confidence and esteem]

Assume responsibility for personal improvement in the areas listed in the criteria group

The first of these standards reflected the expectation that teachers would be able to function as independent decision makers. The second and third signaled an expectation that their decision making would reflect an understanding of substantive and process knowledge relevant to their teaching. The fourth and fifth reflected the teacher's twin responsibilities to respect the needs of individual students and the policies of his or her employer: Neither was given precedence. The sixth standard represented the task force's effort to encourage attention to the lessons of research on effective teaching. The point was to frame a standard that encouraged teachers to use those lessons as guides rather than as a simplistic checklist of "do's" and "don'ts." As written, the standard focused not on the teacher's adherence to particular principles in each and every pedagogical decision but on the negative consequences that are likely to result when a consistent pattern of ignoring those principles develops. The seventh of these basic standards reflected the expectation of continuous improvement, suggesting that the teacher him- or herself will take the lead in identifying areas where improvement might be needed.

As the Bridgeport task force designed the system, evaluators would ask this set of questions for each of the evaluation's four criteria groups: the teacher's planning, classroom management, instruction, and assessment responsibilities. The question, in each case, was whether the teacher did or did not meet the standard in question. If not, the evaluator would detail his or her reasons for believing that the standard had not been met and he or she and the teacher would discuss the issue. No finer distinctions (between "outstanding" and "satisfactory," for example) would be drawn.

But the Bridgeport system does draw a different set of distinctions. The standards listed above are considered *basic* expectations: All teachers are expected to meet them. Two other sets of standards were developed to reflect the expectation of growth in a person's knowledge and skills. Drawing on the research on later career stages in teaching (summarized above), a set of standards was developed to reflect the variety and adaptability expected of more experienced teachers, who could be expected to

> Demonstrate the capacity to draw on a repertoire of approaches in the exercise of each responsibility listed in the criteria group
>
> Develop and implement [plans] that address simultaneously the different needs, abilities, or learning styles of individual students and groups of students
>
> Develop and implement [plans] that serve several purposes at once
>
> Anticipate likely instructional or behavioral problems/developments, and plan contingencies to address them
>
> Monitor student behavior and progress while class is in session, and adjust [plans] to changing/unforeseen situations

Teachers are not expected to be able to fully meet each of them, as they are in the first set of standards. Assuming that they do fully satisfy the first set, they and their supervisors are expected to treat the second set as *targets* for identifying and making provision for opportunities for improvement.

A final set of three standards is specified, reflecting yet another set of targets:

> Develops innovative approaches to the exercise of some or all of the responsibilities listed in the criteria group
>
> Conducts personal research or takes other steps to broaden

the knowledge base that supports one's own and others' teaching in the areas listed

Draws on one's own experience, knowledge, or skills to support and provide leadership to colleagues in the exercise of their responsibilities in the areas listed

Obviously, a teacher who fails to meet any of the basic standards in the first set, or who has not made much progress toward developing the facility reflected in the second, is not likely to demonstrate the creativity and leadership reflected in this third set. But all teachers are encouraged to think of these three standards as additional targets, and their contributions are explicitly acknowledged, if and when they do meet them. But because the standards are applied to each set of criteria, the focus continues to be on strengthening one's own classroom teaching, as well as the teaching of others. There is no incentive to move away from the classroom.

Although it is too soon to pronounce the Bridgeport system a success, preliminary evidence is promising. The system's three basic features—criteria that focus on classroom teaching, standards that are worded objectively in behavioral terms, and the arrangement of standards into three groups reflecting a progression from basic to proficient to mastery—reflect respect for the complexity of teaching and the professionalism of individual teachers. They also provide the basis for substantive dialogues around the problems of practice. Indeed, they provide both teachers and their supervisors with grounds for *insisting* on such a dialogue, if either should be reluctant to engage in one. They provide the basis, that is, for a new system of mutual, professional accountability in public schools: a system that not only satisfies but actively promotes both teachers' exercise of discretion and efforts to hold them responsible for the decisions they make and the growth they pursue.

We suggested earlier that every teacher, at some point in his or her career, usually faces a choice between continuously improving (or trying to improve) his or her knowledge and skills and leveling off and stabilizing at some level of proficiency. Like others, we suggested that the choice between these two orientations depends largely on the culture and organizational processes of a school. Schools that couple a "norm of continuous development" with a

"norm of collegiality," making skill development and school improvement collective rather than merely individual imperatives, can
tap each teacher's natural interest and personal growth and generate
a receptivity to innovation and change. Schools in which teachers
remain isolated—and insulated—from each other and from administrators encourage the opposite orientation (Lortie, 1975; Rosenholtz, 1985).

Notes

1. For a discussion of the "human relations" tradition that devel-
    oped such general propositions, see Bacharach, Lipsky, and
    Shedd, 1983, pp. 182–196.
2. Autonomy and variety were correlated with ratings on quality
    of performance and overall effectiveness. Such a relationship
    did *not* hold for ratings on the quantity of work turned in, nor
    for the core dimensions of task identity and feedback. The au-
    thors noted that one of the jobs included in their study, tele-
    phone operator, was high on both task identity and feedback
    but low on the other two dimensions. That job, therefore,
    tended to be relatively boring and not intrinsically motivating.
3. Hackman and Lawler themselves believe that the motivational
    potential in jobs with their four core dimensions is only attrac-
    tive to people with higher-order needs for personal growth, but
    the evidence to support that argument is ambiguous. They
    found a statistically significant correlation between job com-
    plexity and quality of performance for those workers with high
    growth needs but no such correlation for those with more mod-
    erate growth needs. (Those in complex jobs, with high growth
    needs, also tended to be rated higher in *overall* effectiveness, but
    that relationship was not statistically significant.) But Hack-
    man and Lawler never established whether workers with and
    without high growth needs were in different jobs. In fact, their
    own data suggest that the nature of a worker's job (that is, its
    scores on various job dimensions) was actually a better predic-
    tor of overall supervisory ratings than workers' own self-
    reported "need strength." The possibility still exists, therefore,

that job features with motivation potential actually *generate* the motivation to do well.

4. For another discussion of teaching that uses Hackman and Lawler's framework, see Rosenholtz (1988).

5. Percentages indicated in parentheses are those reporting that they discuss the subject "frequently" or "almost always" with building administrators.

6. Three survey items were combined in a single role ambiguity scale: "I feel certain about how much authority I have," "I know what my responsibilities are," and "I know exactly what is expected of me."

7. Two role conflict measures were constructed following factor analysis. One, measuring *conflict over policies,* included "I often work under incompatible policies and guidelines," "I often have to buck a rule or policy to carry out an assignment," and "I often receive incompatible requests from two or more people." The other, measuring *conflict over resources,* covered "I often receive instructions without adequate resources and materials to execute them," "I often receive extra assignments without adjustment to the ones I already have," and "There isn't enough time during my regular workday to do everything that's expected of me."

8. Percentages in parentheses indicate the difference between the percentage of teachers who say they always, almost always, or often *should* be involved in making decisions on an issue, and the percentage who say they *are* involved that often. The discrepancies for decisions about what to teach, how to teach, and with what texts, range from 22 to 33 percent.

9. To emphasize the importance of general dialogues and ease the practical demands on evaluators, the Bridgeport task force decided to have evaluators apply each standard to each of four *sets* of criteria, rather than to each of the system's nineteen individual criteria.

5

COMPENSATING TEACHERS

Now that we have looked at the work and the job of the individual teacher, it is appropriate to consider how that teacher should be paid. Systems of teacher compensation have been the subject of intense debate in the United States ever since April 1983, when the National Commission on Excellence in Education issued its recommendation calling for performance-based pay systems in public education. Other study commissions, task forces, and scholars issued subsequent reports that also called for changes in the way school systems administer teacher compensation.

Although politicians and members of the general press tend to use "merit pay" as an all-purpose label for these reform proposals, there are significant differences among them. In fact, most of the compensation changes already enacted or being considered do not involve merit pay, at least as that term is generally used, but rather some form of what their proponents call "career ladders." Merit pay is a system that bases some or all of each teacher's compensation on periodic assessments of his or her individual performance. Most career ladder proposals, by contrast, draw salary distinctions based on the duties that different teachers are expected to perform. Both are presented as alternatives to the unified salary schedules that most school systems currently use, which base salaries on teachers' years of experience and level of graduate education (see Bacharach, Lipsky, and Shedd, 1984).

Our purpose here is to consider how each of these compensation systems might affect the management of school systems and either contribute to or detract from the twin purposes of promoting individual initiative and overall coordination.

Merit Pay

Merit Pay and Motivation. Most merit pay plans base assessments of teacher performance on direct administrative observation, evaluation, and (presumed) measurement of a teacher's performance, first by rating the person on a specified set of criteria and then combining these individual ratings in a summary rating of his or her overall performance. Some plans sidestep the difficulties inherent in such a rating process by inferring the quality of a teacher's performance from indirect, narrower, but more objective data like student performance on standardized tests. Both approaches, however, represent performance-based pay systems.

It may be politically astute for advocates of such changes to frame the issue of teacher compensation in terms of whether or not school systems ought to reward merit (Bacharach, Conley, and Shedd, 1990). It may be equally astute for them to assert that their proposal ought to be implemented in public education because they have been proven to "work" in private-sector settings. But neither argument leads to the clear-cut conclusions that their advocates would have people believe.

Experience and training—the criteria that most systems presently use to differentiate salaries—are widely used as criteria for allocating pay in the private sector and are arguably the most reliable and objective, if not necessarily the most precise, measures of an employee's "merit" available. If the argument that one compensation system or another "works" were accepted at face value, the fact that most school systems have based teacher compensation on experience and training for over half a century presumably would have settled the issue of which system works in public education long ago. The fact that many school districts have experimented with merit pay, and some with differentiated staffing, and most have abandoned those systems and returned to the unified salary schedule would be equally persuasive evidence that those other systems do *not* work in public education (Bacharach, Lipsky, and Shedd, 1984).

The importance to teachers of nonmonetary factors derived directly from working with students has been well documented (see Kleinman, 1963; Sergiovanni, 1967; Weissman, 1969). Bishop (1977) and Lortie (1975) present substantial evidence that teachers derive the most satisfaction from positive and successful relationships with students. Lortie (1975), for example, presents straightforward evidence that the "psychic rewards . . . of knowing that [a teacher] has 'reached' students and they have learned" are much more important to most teachers than money or any other extrinsic reward: "Respondents [in Lortie's study] fused the idea of work gratification and the idea of work goals: they made little distinction between deriving satisfaction from their work and reaching classroom objectives. In answering questions which asked specifically about the satisfactions they received from teaching, they overwhelmingly cited task-related outcomes. . . . [T]eaching is satisfying and encouraging when positive things happen in the classroom (Lortie, 1975, pp. 103–104).

There are few experiences more satisfying for teachers than doing well in the classroom, knowing one has done well, and knowing that one's students know so as well. There are few things more humiliating than "bombing" in front of thirty trusting children or twenty-five snickering adolescents. Between those extremes there is plenty of room for teachers' satisfaction to vary, which is to say, there is plenty of incentive to seek the one and avoid the other.

This is the heart of the argument about teaching being intrinsically motivated: The process of teaching is not always rewarding but it is potentially rewarding, and those rewards will vary depending upon a teacher's efforts (Bacharach and Mitchell, forthcoming). If a teacher does not perceive rewards to be available from his or her interactions with students, or does not believe that his or her efforts have much to do with securing them, then there is no reason to believe he or she will be intrinsically motivated at all.

Few compensation theorists maintain that money is the only reason people perform well (or try to do so) at work. Most are willing to acknowledge that some people derive intrinsic satisfaction from performing a job well and that the anticipation of such satisfaction can be a powerful source of motivation. Some theorists, like Lawler (1971), are even prepared to acknowledge that money may be a distinctly secondary source of motivation for some people in some jobs.

Even Casey (1979), who argues at length that teachers are no different from employees in other occupations and that money should be treated as a prime motivator in education, does not suggest that monetary considerations are the only factor that motivates teachers to improve or sustain high performance. In their study of the conditions that may support intrinsic motivation, Hackman and Lawler (1971) concluded that only workers with high growth needs will respond to opportunities to gain intrinsic work rewards. Others may require extrinsic rewards to motivate and sustain their performance. In fact, most compensation theorists argue that linking employee pay to assessments of their performance will supplement intrinsic rewards and thereby provide greater motivation than intrinsic rewards by themselves.

This "supplement" argument proceeds directly from Expectancy Theory, which serves as the basis for most compensation research. Expectancy Theory (Vroom, 1964) asserts that the overall value (or "valence") of pursuing a particular course of action can be expressed as the sum of the values of whatever outcomes are expected to result from such a course of action. Two positive outcomes (for example, a sense of accomplishment and an increase in pay) should each enhance that overall valence. Motivation should therefore be greater in situations where a sense of accomplishment *and* a pay raise are likely outcomes than in situations where only one is available.

As obvious as this argument might seem, it rests on an assumption that is subject to challenge, namely, that the intrinsic motivation to perform particular tasks will not change when a source of extrinsic motivation is added. If a person's intrinsic motivation were to decrease when extrinsic rewards for performing the same tasks became available, the net effect of combining them would be ambiguous and perhaps even negative. Expectancy Theory might still be correct in the sense that overall motivation is a combination of the values of two different outcomes, but the end result would be uncertain.

Two different groups of researchers claim to have tested these questions, each using controlled laboratory experiments as well as field studies, and they have produced what (at first glance) appears to be contradictory evidence. One group of researchers, using reinforcement theory (Skinner, 1969; Ayllon and Azrin, 1968), has generated several hundred studies and a mountain of evidence indicating that people improve their performance on tasks when extrinsic rewards for completing them are made available (for reviews, see Kazdin, 1975; O'Leary and Drabman, 1971). A second group, drawing on a variety of different theories, has produced evidence that extrinsic rewards have detrimental effects on motivation and performance (Deci, 1976; Lepper and Greene, 1978).

The apparent conflict between these two groups of studies is deceptive. McGraw (1978) notes that the tasks typically involved in laboratory and field tests of reinforcement theory almost always have been aversive or uninteresting and have all had "algorithmic" solutions. That is, the subjects knew exactly *what* they were supposed to accomplish and *how* they were supposed to accomplish it as well. The subjects, in other words, had no reason to expect any satisfaction from performing well for its own sake. Under such circumstances, it is hardly surprising that the addition of extrinsic rewards would have a positive effect on performance: There was nothing *else* to motivate them.

In reviewing the studies that found extrinsic rewards to have detrimental effects on performance, McGraw notes that the tasks the subjects were asked to perform (mostly puzzles) were all inherently interesting and had heuristic solutions. That is, subjects in control groups enjoyed doing them without any suggestion that they might be rewarded, and it was not immediately obvious to subjects how to solve them. Performance involved problem solving, rather than just following directions. Subjects who were offered extrinsic rewards to perform such tasks tended to perform more poorly than those to whom such rewards were not offered (Pikulski, 1970; McGraw and McCullers, 1975; also see Condry, 1975).

In reviewing other "negative effects" studies, McGraw notes that when subjects are assigned interesting tasks that have algorithmic solutions, the offer of extrinsic rewards does not appear to have a negative effect on performance. Similarly, once subjects have discovered ways of solving problems with heuristic solutions, the subsequent offer of extrinsic rewards for continued performance does not appear to affect performance adversely. In many cases, the addition of an offer of extrinsic rewards under either of these situations actually seems to improve performance. The presence or absence of problem solving appears to have a major impact on whether extrinsic rewards will have a positive or negative effect on performance.

Although most of these negative effects studies involved impersonal puzzle-solving activities, one that is of particular relevance to teaching involved performance in a social setting. Garbarino (1975) studied the effects of contingent rewards on the behavior of sixth grade students who were asked to teach first graders how to play a complicated but interesting game. Half the sixth graders were individually offered a movie ticket if they could teach the younger child how to play the game; the other half were asked to perform the same task without being offered a reward.

Garbarino found that the emotional tone of the interaction in the reward condition was significantly more negative: Tutors criticized tutees and their mistakes more often, they offered fewer positive evaluations of tutees (and only when they gave the right answers), and they were less likely to engage in laughter. They were also more inclined to volunteer answers if answers were not immediately forthcoming.

The interaction between tutees and tutors who were not offered extrinsic rewards was positive on all these measures. In addition, when tutors in the nonreward condition did make negative content evaluations, they tended to couple their criticisms with positive information about the tutees themselves (for example, "You got that one wrong, but you're really trying."). As for the results of their efforts, nonrewarded tutors were significantly more successful: Their tutees were more likely to achieve mastery of the game and made fewer errors in the process. Offering the reward appears to have encouraged tutors to think of and treat tutees in instrumental terms—as means toward ends—producing low tolerance for frustration, negative feelings toward those who would not cooperate by learning, and, ultimately, less effective performance.

There are two ways of interpreting these findings. Deci (1976) argues that extrinsic rewards actually undermine motivation. He argues that tasks that are interesting and challenging (that is, have heuristic solutions) provide opportunities for gaining self-confidence and a sense of accomplishment. Such intrinsic rewards will diminish, Deci argues, if the individual attributes the reason for performing to an external source. If one concludes that her or his behavior is controlled by someone who is manipulating extrinsic rewards, one's personal stake in performing well "for oneself" will be undermined. Deci and colleagues have conducted a number of studies that suggest that when the controlling aspect of extrinsic rewards is made salient, intrinsic motivation and subsequent performance at such tasks are negatively affected (see Deci, 1975).

The second explanation suggests that extrinsic rewards do not necessarily undermine motivation to perform but that they change *what* people are motivated to perform. Condry and Chambers (1978) argue that when rewards are offered, individuals will concentrate on doing what is necessary to get them: "Attention is focused on the easiest route to [the] goal." When offered a choice between two activities, either of which could produce the same reward but one of which is riskier and less certain, subjects choose the easier route. Once engaged in an activity with a nonobvious (heuristic) solution, subjects who have been offered extrinsic rewards are more likely to focus on getting the answer and thus getting the reward. Subjects who have not been offered rewards are more likely to focus on understanding the problem: They tend to learn more quickly, make more efficient use of negative information (they ask themselves *why* an approach did not produce a solution), and make fewer "wild guesses": "Intrinsically motivated subjects attend to and utilize a wider array of information; they are focused on the *way* to solve the problem rather than the solution. They are, in general, more careful, logical, and coherent in their problem-solving strategies than comparable subjects offered a reward to solve the same problems" (Condry and Chambers, 1978).

Deci, McGraw, Condry and Chambers, Garbarino, and others offer several reasons, therefore, for questioning the use of pay-for-performance systems in work settings that require employees to engage in substantial amounts of problem solving. Garbarino's study raises additional questions about the risks of using such systems in social settings, where a person may need the cooperation of others to reach his or her own objective. Not all of these researchers agree that overall motivation declines when extrinsic rewards are made available, but all of them predict that individuals will perform *differently* when contingent rewards are available. To the extent that performance involves searching for nonobvious solutions and winning the cooperation of others, it will be facilitated when individuals have a sense of personal commitment or stake in the search process itself.

None of these explanations is inconsistent with the assertion that money is a potentially powerful source of motivation. Indeed, as Garbarino's study, in particular, illustrates, extrinsic rewards may be *so* powerful that they can change people's perceptions of their own needs and motives. The argument that individuals who are offered contingent rewards will choose whatever seems to be the easiest and most direct route to those rewards is precisely what most compensation models, especially those grounded in Expectancy Theory (Vroom, 1964), would predict. The observation that contingent rewards facilitate performance when tasks have algorithmic solutions, but not when solutions are heuristic, is also consistent with the advice offered by traditional compensation theorists: The criteria for granting rewards in a pay-for-performance system must be objective and clearly understood and employees must know how to go about reaching those goals (Mahoney, 1979; Lawler, 1971; Milkovich and Newman, 1984).

The only real difference in these perspectives is that most compensation theorists tend to assume that it is always possible for the employer to specify objective outcomes and clear ways of reaching them, while the scholars who have demonstrated that systems of contingent rewards can have negative effects tend to question that assumption (Bacharach, Lipsky, and Shedd, 1984). As their studies illustrate, in some work situations clarifying goals and finding ways of reaching them are part of the process of performing itself. Whether a pay system can serve as an effective source of managerial control and individual motivation ultimately depends, therefore, on the nature of the work performed in the organization and the nature of the interaction among those who perform it.

Merit Pay and the Nature of Teaching. Problem solving and interaction with other people are basic features of many occupations, but as our earlier analysis of teaching pointed out, few occupations combine intensive, nonroutine problem solving and the management of relationships with large numbers of other people. Few occupations involve solutions that are as difficult to come by as those in teaching. Earlier we noted features of teaching that compel teachers to develop skills and standards of competence largely on their own: outcomes, goals, and criteria of assessments that are multiple, ambiguous, and often conflicting; the paucity of research on teaching and the absence of any authoritative body of "how to" knowledge; the lack of a technical vocabulary that might facilitate the exchange of insights and the analysis of problems among colleagues; and entry processes, physical separation, and time limitations that limit opportunities for such exchanges.

Teachers have few opportunities to step back from the concrete details of their classroom experience and organize them into coherent patterns that might yield to solutions. If there is a difference between the role requirements of teaching and the heuristic problem solving required of subjects in the negative effects experiments we discussed in the previous section, it is that the experimental subjects at least had the benefit of knowing what the problem was, even if they were not told how to solve it. Teachers must usually discover for themselves the problems that they are responsible for solving.

Lortie (1975) and others have noted that much of the teacher's role concept—and many of the opportunities for intrinsic satisfaction—are wrapped up in the conviction that he or she can and must develop personal performance criteria. The negative effects research discussed here suggests that this conviction is a critical variable in the problem-solving process and a critical resource that school districts can ill afford to squander.

But these same features of teaching can be characterized as problems—examples of structural looseness, weak feedback mechanisms, and lack of coherence—that need to be corrected. The conviction that a person can "become a teacher by being a teacher" may be a source of reassurance to new teachers and a source of pride for more experienced ones, but it is hardly grounds for public satisfaction. It implies that beginners must undergo an inefficient, trial-and-error process of searching for algorithms of technique and analysis without being able to draw on the insights of others who have already experienced such a process. It implies that more experienced teachers may content themselves with having developed satisfactory solutions to recurring problems, simply because those solutions generate fewer disadvantages than ones that may have been tried in the past and because teachers have no way of knowing how much more (or less) success they might have if they were to try something else.

From the point of view of those responsible for managing overall school systems, the motivational problem is not really that teachers will not want to perform well. It is rather that there is too much opportunity—and too much incentive—for them to define standards of effectiveness that allow them to conclude that they *have* performed well, when more demanding standards and more critical assessments of performance might reveal ways in which they could improve. Indeed, under some circumstances teachers' desire to do well can actually *undermine* efforts to coordinate a school or district's overall program or efforts to increase teachers' sensitivity to the needs of their students. As Lortie (1975) notes, the pursuit of intrinsic satisfaction in the classroom naturally leads teachers to concentrate on doing those things they are most likely to do well, but not necessarily what their administrative superiors want them to do or what their students need them to do.

Merit pay is based on the assumption that it is possible to specify and measure levels of overall teaching performance. Doing so involves more than merely evaluating or making informed judgments about selected aspects of a teacher's performance. It involves specifying criteria that apply to all important aspects of all teachers' duties and specifying standards that permit evaluators to draw objective distinctions between different levels of performance on each of those criteria. Evaluators then have to weigh and combine these separate measurements to produce summary assessments of overall performance that each teacher is prepared to accept. If the evaluations are *not* accepted as being reasonably objective and fair, the perceived links between performance and compensation will be broken and the system will fail on its own terms.

Teacher opposition and general dissatisfaction with evaluations are the two reasons that most often prompt school districts to abandon merit pay schemes, usually after only a handful of years of experience with them.[1] The two reasons are closely connected. Perceptions that merit evaluations are biased, subjective, and generally unfair are more responsible for teacher opposition to merit pay than any other factor (Bacharach, Lipsky, and Shedd, 1984; Bacharach, Conley, and Shedd, 1990).

A few years ago at a conference on merit pay and career ladders, one southeastern state commissioner of education extolled the virtues of the merit compensation system he was about to implement in his state. He dismissed the question by one of the authors about how teachers would be evaluated under this new system by maintaining that the most important thing "was to take action, and worry about the evaluation system when we get to it." He chastised the academics on the panel for worrying too much about "technical" issues. His entire compensation system collapsed within two years, however, because of the failure to seriously consider issues of evaluation.

Unfortunately, the assumption that evaluation is a technical issue is too often used as an excuse for not examining the failures of pay-for-performance systems more carefully. Advocates of merit pay generally acknowledge that teacher confidence in merit pay is essential to a plan's success, and they recognize that weaknesses in an evaluation system are often what destroys such confidence. In fact, they themselves cite such findings to support their contention that teachers would be prepared to accept a carefully conceived and properly administered plan. What they do not acknowledge is that there is any serious weakness in the concept of merit pay itself. The problems that have plagued such plans, they insist, are technical problems that can be overcome with sufficient care in planning, administration, and training of evaluators (Educational Research Service, 1979).

Some of the evaluation problems associated with merit pay undoubtedly are technical. In theory, at least, they might be remedied if a district is careful enough about how it selects and trains evaluators and if it is prepared to devote sufficient time and money to administering the system (Bacharach, Conley, and Shedd, 1990). But a good merit evaluation system is expensive and administratively complex. It is not surprising that funds for administering the system are one of the first things to be slashed, eliminating any possibility of avoiding technical problems.

The real problem with merit evaluations, however, is more fundamental. The fairness and seeming objectivity of an evaluation system assume paramount importance when pay raises hang in the balance, but only the simplest and least demanding aspects of teaching can be reduced to objective criteria and then "measured." Evaluators cannot help making personal judgments and being at least somewhat subjective, because teaching itself requires teachers to make judgments, solve problems, and exercise discretion, while simultaneously managing relationships with large numbers of other people, in situations where cookbook solutions are rarely available.

A merit pay system, to the extent that it is successful, must have the effect of narrowing the criteria by which individual teachers and teachers as a group plan and assess their own efforts (Bacharach, Lipsky, and Shedd, 1984). If teaching higher-order analytic skills is not a criterion used to allocate merit awards, then there is every reason to believe that teachers would deemphasize such considerations in their teaching. The same would hold for any consideration not explicitly measured and given credit in a district's evaluation scheme. The need to reduce teaching effectiveness to a numerical score generates a pressure to focus only on those duties, behaviors, or outputs that are easily observed and measured.

Merit pay thus forces districts to focus attention on those aspects of the job that are least demanding but easiest to evaluate; it gives teachers reasons to perceive anything critical as a threat to their income; it discourages the open, free exchange of information and perspectives that are essential to the evaluation system's effectiveness; and it does so without ever completely eliminating the subjectivity and opportunities for bias that undermine confidence in the system and sour interpersonal relationships.

There are many explanations for the friction that merit pay engenders among teachers. To the extent that merit pay generates comparisons among teachers, either suggesting or proclaiming that some are more effective than others, it runs afoul of the "norm of noninterference" and the "logic of confidence" that dominate relationships in so many school systems (Lortie, 1975; Little, 1982a). More important, in public education merit pay generates quotas. It is well documented that merit pay districts set quotas on the number of teachers who can receive merit stipends. It is equally well documented that those quotas prompt teachers to perceive each other as competitors for scarce merit dollars. Thoughtful advocates of merit pay acknowledge that quotas generate friction, and they sternly warn districts not to use them. But few school districts can afford to heed such advice, given the way that school systems are funded.

In school systems, the money for merit stipends necessarily comes from general revenues and does not increase when a teacher improves his or her performance. The result is that there *has* to be some upper limit—some quota—on the number of merit dollars available, whether or not such a policy is ever formally acknowledged. In private-sector sales occupations and some entrepreneurial professions, where merit pay systems are often used successfully, the employer does not have to set quotas on how many employees can receive merit awards because each employee is individually responsible for generating the income from which his or her incentive payments will be drawn. The more money a person brings in, the more is available for distribution as rewards and the more he or she will get.

Only the wealthiest school districts can afford to set limits that permit all or most of their teachers a realistic chance of getting awards. Teachers in less fortunate districts understand that quotas exist; they understand that their districts cannot afford to let "too many" teachers get high merit ratings; they understand that any colleague who gets a high merit rating automatically diminishes their own chances of getting one; and they are understandably reluctant to cooperate or share job knowledge with each other as a consequence. The nature of school district funding and the inevitability of quotas is not the only reason why merit pay systems generate friction and disharmony among teachers, but it is undoubtedly the most fundamental.

Some advocates note that merit pay also generates competition among employees in the private sector, arguing that a degree of friction and competition might even be healthy. Their argument overlooks another fundamental feature of public education. Merit pay systems work in private-sector settings where it is possible to identify each employee's separate contributions to the organization and where cooperation among employees is not essential (Lawler, 1971). Education, however, is not something that goes on in isolated classrooms, but in *schools*. What ultimately matters is not what one teacher gives to one group of students at one point in time but what students acquire over twelve or thirteen years, as they pass back and forth between classrooms and from grade to grade and building to building. What ultimately matters is how each teacher's efforts fit together with the efforts of others.

Public education is fundamentally a cooperative enterprise, or rather, it *ought* to be a cooperative enterprise. School systems that build and sustain a culture of cooperation, that find ways of overcoming the barriers that separate teacher from teacher, that encourage sharing of job knowledge, and that focus teachers' attention on common, coherent, and challenging sets of goals stand out from others and do a particularly effective job of educating their students (Cohen, 1982; Rosenholtz, 1985). School boards and administrators are acutely aware of this need for more coherence, consistency, and cooperation. Their basic function is to coordinate all that goes on in a school or school system. Their recognition that interpersonal friction and disharmony threaten such coordination is usually what prompts them to abandon merit pay plans.

What is less often appreciated is that the concern for coordination is usually what made merit pay seem so attractive to them in the first place. Its advocates prefer to speak simply of a teacher's motivation "to perform," but such phrases are deceptive. It is more accurate to speak of a teacher's motivation to do what those designing and administering the evaluation system want them to do. *Merit pay is essentially a control mechanism, designed to give teachers incentives to pay more attention to what their administrators want them to do.*

Merit pay plans invariably fail, not because money is unattractive to teachers, or because the plans do not address real needs or potentially serious problems. They fail because money *is* attractive to teachers, and because the needs and problems they address are not as simple as their advocates suppose. In some kinds of work settings, offering money as a reward for performance can change the very meaning of the word "performance," undermining the tolerance for ambiguity and the ability to win the cooperation of others that are essential to its success.

Career and Job Ladders

Merit pay systems base compensation on assessments of performance. Most career ladder proposals, by contrast, draw distinctions among teachers' salaries based on the duties that teachers perform. They differentiate among responsibilities, creating several clusters of duties—in effect, several different jobs—and then rank and pay each job according to some criterion or criteria of relative professional responsibility or importance. Under most proposals, the basic tasks of classroom teaching are grouped in one job and placed at the bottom of the hierarchy; under other more fully differentiated staffing plans, teachers' aides and teaching assistants might occupy the lowest level of the hierarchy while regular classroom teachers occupy the middle.

In either case, those at the highest level or levels of a career ladder continue to spend a portion of their time in the classroom but also have responsibility for functions that traditionally have been assigned to administrators and staff specialists, such as course development, program evaluation, and teacher evaluation and training. Because a person assumes new duties with each promotion, and does not perform new duties *until* he or she is promoted, we will refer to such arrangements as "job ladders."

If the heart of the case for merit pay is that teachers need more incentives to do well in the classroom, the heart of the case for job ladders is that teachers need incentives and opportunities to *improve* their performance. The following are some of the concerns that prompt consideration of career ladders:

- Lack of opportunities for substantive exchange and cooperation among teachers creates serious problems for beginning teachers. Beginners typically find the first few years of teaching to be painful. Education schools and practice teaching do little to prepare them for the practical demands of managing a classroom, and lack of opportunities to draw on the job knowledge of more experienced teachers usually leaves them with no alternative but to learn to teach by trial and error (Lortie, 1975).

- Physical isolation, restrictive time schedules, weak evaluation systems, and inadequate programs of in-service education leave even experienced teachers with few opportunities to step back from their immediate classroom experiences and to consider how they might improve their performance (Little, 1982a).

- The bureaucratic division of labor that affords teachers little voice in decisions beyond their immediate classroom and assigns the highest status to those with the least connection to the classroom poses constant challenges to teachers' sense of professionalism (Bacharach and Conley, 1986).

- Most school systems provide few opportunities for teachers to have a sense of career advancement. The "flat" organizational structure of most school systems, limited opportunities for promotion, and lack of mobility among teaching positions leave many teachers with a sense of career stagnation. As a consequence, many become frustrated and discouraged and leave the profession or go into administration (Chapman and Hutcheson, 1982; Hart and Murphy, 1990).

According to one recent report, at least thirteen states have implemented career ladder programs for teachers either statewide (Missouri, Tennessee, Texas, Utah, Alabama, California, and Florida) or on a pilot/local option basis (Arizona, Indiana, North Carolina, Wisconsin, Colorado, and Vermont) (Southern Regional Education Board Career Ladder Clearinghouse, 1987). It is probably too soon to draw definitive conclusions about these systems' prospects for success, but it is already clear that most of the experiments have run into serious problems. Some, like those in Florida, have already collapsed, while others, like North Carolina's, are the subject of intense political debate (Haac, 1988; "In North Carolina, Career-Ladder Plan Nears a Crossroads," 1989). In most cases, the problems that have plagued career ladders are remarkably similar to those that haunt merit pay plans: They are expensive to administer and they generate dissatisfaction and competition among teachers. In fact, they run into the same basic problems as merit pay experiments for some of the same basic reasons.

That is not how things were supposed to turn out. Many of the early advocates of career ladders, in fact, criticized merit pay plans precisely because they do generate competition and undermine collegiality and cooperation among teachers (see, for example, Rosenholtz and Smylie, 1984). The purpose of career ladders, they argued, was to provide *all* teachers with opportunities for growth in their careers. Advancement would depend upon a teacher's individual qualifications. The opportunity for advancement would encourage each teacher to strengthen his or her knowledge and skills to assume more responsibility for decision making outside his or her classroom.

Whether by intention or accident, the typical career ladder has belied that description. Some plans, like those in Tennessee, Florida, and California, set explicit quotas on the number of higher-level positions open to teachers, meaning that the selection for advancement had to be competitive, no matter what the ostensible selection criteria were. Other proposals made no mention of quotas but incorporated a feature that virtually guarantees that quotas will exist: They specified particular duties that would be assigned to teachers at each level of such a ladder (Hart, 1987).

Under some proposals, higher-level teachers would be assigned formal supervisory or administrative authority over other teachers. Under other proposals, their duties would involve such things as course development, program evaluation, or serving as mentors to beginning teachers. In either case, those who aspire to promotion up a ladder probably think of promotions as advancements in their careers. But if too many people define career progress that way, most of them quickly become disillusioned. Most people are not promoted—cannot be promoted—*not* because they are not qualified to be at the higher level but because there is no vacant position at the higher level or because someone else has beaten them to it. Opportunities for promotions are necessarily limited in a job ladder system by the number of positions at each level and by turnover among people already in those positions. The specification that particular duties "belong" to teachers at particular levels of the system effectively precludes the possibility that advancement would depend solely or even primarily on individual qualifications.

Some career ladder advocates justify differentiation of duties on the grounds of financial feasibility, apparently convinced that the public is only willing to pay truly "professional" salaries to a smaller proportion of teachers, regardless of how many might "objectively" meet the ostensible standards for promotion (see Goodlad, 1983b; Shanker, 1985). Some of these advocates are also convinced that the pursuit of "excellence" necessarily and properly involves the cultivation of an educational elite, capable of infusing school systems with standards of performance that most teachers would not care to support. For these advocates, of course, quotas and competition for advancement are inherent in the very logic of their proposals.

Other career ladder advocates, however, do not appear to have quotas, cost savings, or educational elites in mind when they fashion their recommendations. For some, linking different duties to different career levels seems like a way of providing incentives for teachers to accept more responsibility for exercising leadership and innovation in their schools; for others, differentiation seems like a natural and necessary by-product of other proposals, such as providing mentors for beginning teachers; for still others, differentiation appears to be simply a way of providing opportunities for teachers to assume new responsibilities, with salary increments as recognition of their additional contributions and professional growth. In many cases, it seems, it simply never occurs to anyone that advancement in teaching can take any other form but promotion from one set of duties to another (Bacharach, Conley, and Shedd, 1986).

Some advocates note that existing school structures limit opportunities for promotion, and they point out, correctly, that their proposals would provide more opportunities for promotion than current structures. But the feature of their proposals that allows some teachers to assume new responsibilities is not the changes they would make in the compensation system but the changes that would allow some teachers more time to make such contributions. By limiting the number of higher-level positions available, job ladders actually *restrict* opportunities for teachers to make contributions outside their own classrooms.

The opposite side of this same coin troubles many teachers. Teachers are usually quick to notice that job ladders subtly (or not so subtly) disparage the basic functions of those classroom teachers who are not promoted: Those designated master teachers might continue to do some teaching, but it is their other duties—duties that invariably involve work *outside* the classroom—that justify their higher status and pay. Advocates of job ladders point out, with some justification, that the existing job structure in public education does precisely the same thing, and they note that their plans do not remove master teachers entirely from the classroom. As a round-about way of getting administrators back into the classroom, their approach may have some merit, but it still implies that the functions of classroom teaching are less professional or less important than those reserved for the next level.

A less obvious feature of job ladder plans is that promotions up the ladder cannot be construed as rewards for superior performance or recognition of skills demonstrated at some lower level. A person who is outstanding in the classroom may or may not be qualified to perform the duties reserved for the next level. If a job ladder is run properly, it is a person's qualifications for the *new* job that will govern promotion.

It is not surprising that many people equate "career advancement" with climbing a job ladder; promotion from one job to the next is a typical, if not *the* typical, form of career advancement in most occupational settings. It is the only formal form of career advancement presently available in public education (that is, promotion from teaching to administration).

What is surprising is that such otherwise predictable proposals are surfacing at the same time that the general public and the educational community are paying so much attention to research that is providing new and different images, models, and (sometimes) explanations of organizational effectiveness both in private-sector corporations and in schools themselves. Political leaders who are quick to cite private-sector experience to justify job hierarchies fail to take notice of the evidence of changes now occurring in American managerial practices. The irony is that the new structures (like job ladders) and processes (like merit pay) that are being touted as "reforms" in public education are precisely those that are now being labeled obsolete in other employment settings.

Private-sector organizations that achieve excellence are those that expect excellence from *all* their members and have cultures, processes, and leaders that constantly reinforce that expectation (Hackman and Oldham, 1980; Peters and Waterman, 1982). Parallel evidence from studies in public education consistently documents that schools that are particularly effective are those with high expectations for teachers as well as for students and with cultures, processes, and leaders that constantly reinforce "norms of collegiality" and "norms of continuous improvement" (Wynne, 1981; Little, 1982a; Cohen, 1982). It is incongruous that those responsible for such systems would ever tolerate, much less endorse, a "quota on excellence," or that they would intentionally structure pay relationships in a way that discourages cooperation and sharing of job knowledge among people whose work efforts are interdependent. Yet both notions are inherent in proposals that employ competition to allocate career ladder promotions in public education, just as they are in merit pay systems.

There is also evidence of growing disenchantment in all organizations with what one author calls the "competitive tournament" generated by job structures and their associated pay hierarchies (Sonnenfeld, 1984). When promotion or advancement means climbing a job hierarchy, the promotion system itself must be structured to eliminate larger and larger numbers of employees from consideration, discouraging progressively more people from developing further skills. Career planning that focuses on preparing oneself for a different job can be frustrated by subsequent elimination of that job, which discourages employees from accepting or seeking assignments that pose a high risk of failure. More important, such planning encourages employees to focus attention on developing and demonstrating skills that are unique to particular higher-level jobs—skills that they may never have occasion to use— while it discourages them from focusing attention on skills that they need on their present job: Having already secured that job, there is not much advantage gained by developing these skills further (Sonnenfeld, 1984).

These problems have proven especially serious for organizations that employ large numbers of professional and technical employees (Thompson and Dalton, 1976; Dalton, Thompson, and Price, 1977). Such organizations often create a second technical career ladder, ostensibly to allow such employees opportunities for promotion without having to switch from technical to managerial positions. (In purpose and structure, such technical ladders are much like many of the teacher career ladders presently being proposed.) Although the stated purpose is to hold those with superior technical skills in positions where those skills can continue to be used, these ladders often generate "make work," quasi-technical, or "assistant to" assignments for those at higher levels, simply because employers feel compelled to find different duties for those at higher levels to perform. Such ladders also tend to reinforce sharp distinctions between technical and managerial functions. This discourages employers from assigning duties that are arguably managerial (such as leadership of ongoing projects) to those on the technical ladder and encourages them to create new managerial positions to perform those duties instead (Dalton, Thompson, and Price, 1977).

As general strategies for reforming overall systems, job ladders fail to address the developmental needs of most teachers and schools, for whom lack of improvement is not a matter of inadequate motivation or direction but of insufficient means and opportunity. As Thompson and Dalton (1976), who have focused their attention on the career patterns of professional and technical employees, observe, the problem of so-called "skills obsolescence" is invariably one of organizational obsolescence—organizational structures and processes that create barriers to advancement and discourage initiative, growth, and acquisition of new skills.

The logic of administrative control implicit in the job ladder approach appears to offer the prospect of closer coordination of teachers' separate efforts. In this case it would delegate supervisory responsibilities to a larger number of employees and more clearly delineate what each employee is and is not expected to do. But as with merit pay, such appearances are likely to be illusory. By tying most teachers more closely to the classroom, lowering their status, and implying that decisions made outside the classroom are someone else's business, job ladders only aggravate the problems of isolation and communication that make coordination so difficult in most school systems.

Confusing Ends and Means

As strategies for improving the quality of public education, merit pay and job ladders are based on the assumption that there are serious problems with the performance of individual teachers. On the surface, their advocates tend to characterize the nature and source of those problems differently. Advocates of merit pay emphasize teachers' motivation; advocates of job ladders emphasize teachers' lack of skills and clear direction.

Merit pay advocates assume that teachers who fail to perform well do so largely, if not exclusively, because they lack sufficient motivation; they assume that linking pay to measured performance would be a useful and necessary, if not sufficient, way of motivating teachers. Advocates of job ladders are more likely to attribute poor performance to unclear, conflicting, or unrealistic performance expectations or to a lack of opportunities to develop skills needed to meet those expectations. Their solution is to create a new set of master teacher positions that bridges the gap between classroom and administration, expanding the number of people who perform staff development, evaluation, and quasi-supervisory functions but requiring them to maintain ties to the classroom.

It would be misleading, however, to draw too sharp a distinction between these two sets of assumptions and solutions. Advocates of merit pay acknowledge that performance expectations must be clear and attainable before teachers' performance can be fairly and objectively evaluated. In fact, they argue that fairness and objectivity are such critical considerations when pay raises hang in the balance that putting a merit pay system in place will *force* administrators to clarify expectations and make more opportunities for inservice education available to their teachers.

Similarly, advocates of job ladders acknowledge, albeit somewhat circumspectly, that teachers may need new and stronger incentives, not only to perform their regular classroom responsibilities but also to accept responsibility for the new and different functions that master teachers are expected to perform. Advocates of job ladders tend to characterize "opportunities for advancement" and "assuming wider responsibilities" as incentives, rewards, and forms of recognition in themselves, but they hedge their bets by throwing substantial pay raises into the bargain.

It is difficult, then, to draw sharp distinction between the purposes of compensation systems that focus on measured performance and the purposes of those that focus on levels of duties and responsibilities. The basic reason is that merit pay and job ladders share the same fundamental logic concerning how school systems ought to be managed. Both are devices for organizing and controlling who does what in a school system. The mechanisms are somewhat different: The former uses evaluation systems and performance incentives, the latter promotion procedures, divisions of labor, spans of control, and delegations of supervisory authority. But both represent ways of specifying and communicating what administrative superiors expect of teachers and providing teachers with incentives to comply with those expectations.

There is nothing, however, about the formal structure of the compensation system presently used in public education that prevents school districts from changing their evaluation systems, or providing more useful training, or substantially increasing the salaries of teachers as they advance through their careers. There is nothing that prevents them from recognizing exceptional efforts. Indeed, one study found that teachers who value recognition from administrators are those who tend to remain in teaching (Chapman and Hutcheson, 1982). Some critics claim that the so-called "lockstep" unified salary schedule leads districts to ignore issues of teaching effectiveness and restricts their flexibility in assigning responsibilities. Actually, however, it affords administrators and teachers more latitude in designing evaluation procedures and deciding who will do what in a school system than they would have under either merit pay or a job ladder system.

There is nothing about the unified salary schedules (as there is about merit pay) that requires that evalution procedures be tailored to produce broad, overall, seemingly objective assessments of a teacher's performance. There is nothing about the unified salary schedule that leads teachers to expect that sharing negative information or problems with evaluators and administrative superiors might compromise their chances for a raise in pay. There is nothing about this system that prompts evaluators (and those designing evaluation systems) to concentrate on aspects of a teacher's performance that are easily observed and readily measured, if other, less easily measured aspects of performance happen to be more important or problematic. But such features are inevitable when evaluations are linked to pay.

One feature of current compensation practices in public education, however, does discourage school systems from expanding the roles teachers play outside their classrooms. It is the one feature that comes closest to duplicating the salary differentiation of a job ladder. The differentiation occurs outside the framework of the unified salary schedule, sometimes on an ad hoc basis, and therefore goes unnoticed by most observers. Teachers and their representatives have generally maintained that the compensation provided by the unified salary schedule is for a person's regular teaching responsibilities and that any extra work should receive extra compensation as well.[2] Regular responsibilities vary from one district to the next and are usually defined obliquely or by exception. Thus, a "regular" teaching load is specified as a certain number of class periods or class preparations. Additional classes (teaching summer school, covering classes for absent colleagues, teaching classes that require more than the specified number of lesson preparations, and so on) call for additional compensation. Similarly, duties performed outside the classroom, such as coaching, supervising extracurricular activities, and serving on some committees, are often considered extra, calling for extra stipends. With each additional assignment comes additional compensation.

Such practices are inevitable, of course, as long as the regular teacher workday ends roughly when the normal school day ends and as long as the work year for teachers is approximately the same as the school year. Most teachers devote much more than their required number of work hours to their profession, but much of the additional time (primarily reviewing student work and planning lessons) is spent at home in isolation and goes officially unrecognized (Sizer, 1984). This combination of ad hoc pay and work assignment practices—paying for additional time when extra duties not directly connected to one's classroom have been formally assigned but neither acknowledging nor paying for work that is essential to the performance of one's core responsibilities—represents a real obstacle to developing a broader concept of teacher's basic professional responsibilities. As teachers play more active roles outside their classrooms—working together, learning from and teaching each other, and participating in more organizational decision making—we can expect this combination of practices to come under increasingly sharp attack.

Why do so many reformers insist on changing the way that teachers are compensated? It may be that some of them feel hamstrung by ad hoc pay and assignment practices and mistakenly attribute the resulting inflexibility to the "lockstep" unified salary schedule itself. But the answer is probably simpler. Most of the early reform commission reports seemed to take for granted that school systems ought to use their compensation systems to promote improvements in the quality of public education. In effect, they started by asking not *whether* but rather *how* the pay systems currently used in public education ought to be changed. They did not bother to consider whether or not those systems are in any real sense the cause of the problems to be addressed, whether or not they represent genuine obstacles to overcoming those problems, or whether or not a change in the compensation system would necessarily be an effective way of addressing them.

There are some hidden assumptions and leaps of faith and logical nonsequiturs in such an approach to educational reform, but this thinking still serves a useful purpose. It reminds us that a compensation system is essentially a *tool* for managing the relationships between an organization and the people it employs. Money is too important (to many people and for many reasons) for us to ignore the possibility that a change in a compensation system might be a powerful tool for effecting desired changes in public education. But sometimes money is *too* important, for too many reasons, to be an effective tool of reform.

Advocates of merit pay and job ladders confuse means with ends—they equate controlling individual teachers with achieving coordination among them—and ultimately they undermine their own purposes. Not only do they restrict the discretion and flexibility of individual classroom teachers (which their advocates will readily acknowledge) but they undermine what little incentive exists for teachers to cooperate among themselves.

As long as teaching is thought of exclusively as what is done inside the classroom, boards and administrators will be attracted to pay systems and other devices that allow them to control what teachers do behind their classroom doors. And as long as boards and administrators pursue such purposes, teachers will do whatever they can to preserve their autonomy and keep their doors closed.

In Chapter Four, we discussed ways that individual teachers might be encouraged to expand the scope of their activity beyond their immediate classrooms without sacrificing their central commitment to classroom teaching. Chapter Five has considered the complex role that compensation plays in motivating teachers to do so. Now that we have carefully examined what it is that teachers do individually in their classrooms (and the issue of paying them for what they do), it is time to look more closely at what they might do outside the classroom to strengthen what they and their colleagues do on the inside. Therefore, it is appropriate to consider in Chapter Six how the school system as an organization is set up to utilize the teachers' collective talents and energies.

Notes

1. One survey of school district experience with merit pay found that 10.5 percent of all school districts surveyed either had a merit pay plan in 1977–1978 or else had had such a plan in the past and had abandoned it. Of these, roughly 61.4 percent had dropped the plan and returned to the unified salary schedule after an average of six years experience. Of the remainder, over half had had merit pay for less than six years, suggesting that many of them were probably still candidates for disillusionment (Educational Research Service, 1979).

2. The authors are indebted to Richard Segall, principal of the Englewood (New Jersey) Dwight Morrow High School, for pointing out the importance of this not-so-hidden but usually overlooked feature of compensation practices in public education.

6

STRUCTURING PARTICIPATION

The proposition that teachers should be involved in making decisions for their schools and school districts (as opposed to decisions only for their individual classrooms) is gaining widespread support among public policymakers. Task forces of the National Governors' Association called for giving teachers "a real voice in decision [making]" and for developing "school-site management" that respects the professional judgment of teachers (National Governors' Association, 1986). The Education Commission of the States (ECS, 1986), the Carnegie Corporation's Task Force on Teaching as a Profession (Carnegie Commission, 1986), a task force of deans of schools of education (Holmes Group, 1986), and a prominent state commission (California Commission on the Teaching Profession, 1985) all issued similar calls. The National Education Association and the National Association of Secondary School Principals jointly developed and publicized a "cooperative model for a successful secondary school" that places heavy emphasis on teachers' participation in an expanded agenda of school-level decision making (National Education Association/National Association of Secondary School Principals, 1986). The American Federation of Teachers has repeatedly called for restructuring school systems to give teachers authority over decisions that affect their work (AFT Task Force, 1986).

These recent reports provide a healthy antidote to ones issued just a few years before, which tended to treat teachers and local administrators as the targets of reform rather than initiators and supporters (Bacharach and Conley, 1986). The assumption that these actors have to be *forced* into accepting more responsibility for the quality of education (as well as the assumption that states can devise effective policies to compel them to do so) has started to give way.

Taking its place is the argument that states can most effectively influence reform by establishing the preconditions for improvement, including an environment that enables teachers and administrators to do their jobs effectively and therefore encourages good teachers to remain in teaching (Education Commission of the States, 1986). According to this argument, teachers and school administrators need to be given more authority, more opportunities, and more resources to make decisions concerning the educational programs of their schools and districts.

This chapter examines the rationale for encouraging greater employee participation in decision making, in public education and elsewhere, and then considers the variety of ways in which participation can be structured. Many observers maintain that a wholesale adjustment of decision-making authority, from district offices to schools, is needed to revitalize public education. The authors agree that some shift in authority may be appropriate, but structures that facilitate participation on some kinds of issues today are likely to be obstacles to participation on other kinds tomorrow. The real need is to become less preoccupied with authority and to develop influence structures that can adapt to a constantly changing environment.

The Case for Involvement

The research to support involving teachers in school and district decision making has investigated many possible outcomes associated with that involvement. The direct research on teacher participation tends to parallel the research on participation in other settings (summarized in Chapter One). That is, most (but not all) studies indicate an association between teacher participation and job satisfaction (Conway, 1984; Warner, 1981; Flannery, 1980; Thierbach, 1980). Other studies provide credible grounds for believing that teacher participation can help reduce role conflict (Alutto and Belasco, 1973; Bacharach, Bamberger, and Mitchell, forthcoming), raise morale and trust for school leaders (Conway, 1984), and reduce teacher stress and burnout (Bacharach, Conley, and Bauer, 1986). Several studies suggest that lack of opportunities to participate in decision making is a factor in many teachers' decisions to leave the profession (Chapman and Hutcheson, 1982; Vance and Schlechty, 1982; Bacharach, Bauer, and Shedd, 1986; Bacharach and Bamberger, 1990).

Purkey and Smith's (1983) detailed review of the research on school effectiveness cites only two studies that suggest that participation in decision making might contribute to school effectiveness, but the school effectiveness research was not designed to test the effects of participation or even determine how schools might have become effective. On the other hand, that research does lend strong support for the proposition that teachers and administrators in more effective schools work closely together. Teachers (as well as principals) in effective schools sometimes provide instructional leadership, and instructional leadership is needed at the school as well as district level (Edmonds, 1979; Rosenholtz, 1985).

The extensive research on the factors affecting organizational and policy changes in public education, and particularly factors affecting teacher acceptance of change, indicates that teacher participation in decision making is certainly helpful—and probably crucial—to the success of any change effort (Berman and McLaughlin, 1980; Runkel and Harris, 1983; Daft and Becker, 1978). Because adaptation to change is a critical issue in organizations that combine high levels of employee discretion and close coordination of employee efforts, this literature lends important support for efforts to promote greater teacher participation.

Studies of innovation in school systems have also generated conclusions that are supportive of participation. Schools that are particularly innovative have been found to have "norms of collegiality" and "norms of continuous improvement" (see Chapters Four and Five) that minimize status differences between administrators and teachers, engage all staff members in planning new pro-

grams, and cultivate an ongoing dialogue about how school programs and individual performance might be improved (Little,
1982a). Other studies have documented the fact that new school
programs have a much greater chance of success (judged by a
number of different criteria) when teachers are involved in their
initiation, development, and implementation (as opposed to only
their implementation) (McLaughlin and Berman, 1975). Studies of
schools as political and cultural systems have generated similar conclusions about the potential value of involving teachers in school
and district decision making (Weatherley and Lipsky, 1977; Wolcott, 1977; McDonald, 1988; Bacharach and Mitchell, 1986).

Researchers who have actually asked teachers whether they
think they should be more involved in decision making have documented two distinctly different kinds of responses, depending upon how the question is worded. If the question is posed abstractly,
teachers consistently indicate that they do think they should be
more involved in school and district decision making (Bacharach,
Bauer, and Shedd, 1986; Corcoran, 1987), especially on issues with
direct relevance to their own teaching responsibilities (Bacharach,
Bamberger, Conley, and Bauer, 1990; Mohrman, Cooke, and Mohrman, 1978).

When the question is posed more concretely, however, teachers express skepticism about whether "involvement" provides them
with any real influence. One study found that teachers were reluctant to take advantage of apparent opportunities for involvement.
This was not because they did not believe involvement might have
some benefits or were troubled by its potential costs but because past
experience convinced them that most invitations to become involved in decision making were merely efforts to secure their assent
to decisions that administrators had already made. At best, they were
invitations to help managers "fill in the details" (Duke, Showers,
and Imber, 1980). Corcoran (1987) observed similar teacher reactions
to the most frequently employed mechanisms for teacher participation: departmental structures, schoolwide councils, and ad hoc committees (Hart, 1990).

Some of the recent interest in employee involvement in public education can be attributed to the growing popularity of the
same theme in the private sector, although teachers generally have

had more formal opportunities for involvement—and more support for the *idea* of involvement—than their private-sector counterparts. Private-sector corporations, beset by declining productivity, increasingly vulnerable to foreign competition, disillusioned with strategies aimed at enhancing direct control over a restive workforce, and impressed with the apparent effectiveness of Japanese management techniques, such as quality circles, are showing increasing interest in strategies for enhancing employee involvement in decision making (Walton, 1985).

One 1982 report estimated that one-third of the nation's 500 largest corporations had found some form of participatory management or "quality of work life" program to be effective in their organizations (New York Stock Exchange, 1982). Leading business journals and scholars have hailed the advent of a "new industrial relations," claiming that the new job enrichment and participation strategies represent "a fundamentally different way of managing people" ("The New Industrial Relations," 1981; Walton, 1985). Donald Peterson, the president of the Ford Motor Company, declared participatory management "our second bottom line" (quoted in United States Department of Labor, 1986). The president of General Motors followed suit ("GM Woos Employees . . . ," 1989).

It is not surprising that public policymakers are prescribing the same strategies for public education. Private-sector management techniques have always been attractive to policymakers and managers of educational systems, if only because they came with a presumed legitimacy for their policies and approaches that neither the public nor other educators could easily challenge (Callahan, 1962; Tyack and Hansot, 1982). But is educators' interest in employee involvement anything more than infatuation with the latest private-sector fad?

At least with respect to private-sector developments, there are reasons to believe that recent high-profile affirmations of support for involving employees in decision making are genuine. More and more managers are concluding that they do need to make better use of their employees' knowledge, skills, and opinions. Two new arguments for involvement are emerging:

1. *Involvement improves the quality of an organization's management decisions.* It does so by making full use of the knowl-

edge of those who have the closest contact with the organization's clients or customers and the knowledge of those who are most familiar with existing or potential problems in the work process itself. The quality of the organization's products or services and the processes by which they are produced or delivered is thereby improved. Such organizations also increase the number of sources of ideas and information that they consider in reaching management decisions, increasing the likelihood that those decisions will take different perspectives into account and will be more creative and less anchored to conventional wisdoms (Kanter, 1983; Peters and Waterman, 1982; Ouchi, 1981).

2. *Involvement enhances effectiveness, efficiency, and productivity by improving the organization's ability to respond rapidly to problems or opportunities in its environment.* Control mechanisms may provide needed coordination among different organizational members, but only at the expense of flexibility, upward communication, cooperation, openness to new ideas, and openness to change itself. By drawing employees into the process of making decisions, involvement—as a general strategy of management—allows organizations to reduce their dependence upon hierarchical control mechanisms (Peters and Waterman, 1982; Argyris, 1982).

Accompanying the emergence of these two arguments (and to some extent prompting them) has been a wavering of confidence in the principles of hierarchical control and scientific management that have governed much of the thinking of private-sector managers for three-quarters of a century. The principles of hierarchical control of work processes were not developed in a vacuum. Rather, they were designed to meet the particular demands of managing enterprises engaged in the mass production of standardized products (Piore, 1982; Taylor, [1911] 1967). The logic of a detailed, explicit division of labor and centralized planning and control of managerial decisions was premised on the assumption that the products being produced—and the technologies used to produce them—would remain relatively stable for extended periods of time.

American manufacturers, challenged in mass production markets by foreign competition, are now under increasing pressure to shift from the production of standardized products for mass markets to the production of smaller batches of specialized products tailored to the needs of particular groups of customers. New and adaptable computerized technologies are making it technically feasible for manufacturers to carve out such niches. Geographic proximity to specialized markets allows them to protect these advantages from foreign producers.

But manufacturers cannot take advantage of these market opportunities and technical wherewithal unless they also change how they organize and manage their *human* resources. The more specialized, varied, and changeable the products an organization produces and the fewer of each product it produces, the more likely it is that the tasks necessary to produce the products will constantly change. As that happens, it becomes less feasible to assign each employee a discrete set of duties that will remain constant for an extended period of time. That, in turn, means that it will become increasingly difficult for staff experts at higher organizational levels to anticipate and decide what all those tasks and duties should be. Instead, management must place increasing reliance on its line workers—those who have detailed knowledge of production processes and customer needs—to specify how their separate and collective efforts ought to be organized (Piore, 1982; Kochan, Katz, and Mower, 1985). Management expects workers and their immediate supervisors to exercise much more discretion over which problems they refer to higher management and which ones they resolve for themselves.

Economies of scale (or the lack of them) can also affect the appropriateness of different management approaches. The fewer of any one product an organization produces, the more important it is for it to anticipate and avoid mistakes that might occur in the production process before production begins. For example, an organization that intends to make a million widgets can afford to catch mistakes in its production process after production has been initiated and can assign responsibility for catching and correcting them to the staff experts who initially designed the process. The costs of wasted materials and time can be passed on to a million consumers without any appreciable impact on the price of the widgets. On the other hand, an organization that intends to make ten highly specialized widgets for a select group of customers must catch and correct mistakes before production begins, or else the costs, in terms of lost time, materials, and (ultimately) market position can be disastrous. The managers of American corporations are finding employee involvement strategies attractive because they provide management with *information* about production processes that is vital to their firms' productive efficiency, because they provide management with needed *flexibility* in the way work is organized and managed, and because they allow the organization quick *adapability* to new circumstances and problems (Piore, 1982; Ouchi, 1981; Peters and Waterman, 1982; Kanter, 1983).

If this line of reasoning is correct, then industrial employers are becoming increasingly dependent on their workers' detailed knowledge of work processes, on their workers' willingness and ability to exercise discretion and judgment, and on their workers' willingness to work cooperatively with one another in the face of constantly changing work situations. Thus, there are reasons to believe that employee involvement is becoming a necessary strategy (rather than just an occasionally helpful tactic) for managing at least some industrial enterprises. The same reasons suggest that employees are more likely to be afforded real discretion or influence under such circumstances. Without much fanfare (but with profound implications for how organizations and their relationships with employees are managed), "involvement in decision making" has shifted from being something that managers give to their employees, to something that they get from them.

In structural terms, the pressures on school systems to provide a high-quality education for large numbers of students, while remaining flexible enough to adjust to the needs and abilities of individual students, are remarkably similar to the pressures on American manufacturers to meet the specialized needs of large numbers of customers while improving quality across the board.

Better Decisions. The most straightforward argument for enhancing teacher participation, then, is simply that doing so will improve the quality of decisions made at the school or district level. As the only employees with direct, ongoing contact with students—and day-to-day responsibility for their instruction—teachers are a school system's primary reservoir of organizational knowledge about means and ends (Bacharach and Conley, 1988). Like private-sector organizations facing the demand for specialization, school systems can no longer maintain that they have a single, readily defined "product" that can be mass-produced. As they abandon that pretense, they are forced to turn more and more often to those with direct knowledge of students' needs and abilities.

The fact that individual teachers may not fully appreciate or be able to act on their knowledge does not make their collective knowledge any less critical to organizational effectiveness. The hitch, of course, is that someone has to *collect* collective knowledge before it can be put to use. Much of the management of school systems involves the collection (or attempted collection) of the student, class, or situation-specific information needed to make broader organizational decisions. In this context, those with primary responsibility for school and district decision making need the advice and information of those who are most knowledgeable about students and actual work processes. Participation strategies shift responsibility for identifying and volunteering information with systemwide implications to those with direct access to that information, without burying them under piles of report forms.

Overcoming Isolation. Teacher participation also promotes horizontal integration among teachers and the decisions that each of them, individually, makes. Most studies confirm that teachers have few opportunities to engage in substantive dialogue and exchange of information, even though their pedagogical knowledge, skills, and information about students are arguably a school system's most valuable resources. The solitary nature of most teaching assignments, the physical layout of school facilities, and restrictive time schedules usually preclude such interaction (Lortie, 1975). So do organizational norms that discourage advice giving or seeking and treat "work" as something necessarily and exclusively done in the classroom (Little, 1982a).

All too often, teachers define their need for discretion as a right to autonomy, buttressed by an "ideology of noninterference" that regulates interactions among teachers as well as between teachers and administrators (Ashton, Webb, and Doda, 1982, p. 240). This norm of noninterference tends to make peer criticism "unprofessional" (McLaughlin, 1984, p. 197) and casts requests for peer assistance as indications of incompetence (Rosenholtz, 1985). As Bishop (1977) observes, "The basic isolation which is imposed on the teacher by self-contained classroom organization . . . is extended by her [or him] to become a broader right of isolation from colleagues and their opinions and evaluations. Isolation becomes positively valued . . ." (p. 178).

Closely linked to this norm of noninterference is an egalitarian norm among teachers. Lortie, for example, indicated (as of 1969) that teachers were unenthusiastic about current differentiations (such as grade and departmental chairperson positions) and expressed no interest in additional ranks (Lortie, 1969). Various case studies have indicated that teachers believe that (1) they should have equal status and (2) requesting or proffering advice confers superior status upon the advice giver (Glidewell, 1983).

A combination of structural and normative factors, then, isolates teachers from each other and prevents them from sharing the reservoir of skills, knowledge, information, and resources that, as individuals, they have acquired through the daily demands of continuous classroom decision making. School systems that are supposedly strapped for time waste enormous amounts reinventing wheels that have been invented and reinvented countless times before. In doing so, they not only deny individuals the opportunity to learn from each other, but they deny themselves, as systems, the opportunity to cultivate a continuously expanding body of professional and institutional knowledge that each individual can supplement, reinforce, and pass on to others.

Coordination of Management. The need for greater coordination of teachers' separate activities constitutes another reason for involving teachers in school and district decision making. Mohrman, Cooke, and Mohrman (1978) found that teachers wanted to participate in technical decisions—those with a direct effect on teaching—but not in what the researchers called managerial issues, such as hiring, budgets, and overall building assignments. Data from the NEA's CART survey confirm that teachers are most insistent that they be involved in decisions that directly affect their classroom activities, such as how to teach, what to teach, and which texts are available and actually used. As we have already noted, however, the same data indicate that the discrepancy that teachers perceive between desired and actual participation is greatest in areas that fall on the borderline between classroom and school: grading policies, student discipline codes, student rights, student class assignments, and (above all) standardized testing policies. Teachers are most likely to feel the effects of each others' teaching in areas like these. Different expectations of students can generate confusion and provoke charges of inconsistency or unfairness. If we are reading the NEA data correctly, teachers feel least excluded from areas that are most important to their daily activities, but they feel most severely "cut out" of decision making in those areas that regulate the relationships between their students and the rest of the school system (National Education Association, 1988).

Setting formal policies is only one element in managing an organization. Translating general policies into group and individual assignments; orchestrating different activities; setting and adjusting time achedules; reconciling conflicting priorities; developing human resources; securing material and other resources; and monitoring the progress of programs, staff members, and students are also managerial functions that can benefit from teacher participation.

Because these kinds of decisions involve direct coordination of activities, they necessarily require communication with those whose activities are being coordinated. In fact, many of the responsibilities that are typically reserved for district and school administrators represent nothing more than roundabout ways of coordinating the activities of teachers in adjacent classrooms. Studies of schools as "loosely coupled systems" suggest that overreliance on administrators to serve as coordinators, initiators, and conduits of information between staff members (among other things) aggravates the very "looseness" that hierarchical strategies are supposedly so good at overcoming (Weick, 1982). Providing more opportunities for teachers to work—and talk—together can improve both the quality and efficiency of coordination in a school system.

Given the nature of teachers' work, it is misleading to frame the issue of participation as a question of whether teachers should be involved in school management. Their day-to-day decision making within their individual classrooms involves the definition and balancing of goals; the translation of goals into particular activities; the securing of resources and their commitment to particular purposes; and the monitoring, evaluation, and adjustment of the performance of individuals, groups, and the teacher him- or herself. Despite their sometimes low status in the eyes of the public, teachers are, in fact, managers, performing managerial functions (Bacharach, Conley, and Shedd, 1987; Berliner, 1983).

But teachers' involvement in decision making is almost entirely that of exercising delegated authority within the context and constraints of policies and resource allocations over which most teachers, in most systems, have little influence. The issue of participation, then, is properly framed as one of closer *integration* of management decision making at district, school, and classroom levels. The more teachers are involved in planning, organizing, and evaluating school and district policies, programs, and resources, the more influence the school and the district can be expected to have on the classroom.

One of the greatest strengths of participation, as a means of coordination, is that it need not be exercised through more directive supervision or more detailed bureaucratic prescriptions. By building consensus on goals and agreement on priorities, it allows the relaxation of controls over the means that individuals will use to serve those ends (Argyris, 1982; Kanter, 1983; Bacharach and Conley, 1988). Broader involvement in centralized planning and assessment of policy permits more decentralized responsibility for execution. Recent research on school effectiveness ascribes great importance to goal consensus and a sense of school mission (Wynne, 1981; Rosenholtz, 1985) and the undeniable need to allow teachers wide discretion over how they orchestrate their classroom activities (Lortie, 1969; Bacharach, Conley, and Shedd, 1986). No more persuasive argument exists, therefore, for increasing teacher participation in school and district decision making.

Private-sector developments support the contention that participation strategies might afford school systems opportunities to give their teachers even more discretion than they presently exercise—particularly over *how* they plan, execute, and evaluate their instructional efforts—and yet allow the systems to improve coordination of teachers' separate efforts. In professional settings, like other settings requiring constant adjustment to the needs of groups and the needs of particular clients or customers, participatory management is best understood as an approach to the coordination of different individuals' efforts rather than to the supervision of individuals. The case for participation ultimately rests on the need for a closer, more organic integration of strategic and operational, technical and managerial decisions throughout a school system.

Forms of Participation

Different people have different conceptions of what it means to involve teachers in decision making. Depending on who is asked, "involvement" can mean anything from occasional solicitation of opinions to a wholesale redefinition of who makes what decisions in a school district. Proposals for restructuring school systems typically focus on shifting authority on selected issues from district offices to schools and establishing some form of governing council that includes teachers and (often) parents, as well as administrators: so-called "school-site management." But other forms of participation have received attention, as well, such as "school improvement teams" and similar task forces, charged with making recommendations to their districts' boards of education for changes.

These differences may be one reason administrators and teachers have such different assessments of the present state of collaboration in their districts. Ninety-three percent of the building principals responding to a recent survey indicated that "decision making in my school is a collaborative process," whereas only 32 percent of the teachers in their schools agreed with the same statement (see Organizational Analysis and Practice, 1989). Follow-up discussions of these data indicated that the two groups defined collaboration differently. Principals believed that teachers were involved in decision making if some teachers were given the opportunity to voice their opinions about particular decisions. Teachers dismissed mere consultation, particularly if it involved a handpicked group of teachers, and insisted that genuine involvement carries with it the right to make decisions without prior approval.

These differences illustrate an important distinction. Employees can be involved in decision making in either of two ways: They can actually make decisions themselves, or they can participate in decisions made by others. Some researchers protest that these two forms of involvement—the one based on the *exercise of author-ity,* the other based on the *exercise of influence*—are so different that they cannot be usefully compared (see Locke and Schweiger, 1979). Others insist that the two forms must be considered together, treat-ing the exercise of delegated authority as one end of a relative-influence continuum and those situations in which superiors exer-cise unilateral authority without input or influence from employees as the other end (Nightingale, 1982; Susman, 1979). In between (they argue) are situations in which one or the other provides (1) information or (2) information and opinions to the decision maker. The midpoint of such a continuum would be represented by situa-tions in which each party has a veto over any decision reached and in which decision making is therefore shared equally by both.

Both of these arguments raise important issues, but both are misleading. The exercise of delegated authority to make certain decisions and the exercise of influence over someone else's decision making both represent ways of exercising "voice" in decisions in an organization concerning who will do what, with what resources, and toward what ends. All else being equal, employees who have been given the authority to make certain decisions probably have more voice over those decisions than those who have opportunities to influence such decisions. But we all know of occasions when persons with crucial information or authoritative opinions have exercised more real influence over decisions than those with the ostensible authority to make them. The differences between the ex-ercise of authority and the exercise of influence, therefore, are not simply ones of degree.

Authority (the acknowledged right to make a final decision with respect to some matter) is a finite quantity. Its exercise may be circumscribed, revoked, prohibited, or even shared; but the more authority one person or party has in a particular situation the less is available to others. *Influence,* on the other hand, need not be framed in "fixed-sum" terms. Two parties may each have "a lot" of influence over each other's decisions, "a little" influence, or equal or various amounts of influence in between (see Bacharach and Lawler, 1981). Providing employees with more influence over decisions reached at higher levels of the organization does not nec-essarily decrease higher management's own influence, but doing so might provide all parties with more influence over each other's decisions.

Individuals can exercise delegated authority as individuals, in groups, or as representatives of other (usually larger) groups, or they can participate in higher-level decisions on any of those terms.

- *Individual employees* can be given authority to define their own responsibilities, determine and secure their own resources, and monitor their own performance, or they can participate in decisions made by others with respect to such matters.
- *Groups of employees* can be given the collective authority to define at least some of the parameters of their own work, divide responsibilities and allocate resources among their own members, or, acting together, have various levels of input into such decisions.
- *Employee representatives* can be given the authority to veto or agree to changes in managerial policies that affect other employees (that is, more employees than those directly involved in the discussions concerning such policies), or employee representatives can participate in higher-level decisions on behalf of a still wider group.

As Table 5 indicates, each of these approaches can be used to increase employee involvement in decision making:

Table 5. Strategies for Involving Employees in Decision Making.

Level of Decisions	General Strategy	
	Delegation	*Participation*
Individual	Job enrichment	Management by objectives
Group	Autonomous work groups	Quality circles
Representative	Works councils	Labor-management committees

Note: Approaches listed in cells are examples of more general strategies.

Management by objectives is a participation strategy that relies upon periodic negotiations between individuals and their supervisors to set measurable objectives that will provide direction for each individual's efforts over a specified period of time, thereby allowing the individual more discretion over *how* he or she will perform the work (what we have termed "performance decisions") (Blake and Mouton, 1964).

Quality circles are small groups of employees, generally from the same work areas, who meet on a regular basis to identify, analyze, and generate solutions to problems in their work environment, either in the work process itself or in any of the immediate organizational or interpersonal contexts that affect performance. They represent a participation strategy, since immediate supervisors are either circle members themselves or must agree to any solutions proposed by a circle (Thompson, 1982).

Labor-management committees are groups of employee and management representatives who meet periodically to address problems outside the context of formal contract negotiations or grievance procedures. They may be formed to address particular issues, such as employee health and safety, or they may serve as forums for discussing whatever issues one or the other party chooses to raise (Kochan, Katz, and Mower, 1985; Nurick, 1985).

Job enrichment is a delegation strategy that assigns to individual employees more responsibility for whole products or services, thereby requiring less direct supervision of individuals and less coordination among employees and providing employees with a greater sense of accomplishment in their work (Hackman and Oldham, 1980).

Autonomous work groups replicate, at the group level, the delegation strategy of providing employees with more responsibility for making management decisions with respect to complete products or services. They are used in situations where it is impractical to assign a single person such responsibility but possible to assign it to a relatively small group of employees performing interdependent tasks (Trist, 1981; Weisbord, 1985).

Works councils are groups of employee representatives who have formal authority to veto or approve certain management policies, generally ones with an impact on terms and conditions of employment. This is a delegation strategy widely employed in Europe; the closest parallels in the United States would be employee representation on boards of directors of worker-owned firms and agreements by employers (generally in craft settings) to abide by union-established work rules, rather than insisting on joint negotiation of such rules (Jain, 1980).

The particular approaches listed in Table 5 are illustrations of the six more general structures that result when either delegation or participation is used as a means of involving individuals, groups, or employee representatives in decision making. Each of these approaches, in turn, can be distinguished by the *scope* of employees' involvement, the *formal structure* of their involvement, the *processes* employed as means of exercising either authority or influence, and the kinds of *support* the employer provides to sustain the efforts (Shedd, 1987).

What follow are brief summaries of characteristics that fall under each of these categories, together with indications of why each might be an important criterion for distinguishing among efforts to involve teachers in decision making.

Scope. This concerns the nature of the subjects that participants address. The first and most obvious dimension of scope is the kinds of issues addressed. Some "involvement" programs are explicitly designed to address educational policy issues; others are meant to address what might be termed climate issues. The former concern the substance of a school system's instructional program, the latter the relationships and decision-making processes that support such a program. These distinctions often blur in practice, however, since most programs allow participants some leeway in deciding which issues they will address. In fact, some of the most important scope questions concern how participants and others go about determining which issues will be addressed.

One way that some programs answer this question is to spell out specific goals in advance for the program. Alternatively, a procedure may be specified by which participants set their own goals, either at the outset or at a specific time after they have begun working with one another. Many "effective schools" programs, for example, work within a framework of goals supplied by school effectiveness researchers, whereas many problem-solving programs are defined by their standard processes rather than their fixed goals.

Another way of defining the scope issue is to determine who sets the agenda of subjects to be discussed. In some instances, management defines the basic agenda in instituting the process, as is often the case with task forces or committees. In other instances, definition of an agenda is left to participants themselves.

Yet another dimension of scope concerns the limitations that are placed on discussions, either in terms of discussions themselves or (more often) in terms of their results. The three most frequently employed kinds of limitations are (1) prohibitions on taking up issues or making recommendations that go beyond the authority of those sitting on the committee; (2) prohibitions on discussing or submitting recommendations that would require some other department or agency to take action; and (3) prohibitions on discussion of issues that might be framed as grievances under a negotiated labor agreement, or recommendations that would require changes in such an agreement. In more general terms, the issue is whether those involved in a committee or group have the formal authority to make final decisions in any areas or whether they have to seek approval for any or all of the plans they develop.

Formal Structure. The structure of a participation program defines who does what and who deals with whom. First, which groups participate and what is the mix of participants? Which groups are involved (for example, teachers, specialists, principals, central office staff, superintendent, board members, parents, other community members, students)? Are participants drawn from one level or more than one level of the organization? The decision to establish homogeneous groups (which must submit recommendations to higher levels of the school system) or heterogeneous groups (which often have officials with approval authority physically present) is probably the most significant structural decision to be made.

Second, is the immediate program structure broad and inclusive or narrow and selective? Is it designed to provide all faculty members or staff members with a vehicle for participation in decision making, such as departmental structures or suggestions systems open to all? Or does it directly involve only a limited number of staff members, such as faculty councils, permanent committees, or ad hoc task forces? Those who extol participation as a new concept in public education overlook the fact that some long-standing structures, like secondary school departments and middle school faculty teams, provide opportunities for broader participation than many more recent experiments (Corcoran, 1987).

The third structural issue (closely related to the second) is whether individuals participate as individuals or as group representatives. In immediate terms, the distinction implies different kinds of selection processes and different arrangements for replacing members who withdraw from the program. In broader terms, it implies less or more obligation to represent the interests or opinions of others not directly involved and different degrees of urgency to the issue of communicating with others.

Fourth, how are participants selected? Can anyone participate at his or her own initiative? Are participants elected? Appointed? Are all members of a given group (all principals, all faculty members in a given school, and so on) automatically participants (as they would be in most broad-based programs)?

Fifth, does the program consist of group discussions at one level of the system or is there a structure of simultaneous discussions at more than one level (that is, a districtwide committee, school-level committee(s), or both)? One program that worked with homogeneous groups comparable to private-sector quality circles owed much of its success to the fact that building principals who acted as approving officials for teams of their own teachers also had a team of their own, which submitted recommendations to the superintendent.

Sixth, do the groups themselves have designated leaders for their discussions, and if so, how and by whom are they selected and according to what criteria? Is leadership an expected part of their job responsibilities or an additional responsibility, added without adjustments to their other responsibilities?

Seventh, what provisions have been made for overall coordination of the program? Is someone designated as program coordinator? If so, is that function one of his or her regular duties or an additional responsibility? Is there a steering committee, and if so, how are its members selected and what are its responsibilities?

Processes. Process issues concern how participants go about making decisions. First, and most significant, are discussions conducted according to a structured, preestablished approach, or is it up to participants to determine on an ad hoc basis how they will conduct their discussions? Some researchers contend that a structured process is essential; others hardly mention it. Our own conviction (discussed below) is that the need for a well-defined decision-making process varies, depending upon other features of an involvement program: The broader and less well defined the scope of a group's activities, the more important it appears to be that it have a well-defined process by which to make its decisions.

Second, which stages of decision making are participants involved in? Do they generate solutions to already defined problems, or are they responsible for identifying and defining problems or issues as well? Do they engage in detailed analysis of problems, or do the causes and solutions of problems tend to be obvious, once the problems themselves have been identified? Do they generate possible solutions? Are they responsible for selecting one or more recommended solutions, or do they decide the solution(s) to be implemented? Are they charged with implementing the solution(s) selected? Will they monitor the implementation process over time?

Third, what forms of input do participants have into school or district decision making? Do they gather and provide information to be used in decision making, and if so, do they employ systematic data-gathering techniques such as employee surveys to do so? Do they have a hand in interpreting the survey data? Do they make recommendations on policy alternatives submitted by others? Do they generate and make policy recommendations on their own initiative? Do they have the authority to make decisions on policies or programs, without reference to any higher authority? Do they have the authority/responsibility for implementing decisions themselves (and must their decisions be made with that responsibility in mind), or can implementation be assigned to some other individual or group?

Fourth, how do participants finally make their decisions (by majority vote? by consensus? by some other decision-making technique?)? Most researchers who address the question suggest using decision by consensus, since that approach reassures individuals that their opinions will be given serious consideration and at the same time encourages them to accept personal responsibility for respecting the integrity of group processes. But clearly, the answer to this question may differ, depending upon the nature of the issues addressed and whether people participate as individuals or as representatives of larger groups.

Support. All researchers agree that participation programs must have strong support from top management in order to succeed. Verbal support is rarely, if ever, sufficient. Other forms include some form of personal involvement of top managers, clear evidence that they intend to monitor implementation of the program, evidence that they intend to reward commitment to the effort, evidence that they will not insist upon instant results, and evidence that they recognize that new programs entail risks and that risks require some tolerance for failure.

Second, most observers agree that one of the most important contributions top managers can make to the success of a participation program is to practice what they preach: They must provide their own subordinate managers with the kinds of opportunities to participate in decision making that those managers are expected to provide to their subordinates. In a recent study of building principals' attitudes toward teacher participation in decision making, for example, Mitchell and his colleagues (Organizational Analysis and Practice, 1989) found that evidence of a double standard can undermine middle managers' support for participatory management more quickly than nearly anything else.

A third form of support that may be necessary in some situations is a willingness to make certain basic guarantees to employees who participate in the program. If one of the purposes of the program is to identify ways of improving productivity and efficiency, managers may have to offer employees a guarantee that no one will be laid off as a result of identified savings. Guarantees that participating schools or departments will be able to retain all or some of the resources they save can provide a powerful incentive to look for such savings.

Fourth, a participation program that is assured of top management's support must also cultivate support from managers and employees. Besides the previously noted admonition to involve middle managers in higher-level decision making, the three elements most often cited by researchers as parts of such cultivation are (1) detailed communications about the program and its purposes to all managers and employees, including an open acknowledgment of any management objectives that might not be particularly attractive to employees (such as improving efficiency); (2) involvement of any employees or managers who are likely to be affected by the program, especially if the program appears to challenge the traditional roles they have played in the organization (for example, first-line supervisors, staff experts, union representatives, and so on), and (3) assurances that participation will be voluntary and that nonparticipation will not be penalized.

A fifth prerequisite, cited by every researcher, is the need for adequate resources to support the program. The most important resource is generally *time* for participants to engage in participation activities, paying attention to the ripple effects of removing teachers from the classroom and providing substitutes for their classes. Many school programs try to avoid scheduling meetings during school hours, but scheduling meetings after hours is sometimes interpreted as an indication that a school system regards participation as a frill. Some programs pay teachers for their participation; others schedule meetings to fall on days when schools are open only half a day. Other resources that are potentially important include *access to information* pertaining to subjects under discussion, and *access to specialized expertise* for the analysis of issues or the preparation of certain kinds of program recommendations.

Sixth, and closely linked to the need for resources, is the need for training in procedures employed or skills needed by participants. Training might focus on the substantive issues that participants are meant to address, such as school improvement or dimensions of school effectiveness; it might focus on technical skills such as problem identification and analysis of educational data; or it might focus on building interpersonal sensitivity and communication skills. (Conceivably, it might involve some combination of all three, although it is easy to overlook the need for them all, as we will note below.) As for the training approach, it is generally agreed that some classroom training may be necessary but that the most effective training in participation skills is acquired in the course of working on the actual business of the program.

The Cooperative Relationships Project

Some efforts to promote greater teacher involvement in decision making give explicit attention to questions about scope, structure, process, and support. Our general impression, however, is that most reformers adopt whatever model is readily at hand and neglect to consider the alternatives that may be open to them. One program that has avoided this particular pitfall is the Cooperative Relationships Project (CRP), initiated in 1987 by New Jersey governor Thomas Kean and the New Jersey State Department of Education.

The authors and their colleagues at Organizational Analysis and Practice (OAP) helped the state design the program, together with state associations representing New Jersey's teachers, principals, superintendents, and school boards. One of the keys to the program's three-year success, however, has been that most of the decisions regarding scope, structure, and support have been left to the teachers, administrators, and board members in participating school districts. Only the process for making decisions has been carefully specified, and even these specifications have been relaxed as local parties have refined their own conception of what they want to accomplish.

As originally designed, CRP has three basic purposes:

- To increase teachers' empowerment in decision making that affects the classroom
- To identify specific ways of improving the working and learning environments of public schools
- To develop ways of promoting ongoing, cooperative change in school systems

Like most other involvement programs, CRP is based on the premise that teachers should have a powerful voice in decisions that affect their work. But unlike some other programs, CRP does not assume that the influence of other actors must necessarily diminish in order for teachers to secure such a voice. In fact, the project assumes that principals, support personnel, district administrators, and school board members play vital roles in coordinating and supporting the activities of teachers and students, and that, as such, each contributes different but important perspectives and invaluable information on student needs and system problems. CRP is based on the assumption that the key to a school system's success lies in making the best possible use of all these perspectives.

Some New Jersey observers have scoffed at this "teachers win but nobody loses" formula, claiming that it is the kind of unrealistic dictum that state-level interest groups are bound to negotiate and that parties at the local level are bound to find unworkable. Those involved in the program acknowledge that it was politically expedient for state policymakers and association representatives to agree on such a formula, but they insist that the formula has helped win support for the program at the local level as well. Indeed, one of CRP's greatest strenghts is that board members, central administrators, and (most important of all) building principals have proven to be as enthusiastic about the program as teachers. The key, it appears, is that the combination of several program features— features like those summarized in the previous section—allows participants to give practical effect to what might otherwise sound like an impractical premise.

Structure. In each of nine pilot districts, problem-solving committees composed of teachers, other staff members, principals, district administrators, and school board members assumed responsibility for identifying, selecting, and solving issues. A districtwide committee addresses issues that affect more than one school and serves as a steering committee for committees of principals, teachers, staff members, and (in some cases) parents that operate at individual schools.

Each stakeholder group is responsible for deciding how members of its group will be selected to serve on committees. (Thus far, teacher unions have chosen to appoint members to all nine district committees but usually elect members to school committees.) Once selected, members sometimes act as representatives of their respective groups and sometimes speak as individuals: The choice of roles is up to each member and is usually treated as a practical question whose answer varies from one situation to the next. Superintendents usually choose to represent their central administration, and teacher union presidents are sometimes called on to speak or act for their organizations and constituents. But board members, principals, and other teachers who serve on CRP committees confront such situations less frequently. In practical terms, the important issue usually is not whether any one person speaks as an individual or as a representative but whether each group of members and the committee as a whole communicate effectively with others in their schools and districts.

The Cooperative Relationships Project makes use of facilitators to assist committees in their deliberations. At the outset, these facilitators work for the State Education Department or for Organizational Analysis and Practice, but members of district problem-solving committees (and some school committees) have been specially trained to train and then facilitate committees in individual schools. Still others are participants who serve periodically as facilitators for their own committees.

Facilitators play an important role in teaching committees how to use CRP's process of cooperative problem solving and subsequently in guiding them through that process (see below). In these respects, they chair CRP meetings, just as other committee chairpersons would do. Given the importance of the project's steps and guidelines, at least at the outset, facilitators play a critical function in the project.

But CRP's facilitators play little or no role in the substantive decisions that committees make. Even when they are committee members, their role as facilitator gives them no special voice in those decisions. Committee members are considered the experts on the problems in their school or district and are expected to take responsibility for identifying, analyzing, and generating solutions to those problems.

Scope. Each CRP committee is free to decide for itself what sorts of issues it will and will not address. Committees tend to avoid issues that can readily be addressed in some other forum (such as collective bargaining) or that fall completely outside the authority of everyone on their committee (such as legal issues). But there is no formal limitation on what a committee can either discuss or recommend, and any member can raise any issue for possible consideration.

While there are no formal restrictions or prescriptions on

what issues a CRP committee should address, members are encouraged to focus on issues of importance to a school or district's educational programs. As part of their initial training, committees receive
detailed summaries of teachers' responses to an organizational climate survey, completed by all members of a school district's faculty.
The surveys, developed by OAP consultants, draw on a variety of
perspectives, integrated by the basic premise that teachers care about
the quality of the education they provide to their students and are
in the best position to identify organizational obstacles or problems
that limit its effectiveness. The surveys are diagnostic, in that they
are designed to be used as starting points for identifying and prior-
itizing issues, rather than as devices to point fingers or to draw
automatic conclusions about which district conditions are "good"
or "bad." Committee members receive training in survey analysis
and are responsible for interpreting survey results themselves.

Two other features also affect the scope of CRP committees'
deliberations. First, all committee decisions are made by consensus,
which means that no decision is adopted unless every member is
willing to accept and support it. Second, CRP committees have no
authority or resources of their own, at least at the outset. Unless
decisions happen to fall within the authority and available resources of their own members, they must secure the agreement and support of those who do have such authority and resources. Both of
these features impose practical constraints on the scope of committee discussions.

Committees have used the flexibility that CRP affords to
address a variety of issues and solutions. District committees have
played important roles in defining future directions for their districts, improving relationships with parents and the public, enhancing the professional development of teachers, and adjusting relationships between district offices and schools. Several teams, for
example, have sought to involve community members, parents, faculty, and staff members in defining future directions for their districts, taking steps such as:

- Orchestrating the development of district mission statements
- Analyzing the long-term implications of demographic, techno-

logical, and economic trends for the district's future programs and its ability to attract students
- Meeting jointly with the district's board of education to develop five-year goals for the district

Teams in several districts and schools have worked on improving relationships with parents, other districts, and the general public in a number of ways, such as:

- Increasing public recognition of students' academic achievements
- Improving communication between parents and teachers
- Working with civic leaders to temporarily relieve crowding in an elementary school, then identifying a site for a new school
- Improving curriculum coordination with sending districts
- Opening in-service programs to faculty in neighboring districts
- Hiring a specialist to disseminate program information to guidance counselors and potential students in sending districts
- Creating a faculty speakers bureau
- Developing videotapes about their districts
- Improving the information provided to the public prior to budget and bond referendums

Several teams have focused on improving the professional skills of staff members and increasing the recognition for teachers' efforts. These include:

- Initiating in-service programs in areas such as student discipline, mainstreaming, time management, job stress, and the effect of teachers' expectations on students
- Increasing the district's pool of qualified substitute teachers and improving the scheduling of their time
- Developing procedures for the selection of teachers for the governor's teacher recognition program
- Revising a district's procedures and criteria for evaluating the performance of its professional staff members
- Changing procedures for hiring and orienting new teachers
- Creating a professional library for teachers

Other teams have taken steps to shift more decision making to individual schools and to improve coordination among them. Such steps have included:

- Arranging for the district office to shift responsibility for student placements to a team of teachers in each elementary school
- Increasing communication between teachers at different grades about students' needs and abilities
- Establishing a task force to review the articulation of curriculum between elementary, middle, and high schools
- Developing a procedure to involve faculty and school administrators in setting the district's budget priorities
- Conducting a comprehensive review and revision of all district policies, covering curriculum and instruction as well as personnel and administrative issues
- Eliminating unnecessary administrative paperwork
- Streamlining the reporting of maintenance requests
- Establishing a computerized district calendar

Although each committee is free to decide which issues it will address and how it will address them—and thus to define the kind of role it will play in the district—committees have tended to adopt one or some combination of three different roles. Some teams have chosen to act as in-house troubleshooters, focusing on particular problems in the learning, teaching, and working environments of their respective districts and schools. Others have assumed responsibility for orchestrating more comprehensive goal-setting and improvement processes. Still others have taken on specific responsibilities (in the budget-setting process, for example) or have arranged to have specific responsibilities delegated to new groups at the district or school level.

Committees can and usually do play more than one of these roles. Those that have chosen to play the last role have served as vehicles for a process of *restructuring* that CRP facilitates but does not require. Teams must decide for themselves whether specific problems or concerns can be addressed effectively within their district's existing structures or whether changes in those structures themselves may be needed.

This flexibility does not, in itself, give teams the right to preempt the authority of other officials or groups, such as boards of education or teacher associations. Nor does it give teams the right to demand support from those who may be affected by the plans it develops. Rather, CRP teams must *win* support for the solutions they develop. Whether a team's solution involves mobilizing resources, changing specific policies, or making fundamental changes in who makes what decisions in a district, its members must develop ways of building an ever broader consensus around each issue that they address.

What enables committees to choose among these roles, and forge these kinds of consensus, is the specific process that they employ in making their decisions.

Process. CRP committees use a distinctive decision-making process that promotes cooperation, creative problem solving, and commitment to the decisions eventually reached. The process is structured to give participants maximum control over their own decision making.

- Participants have complete responsibility for setting their own agendas and for deciding which problems or issues they will address.
- Problem identification, causal analysis, solution development, and action planning are addressed separately in order to build a firm base for cooperation and to promote an analytical approach to issues.
- At each stage, committees employ a combination of idea-generating, analysis, and agreement-building techniques that involves all committee members and takes advantage of their different skills.
- All major decisions, including the selection of issues to be considered, are made by consensus. No decision is final until every committee member is prepared to say that he or she understands, accepts, and is prepared to support that decision.

At the heart of the cooperative problem-solving process is a decision cycle consisting of several steps, each employing a different, well-tested decision-making technique. The steps are arranged in an order that helps committee members generate ideas, refine and analyze them, and move toward agreement.

- *Brainstorming* enables members to generate as many ideas as possible for initial consideration.
- *Clarification* ensures that everyone understands the basic ideas listed.
- The *first cut* allows the group to pare down the list of ideas so that subsequent discussion can focus on those that deserve serious attention.
- *Force field analysis* enables group members to identify the arguments for and against each idea and to distinguish between value judgments and factual arguments.
- *Data gathering* (if needed) resolves any factual disagreements that may have emerged during force field analysis.
- *Discussion to consensus* continues until all members are satisfied with the decision the committee plans to make.

CRP committees use this decision cycle at least three times when dealing with a particular issue: to select a problem to work on, to decide which of the problem's causes they will address, and to select a solution that addresses the problem and its cause(s).

This combination of steps, stages, and procedural ground rules serves a number of functions. First, it sets all committee members on an equal footing and guarantees that each person's opinions are given careful attention, without compromising the formal authority of school boards and administrators or the bargaining rights of teachers and principals. School boards and administrators who might otherwise balk at the wide-open scope of discussions, as well as associations that might be wary of compromising hard-won bargaining gains, are reassured by the requirement that every committee member must agree to accept and support a decision before it becomes final. (Debates over how many people will represent each stakeholder group on the committee are thereby avoided as well.)

Second, the structured decision-making process promotes cooperation, teamwork, and interpersonal trust. Its analytical approach allows committees to avoid the traps that other groups often fall into when making decisions, such as defining their problems in terms of too obvious solutions (for example, "Our problem is we don't have enough money to . . .") or failing to appreciate the value of different perspectives derived from different roles played in the school system.

Like other kinds of decision-making groups, CRP committees face the need to build a working relationship among members. The issue is particularly important for new CRP committees because they typically lack the homogeneous membership or clear upfront objectives that hold other kinds of groups together. Initial adherence to a set of procedures allows members to get right to work identifying and solving specific issues of mutual concern, and to work out an overall sense of direction for their committee more gradually. The structured process buys them time to get used to their new roles and relationships.

Third, CRP's structured process allows each committee to make the most effective use of each member's distinctive information and skills, allowing individuals opportunities to develop new skills as well. To operate smoothly, decision-making groups need members who perform a variety of different roles, including initiating, information/opinion seeking, information/opinion giving, clarifying, elaborating, checking, summarizing, gatekeeping, harmonizing, encouraging, and diagnosing problems of the group itself (Miller, 1984).

Some of these roles emphasize getting the immediate job done; others are directed more toward maintaining the energy, cohesion, and continuity of the group itself. But all of them actually serve both purposes. In any decision-making group, each member is likely to have particular skills and is likely to be most comfortable performing roles that match those skills. As anyone who has ever chaired a committee knows, the challenge is to structure a process that ensures that all roles are served and to guarantee that no one with one set of skills dominates the entire process. At the same time, if decision-making groups are to make the best possible use of each member's potential, they should try to avoid the assumption that particular people can perform only certain roles. The Cooperative Relationships Project's structured process encourages all members to perform all sorts of functions in the course of dealing with a particular issue.

Support. The most important signal of management support for the efforts of CRP committees is the fact that school board members sit on all nine district committees and superintendents sit on all but two of them. District committees, moreover, were initiated at least one year before school-level committees were formed. Several observers and participants have questioned whether so much lead time was necessary, but one payoff is clear. Principals— who at the outset were generally the most skeptical about district officials' commitment to the process and were the most wary of being held to a double standard—are now among the project's strongest advocates. The direct involvement of district officials gave principals opportunities to see district officials "practice what they preach," and gave top managers a more realistic understanding of the practical demands that employee participation can make on administrators. It also gave principals a chance to gain new influence themselves in district-level decision making.

As a result, principals have come to play pivotal roles on most district committees. As the ones in the best position to understand and translate the differing perspectives that teachers and district officials have on organizational problems, they have gained the respect of their fellow members. And their support has proven invaluable in the subsequent initiation of school-level committees. The support of middle management—the most problematic link in many participation and organizational improvement programs, especially in education—is one of the Cooperative Relationship Project's greatest strengths.

As important as general management commitment is, however, it must be supplemented with other, more concrete forms of support. At the outset of the project, a representative of the State Education Department and one or more OAP consultants provided district committee members with intensive training in group decision making, then facilitated their monthly or biweekly meetings for the remainder of the school year. One year later, they began training several committee members in each district to take on these roles themselves. As expected, the teachers and administrators who received this additional training quickly assumed responsibility for leadership and facilitation on their own committees, as well as providing training and support for the newly formed school-level committees. When a severe budget crisis forced the state to terminate its financial support for CRP in June 1990, committees in eight of the nine pilot districts decided they would be able to continue performing these functions on their own, with only occasional facilitator training support from OAP.

It is too soon to make any definitive judgments about CRP. District and school teams have successfully implemented many of their action plans, but a few of their plans have not been successful, and many others are still being implemented. Besides developing the capacity to train and facilitate their own activities, a recent survey of participants indicates that teams in all nine pilot districts have made progress in each of the following areas:

- Most teams began by addressing narrowly defined issues that focused on relationships among adults, and gradually they shifted toward longer-term, broader issues with more direct impact on students and a district's educational programs.
- All teams have experienced increasing levels of trust and cooperation among their own members. Some (but not all) have seen the gradual improvement of relationships among teachers, administrators, and board members generally.
- Boards of education and administrators are increasingly committed to involving teachers and other staff members in decisions that affect their work. This shift has been especially pronounced among principals, who initially were the most skeptical about CRP and are now among its strongest supporters.

Preliminary discussions with project participants suggest that no one feature is responsible for these kinds of progress. Instead, the key appears to be the *internal consistency* of different project features and their *external congruence* with other organizational and political elements in their respective districts.

The issue of *internal consistency* focuses attention on how a program's features complement or conflict with one another. Take, for example, CRP's wide-open scope, its requirement that all decisions be made by consensus, and the fact that committees have no state-mandated authority or specific objectives. With no fixed responsibilities or formal authority, CRP committees all began their work as ad hoc "change agents," identifying and developing solutions to address them. The open-endedness of the process allowed them to focus on issues that were of particular concern to the various constituencies in their respective districts. But the same open-endedness raised the danger of aimlessness, as committees moved from one discrete problem to another without any overall sense of direction. At the outset, CRP's highly structured process compensated for this lack of direction. But most committees lost momentum in their second year and did not regain it until they took steps to set goals or long-term agendas for themselves. Once long-term targets were established, committees discovered that they could relax their adherence to some of the project's procedural rules.

Internal consistency is also illustrated by how the composition of committees and the structure of decision making complement each other. Different groups of participants are attracted to different features of the overall process and are prepared to accept features that they do *not* find particularly attractive because the features fit so well together.

Teachers like the fact that problem selection and causal analysis are treated as discrete decisions (as opposed to being combined with solution development in a single needs analysis). Treating the steps separately gives committees effective control over their own agendas and distinguishes them from other kinds of administration-appointed committees. Administrators sometimes express frustration about the time that such steps add to the decision-making process. But they are pleased that committees are expected to take responsibility for implementing their own decisions, including identifying needed resources, marshaling support, and deciding who will do what to put their solutions into effect. It is these features, they note, that force committees to consider the administrative feasibility of their decisions and to hold themselves accountable for the decisions they make. Teachers, in turn, sometimes express impatience with the details of action planning and indicate that they would just as soon delegate them to individuals (more often than not, to administrators) to resolve. But most of them have come to accept the responsibility for follow-through as part of the overall "deal."

The issue of *external congruence* raises similar questions about how particular features of CRP (or any participation program) "fit" with other features of a particular school system. Take, again, CRP's committees' combination of broad scope, consensus requirement, and lack of formal authority and resources of their own. Neither school boards nor administrators in many districts would have accepted the program's unlimited scope of discussions if the consensus requirement did not give each individual member the right to veto committee decisions. Many observers initially predicted that this combination of features would either paralyze CRP committees or else render them pawns of the administrators who sat on them. But participants now cite broad scope, committee composition, and the consensus requirement as the project's three most valuable features, and only a handful (less than 10 percent) believe that the selection of issues has been manipulated to serve board or administration purposes.

Our own interpretation of these results suggests that the same features that protect the authority of boards and central administrators have enabled principals and teachers to gain new power in the decision-making process. By leaving board and central office authority intact, CRP removes any excuse those actors might otherwise have to avoid talking about issues that fall within their authority. In the process, they permit teachers and principals to use their detailed knowledge of classroom and school conditions (of problems that need attention and solutions that will or will not work) and the power that comes with the ability to forge consensus around particular strategies in decision making. Given that power, most CRP committees have found boards of education and central administrators reluctant to challenge the decisions that their district CRP committees generate, even those they have the formal authority to challenge.

The exceptions to this rule have served to reinforce it. Boards of education rejected the recommendations of CRP committees in only two instances over the first three years of the project. In one case, a board took a committee's recommended budget priorities "under advisement," but eventually accepted only some of them. In another, a board rejected a committee's recommendations for relieving crowded conditions in the district's elementary school and fashioned a new solution of its own. In both cases, the conflicts that erupted between the board and the district CRP committee prompted the parties to reassess their relationships and forge new ground rules for working with each other. The authors' discussions with individual committee and board members suggest that the committees now accept the need to sell their recommendations to their boards, and their boards now recognize that they have a reciprocal obligation to engage in a dialogue with their staff members before rejecting or modifying carefully considered recommendations.

In these respects, the lessons of the Cooperative Relationships Project are similar to those we have drawn from the research summarized in previous chapters on teacher compensation and the work of individual teachers: School systems should be wary of the temptation to create new authority structures in order to compensate for the apparent weaknesses of old ones. Given the growing need for flexibility and adaptability in the development and administration of school programs, new structures are likely to be outdated almost as soon as they have been put in place. What are needed are not so much new structures but less reliance on structures to dictate who is responsible for what.

If school organizations are to harness the collective energy of teachers in more flexible ways, using new structures of participation (as this chapter has argued), then it is vital to reconsider the role of the already existing structure of collective action—the teachers' unions. Chapter Seven discusses the image and role of teachers' unions and the collective bargaining process.

7

THE CHANGING ROLE
OF UNIONS

As collective bargaining in public education enters its third decade, and as recent efforts to reform public schools near the ten-year mark, policymakers and scholars are raising questions about the relationships between the two developments and about their impact on the management of public school systems (Kerchner and Mitchell, 1988; Bacharach and Shedd, 1989; Shedd, 1990). Some observers insist that collective bargaining poses a serious threat to the management of school systems and to efforts to reform public education. Others acknowledge that teacher unions have forced school boards and administrators to change the ways in which they manage, but they claim that school management may have been strengthened in the process. Still others argue that teacher unions and school management are undergoing fundamental changes as both struggle to adapt to the new public expectations reflected in the current reform movement.

Unlike studies published in the mid-seventies, which focused almost exclusively on the wage effects of teacher unionism, more recent studies have focused on the ways that collective bargaining has affected the work of teachers, the management of school districts, and educational policymaking. Most recent studies conclude that collective bargaining has had much more of an impact on educational programs and the management of school districts than earlier observers had expected, but descriptions, interpretations, and explanations of that impact vary widely.

We argue in this chapter that collective bargaining has both affected and been affected by many of the same pressures evidenced in the current efforts to reform public education. The most distinctive pressure is to include teachers in the formulation of educational policies and programs, which necessarily involves a redefinition of the roles that boards of education, administrators, teachers, and their representatives play in the management of school systems.

Conflicting Evidence?

The evidence on collective bargaining's effects is confusing. Some observers insist that bargaining has introduced rigidity into the management of school systems and has reduced the capacity of school managers to respond to changing public demands (Grimshaw, 1979; Kearney, 1984; Goldschmidt and Stuart, 1986). Others agree that bargaining has changed the way in which schools are managed. Teachers now have new leverage to insist that they be included in school and district decision making (Kerchner and Mitchell, 1988; Johnson, 1983). On the other hand, these changes may have actually enhanced the flexibility of school systems by providing administrators with new mechanisms for securing their teachers' cooperation.

Some observers have suggested that bargaining has resulted in the centralization of authority in district offices and has sharply curtailed the authority of building principals (Goldschmidt, Bowers, and Stuart, 1984). Others have concluded that principals continue to play a pivotal role in the management of school systems and retain plenty of influence if they care to exercise it (Johnson, 1983). Some have concluded that collective bargaining has encouraged teachers to think of themselves as "laborers," with a diminished sense of responsibility for the quality of education and the welfare of their students (Lieberman, 1980); others insist that bargaining has enhanced the professionalism of teachers, encouraging them to accept more responsibility for the quality of educational programs (Kerchner and Mitchell, 1988; McDonnell and Pascal, 1988).

A few scholars have begun to develop a thesis that may help reconcile these seemingly contradictory observations. Kerchner and Mitchell (1986) and Johnson (1987) suggest that collective bargaining in education is itself undergoing a major change, from a system borrowed from and structured along the lines of traditional private-sector labor-management relations to one specifically adapted to public education, in which both parties make explicit use of bargaining to address issues of educational policy.

If that is indeed what is happening, then it is possible that the seemingly contradictory evidence of bargaining effects may be drawn from school systems at different points in such a transition. The evidence that collective bargaining has produced rigidity, centralization, diminished supervisory authority, and a "laboring" conception of the teacher's role may be drawn from settings where a traditional (industrial) model of collective bargaining continues to predominate. The evidence that bargaining has produced increased flexibility, responsiveness to public concerns, respect for the leadership role of building principals, and teacher involvement in professional decision making may reflect labor-management relationships in settings where the parties have made the transition to a newer form of collective decision making. The evidence of increased conflict and bitterness in education bargaining may be characteristic of relationships in transition between these two approaches, as one party struggles to reconstruct the labor-management relationship along lines that the other refuses to accept.

The basic outlines of this argument are sound. It is well documented in the general research on industrial relations that the parties to collective bargaining relationships tend to adopt substantive and procedural rules that reflect the characteristics of their particular industry (Dunlop, 1958; Kochan, 1980). It is equally well documented that the most serious conflicts in labor-management relations tend to occur when one or the other party attempts to change the structures and processes of bargaining itself (Weber, 1964; Chamberlain and Kuhn, 1965). There are good reasons to believe that school managers and teacher unions are, in fact, creating a new set of rules to govern their relationships—a set of rules uniquely tailored to their particular environment. Much of the acrimony attributed to traditional collective bargaining may be, in fact, a sign of tension between different approaches rather than a characteristic of traditional labor relations itself.

But these arguments raise as many questions as they answer. If unions and employers tend to adopt rules that reflect the particular characteristics of their industry, why would the most distinctive feature of this new generation of labor relations in public education be teachers' collective participation in school and district education policymaking? (If true, that would represent a dramatic change in the way school systems have typically been administered.) If teacher unions are prepared to insist upon such participation to the point of provoking serious labor-management conflicts, is it accurate to suggest that professional unions are more likely to pursue cooperative strategies for dealing with their employers than are other unions? If teacher unions are particularly concerned with "process" issues—issues of participation, authority, power, and change—is it possible that school bargainers will never achieve the level of cooperation that characterized private-sector labor-management relationships in, say, the 1950s? At that time the structure of bargaining and division of responsibilities between union and management were relatively clear and stable.

Much of the speculation about what new teacher unions will be like is still dominated by conventional images of the old ones (Bacharach and Shedd, 1989): Rather than being adversarial and concerned with preserving their own power, the new unions will be cooperative and nonconfrontational. Rather than opposing efforts to improve the quality of teaching, they will actually assume responsibility for the quality and quantity of their members' efforts. Rather than negotiating rules that restrict flexibility, they will look for ways to relax restrictions on both teachers and administrators. Rather than insisting that teachers' rights and benefits be allocated equally or else on the basis of seniority, they will insist that the responsibility and compensation of teachers be differentiated, ordered hierarchically, and allocated on the basis of professional competence.

Some of these assertions probably will prove to be accurate simply because people expect them to be. No doubt many policymakers, school board members, administrators, teachers, and their hired or elected representatives have believed that unions are necessarily adversarial, that they are invariably opposed to efforts to improve their members' performance, and so forth. As active metaphors or "institutional myths" (Dowling and Pfeffer, 1975; Meyer and Rowan, 1977), such convictions have played an important role in shaping the behavior of unions and employers in public education, even if the evidence to support them has been ambiguous. There is no reason why a new set of myths should not have similar influence, even if some of them have been created by holding a mirror up to the old ones.

But the argument that conflict and lack of cooperation are defining characteristics of traditional labor-management relations—as opposed to particular labor-management relationships—is open to serious challenge, and the conviction that cooperativeness will be a defining characteristic of the new labor-management relations in public education is probably misleading as well. A bargaining system tailored to the markets, work processes, and management systems of public education undoubtedly will remove some of the present sources of conflict in teacher bargaining. But such a system will almost certainly expose other sources of conflict that until recently have been sheltered behind assertions of management prerogatives and union indifference.

Changes in collective bargaining in public education are unlikely to occur (or survive) unless union leaders and school managers are prepared to accommodate each other's concerns and cooperate in the search for innovative solutions to these potential conflicts. But accommodation and cooperation have always been available options, for education and noneducation bargainers alike. Indeed, as we argue in the next section, they have been and almost certainly will continue to be the parties' most reliable and powerful sources of leverage upon each other.

Conflict and Cooperation in Traditional Bargaining

Perhaps the most frequent charge leveled at collective bargaining in education is that it has generated an adversarial relationship among school boards, administrators, and teachers (Bacharach and Shedd, 1989). This adversarial relationship is thought to undermine the effective administration of public education and prevent cooperative efforts to improve the system's performance. Advocates of bargaining argue that bargaining more often serves to reveal (rather than to generate) conflict in the employment relationship, but they tend to accept the adversarial label itself.

As appropriate as that label may sometimes seem, other evidence suggests that it is misleading. One of the most distinctive features of collective bargaining is that it *combines* elements of conflict and cooperation, providing incentives for the parties to cooperate by posing conflict as an alternative. It is a mistake to assume that threats of strikes or similar coercive tactics are the basic source of leverage in collective bargaining, even in traditional private-sector settings. In fact, the trade-off—the offer to accommodate another party's interests in some areas in return for accommodation of one's own interests in others—is usually a much more effective source of power in bargaining (Bacharach and Lawler, 1981).

Much of what appears (to outsiders) to be senseless maneuvering and bargaining ritual often represents the careful search for just such sources of bargaining leverage. The process is not reassuring to those who equate cooperation with orderly discourse or a willingness to sacrifice personal interest for the common good. But those who are prepared to look beyond the messiness of the process can hardly dismiss the fundamentally cooperative nature of an arrangement that encourages self-interested parties to search for ways of accommodating each other's concerns. As several scholars of American collective bargaining have pointed out, the argument that structural arrangements can turn potentially divisive interests into sources of cooperation is not unique to industrial relations. It is essentially the same as the argument on which our constitutional system of government is based (Commons and others, 1958).

The catch in this argument is that it assumes that each party has something the other party wants (Bacharach and Lawler, 1981). A party cannot offer to accommodate another party's interest if it has nothing to accommodate *with*. Until recently, we would argue, that has been the real source of weakness—and friction—in the system of collective bargaining employed in public education: Teacher unions have had very little to withhold from or offer to their management counterparts. Private-sector structural arrangements and legal principles have served the interests of both labor and management in industrial settings because they have ensured that each has "something the other party wants," and thus, something to trade. The same structures and principles have had the opposite effect in public education, actually undermining opportunities for trade-offs in bargaining. With little to offer each other, it is not surprising that education bargainers so often find themselves using threats of conflict, rather than offers of accommodation, as their principal source of leverage.

The Microstructure of Industrial Unionism

Except for restrictions on the right to strike and the substitution of various third-party impasse procedures, most of the features of collective bargaining in public education were originally borrowed from the private sector: districtwide bargaining units; the periodic negotiation of comprehensive agreements that last for fixed periods of time; legal restrictions that limit bargaining to so-called "bread-and-butter" issues and that require the parties to negotiate "in good faith"; multistep grievance procedures for the resolution of disagreements that may arise during the life of an agreement; and the use of binding arbitration to resolve such midcontract disputes if the parties are unable to resolve them on their own.

These features are so common in the private sector today that it is easy to forget that seventy years ago, in the 1920s, knowledgeable observers were proclaiming that another traditional form of collective bargaining was obsolete and that workers no longer needed outside unions. Scientific management and more sophisticated personnel practices were said to be ushering in a new age of industrial harmony in which employers would willingly sit down with company unions and discuss problems rationally and openly, without workers having to use power tactics to make themselves heard (Taft, 1964; Dulles, 1966). Yet only a few years later, America saw an explosion of militant unionism that turned the predictions of those knowledgeable observers on their heads. In the short space of five or six years in the mid-1930s, the smokestack industries that experts thought were impenetrable were swiftly unionized and the number of American workers represented by unions more than doubled.

From the vantage point of history, it is easy to dismiss the predictions that unions and collective bargaining were on the verge of extinction in the 1920s. But there was actually plenty of solid evidence, derived from nearly twenty years of failed organizing efforts, to "prove" that unions would never establish a foothold in the smokestack industries. True, most American labor leaders showed only occasional interest in organizing those industries, but given the conventional wisdom about what made for a successful union, there were solid explanations to justify their pessimism.

Craft unionism, the traditional form of unionism at the time, was based on principles that were fundamentally inconsistent with the factory system: (1) Workers had to be members of a union before they could be hired, (2) it was the union's responsibility to train workers and to certify when they were ready to be employed, (3) foremen or immediate supervisors had to be members of the union and subject to union discipline, and (4) the union would control the work process through its unilateral specification of work rules. All four of these principles were fundamentally incompatible with the unskilled labor markets, standardized mass-product markets, machine technologies, and hierarchical managerial systems on which factory systems were based. As long as union leaders clung to those principles, the prediction that they could never break into the factory sector was fundamentally correct.

What the observers of the 1920s were not counting on was that the workers in smokestack industries (with the help of some union leaders) would reinvent the concepts of "collective bargaining" and "union." They abandoned the notion that a "real" union must control hiring, training, immediate supervision, and the work process itself, acknowledging (however grudgingly at first) that control of such processes was the prerogative of management. Eventually, that acknowledgment was elevated to a set of principles. It was "management's job to manage," it was said, and the union's job to negotiate and then police protections against management's arbitrary exercise of that authority. Unions that crossed the line and got too involved in making managerial decisions only compromised their members' interests and undermined their own power base. It is not surprising that management heartily embraced these new principles.

What industrial unions got were somewhat higher wages than in comparable nonunion settings and increasingly detailed agreements, negotiated for fixed periods of time, with grievance procedures that culminated in binding arbitration for the resolution of disputes that might arise during the life of the agreement. Many of the provisions of these agreements established links between different jobs and pay rates and specified how employees were to be selected, either permanently or temporarily, for those jobs.

Management, in turn, got a stable workforce. The higher wages and benefit packages linked contractually to job ladders and seniority had the effect of lowering quit rates and tying workers with specialized skills to the employer, in what one scholar called a new "industrial feudalism" (Ross, 1958; Block, 1978). Seniority clauses governing reassignments, promotions, and layoffs protected more experienced workers from the threat of competition from junior workers, eliminating an obstacle to the informal sharing of job knowledge among workers (Thurow, 1975). Layoff and recall procedures provided employers with a way of temporarily reducing employment in slack periods without permanently losing the knowledge and skills of the workers who were laid off (Medoff, 1979).

The stability that these various contractual provisions encouraged was an important asset to factory managers and undoubtedly played a key role in securing management's acceptance. Indeed, contrary to popular impressions, research indicates that, at least until recently, unionized firms have often been more productive than nonunionized firms in the same industries (Freeman and Medoff, 1979). It is unlikely, however, that employers would have accepted industrial unionism if these stabilizing arrangements were all that a union had to offer. After all, an employer with sufficient resources could make most of these adjustments without collective bargaining, and many employers intent on avoiding unionization did precisely that.

Paradoxically, the most important concession that industrial unions could make to factory managers was to give them what conventional wisdom suggests unions took away: authority and flexibility. Although the tactics of industrial unions were militant and their leaders' rhetoric sometimes radical, the unionism they invented was essentially an accommodation to the basic features of the factory management system. The employee rights and benefits negotiated by industrial unions imposed restrictions on an employer's ability to direct the workforce, but they actually complemented the factory system of management. The union's insistence on detailed specification of job duties (and the growth of technical personnel staffs to monitor the resulting job structures) complemented Frederick Taylor's system of scientific management, on which much of the design and management of industrial work processes depended (Nadworny, 1955). Management flexibility was restricted by contractual guarantees that job assignments, promotions, and layoffs would be governed partly by seniority and by requirements that work rules must be published in advance before they could be enforced by discipline. But these were largely protections against favoritism and managerial abuse of authority. The actual content of job assignments, job descriptions, and work rules; the structure of job ladders; and the decisions to fill jobs and lay off or recall workers were left to management.

The industrial union's formal acknowledgment of management authority was embodied in several provisions of the parties' negotiated contract. The discipline procedures in industrial union contracts established the principle that a worker's basic obligation to his or her employer was obedience: Insubordination (not incompetence) was the primary grounds for discipline and/or dismissal. The grievance procedures in such contracts provided top management with information about shop-floor problems and first-line supervisory behavior that top managers would never have gotten through their own management hierarchies.

The key to these arrangements was contained in the arbitration procedures of the parties' negotiated agreements, in the often overlooked provision that specified that the terms of their agreement would remain in place for a fixed period of time, and in the union's promise not to call strikes during the life of the agreement. Together, these provisions helped establish the central principle of labor-management relations in the industrial setting, namely, that it is "management's right to manage." Any rights employers have not given up, either by express contract language or by mutually acknowledged past practice, remain rights that employers are free to exercise as they see fit for the duration of the agreement (Elkouri and Elkouri, 1976).

The basic features of these labor-management relationships are so familiar that it is easy to overlook what ought to be the most obvious question: Why would managers be prepared to "pay"—often dearly—for authority they supposedly had all along? First, it is important to note that the structure of the deal between industrial unions and employers reflected a different strategic relationship from the one craft unions and their management counterparts occupied. Craft unions, for the most part, dealt with employers who had no permanent workforces. In fact, they provided employers with their workers, using hiring halls, restrictions on membership, and apprenticeship programs to guarantee that those workers would be qualified to perform the work for which they were temporarily hired. In their dealings with an employer, craft unions occupied the position of sellers of labor; their basic "deal" was an exchange of skilled labor for money.

Industrial unions never occupied such a position. Their members were permanently employed, were given any necessary training after they were hired, and were usually employees before they were members. Because products were standardized, produced in enormous quantities, and required relatively little decision making by the workers who produced them, the employer could afford to separate the planning of work from its execution, giving managers and technical staffs the job of planning the work and giving each line employee a relatively fixed set of duties to perform. In such a setting, the seller of labor is the individual employee, rather than the union, and the control of labor is a management function. The craft union's two sources of leverage were never accessible to the industrial union.

Instead, industrial unions took advantage of the fact that the effective operation of factory systems depended upon the willingness of workers to voluntarily accept directions from their supervisors. The systems were simply too complex (and employers were too dependent upon large numbers of workers) for employers to coerce obedience from each individual, particularly if workers were prepared to act collectively in the face of that coercion. What a unified industrial union could control (or could prevent the employer from securing) was the authority to make the whole elaborate system work. As Chester Barnard, one of the seminal theorists on the functions of the executive, noted in the mid-1930s, authority is always delegated upward (Barnard, 1938). The right to direct workers, to give orders, and to insist on obedience must be acknowledged and respected by those workers or else it is an empty fiction. Managers might prefer to believe that individual employees "give" management the authority to direct them when they accept employment and that workers who want to revoke that authority must quit. But whether managers believe such institutional myths or not is ultimately irrelevant; what matters is whether employees believe them.

The benefits and guarantees that soon began to fill industrial union contracts were the price an employer had to pay to secure workers' obedience. The label "job control unionism" is misleading, therefore, for industrial unions never presumed to control jobs as craft unions had done. Instead, they negotiated limits on the employer's control and acknowledged that workers would respect the employer's authority as long as it stayed within those limits.

The Half-Logic of Industrial Unionism

If the principles and practices of industrial unionism were designed to fit a factory setting, why did *education* bargainers embrace those arrangements? One answer (that would require detailed examination if collective bargaining were the exclusive focus of this book) is that education bargainers may have been only dimly aware of what it is they were embracing. The scholars—like George Taylor, John Dunlop, and Arthur Cole—who helped draft the first public-sector bargaining laws in the 1960s and 1970s were steeped in the conventional wisdom of private-sector unionism and industrial labor law. It is not surprising that they would use familiar blueprints, or that the practitioners for whom the new structures were designed would accept these structures without saying much about the design or construction of the new relationships embedded in them.[1]

But if teachers and their employers did not have much to say about the industrial template that was used to shape their bargaining relationships, teachers at least had some choice about whether they were going to buy the structure at all. And large numbers of them did. In that sense, it is still appropriate to ask why teachers chose to embrace industrial unionism when they first obtained the right to bargain.

We would argue that the basic explanation is that teachers and their unions adopted factory union strategies because the administrators and school boards they faced insisted on acting like factory managers. Indeed, one of the basic reasons so many teachers chose to join unions was that the prevailing logic of education management was itself patterned on the industrial model (Cole, 1969; Callahan, 1962). The structures, processes, and myths of industrial unionism complemented and in some ways even supported the top-down managerial ideology that existed in most school systems when teacher unions first won recognition, just as they fit the factory management systems of the 1930s. If there are grounds—and there are—for believing that unions and employers in public education are now in the process of inventing a new form of collective bargaining, it is because that management ideology itself is under serious attack.

As we noted in an earlier chapter, school boards and administrators have had an on-again, off-again love affair with industrial management models for most of the twentieth century. During the first two decades, school reformers used scientific management principles to give the new discipline of educational administration a body of supposed expertise (Callahan, 1962). In the late 1950s, post-Sputnik reformers issued repeated calls to overhaul the structure and management of school systems along private-sector hierarchical lines. In most systems, what had been collections of largely autonomous units dominated by building principals were now to be rationalized by centralizing the control of educational policies and programs in the hands of district superintendents and central office staff experts (Tyack and Hansot, 1982).

If schools were to be run like factories, with hierarchical controls and centralized mechanisms for planning, evaluation, and policysetting, teacher associations would have to act like factory unions, resorting to roughly the same sorts of strategies for protect-

ing the interests of their members. Like their industrial-sector counterparts, teacher unions often challenged particular management
decisions and insisted upon putting in writing policies that administrators might have preferred to leave to their own discretion. But
at least in the early years of bargaining, teacher unions played essentially the same reactive role as their industrial counterparts, insisting that it was management's job to set policy and manage; the
union's job was to negotiate and then police abuses of that
authority.

In fact, teacher unions have provided district central administrators with many of the same benefits that industrial managers
gained from collective bargaining: access to information about
school-level problems; orderly procedures for disposing of various
personnel issues; and grounds for insisting that school principals
adhere to policies prescribed or agreed to by central administrators.
Indeed, case studies of school district power relationships indicate
that collective bargaining has provided central administrators with
one of their most effective tools for centralizing management authority and power in their own hands. Not only has it helped them
control their subordinate managers; it also has helped them insulate
themselves—and their staffs—from school board interference in
their day-to-day decision making, by insisting that board members
and administrators must present a united front in the face of union
pressure (Bacharach, 1981).

The only features of industrial unionism that teacher unions
did not seem to embrace were the job ladders, pay hierarchies, and
detailed prescriptions of duties associated with different jobs. Indeed, teacher unions have traditionally been strong defenders of
unified salary schedules, which provide pay increments for seniority
and increasing levels of training but which treat teaching as a single
profession rather than a set of divisible tasks to be ranked in a
hierarchy (Bacharach, Lipsky, and Shedd, 1984).

But even this apparent departure from industrial union practice is deceptive. Teacher unions have generally maintained that the
compensation provided by the basic salary schedule is for a specified
number of class periods (and the preparations for them). The important point is that the compensation is only for duties associated
with the classroom, as discussed in Chapter Five. Additional class-

room work (teaching summer school, covering classes for absent colleagues, teaching classes that require more than the specified number of lesson preparations, and so on) and duties performed outside the classroom (coaching, sponsoring extracurricular activities, serving on committees, and so on) are often considered extra, calling for additional compensation. Teacher unions, in these respects, are just as wedded to the basic industrial union principle of "equal pay for equal work"—and its corollary, "extra pay for extra work"—as their counterparts in industry have always been. School boards and administrators, for their part, sometimes complain about how "unprofessional" it is for teachers to demand extra compensation whenever they are asked to assume new duties, but their complaints have been muted. As in the private sector, such union demands represent tacit acknowledgment that it is management's prerogative to assign such duties in the first place.

It is not surprising that so many boards and administrators find top-down models of management so attractive. After all, coordinating the flow of students through the system—and assigning teachers, specialists, support personnel, curriculum requirements, material resources, space, and time schedules to serve students as they pass through—are jobs that have fallen to boards and administrators to perform. At least until recently, top-down models of factory or bureaucratic management were the only ones that offered any coherent explanation of how school systems might meet this need for coordination.

Many of the factors that generate the need for teacher discretion and judgment also generate the need for coordination among teachers as well. Indeed, debates over how school systems should be managed—and debates over how they should be reformed—almost always turn on the tension between the need to allow individual teachers discretion and the need to coordinate their individual efforts. Metaphors and strategies that focus on the former evoke images of autonomous professionals or craftspersons; those that focus on the latter evoke images of assembly lines and purposeful bureaucracies. Neither set of metaphors or strategies captures the truly demanding task of school management, which is somehow to satisfy both sets of needs simultaneously.

The top-down strategies that have ostensibly guided school

management have never made more than partial sense in public education and have never been strictly observed. At one moment teachers are treated like workers on an assembly line, at another like bureaucrats executing general directives, at still another like independent professionals who are expected to figure out for themselves what it is they should be doing.

School boards, administrators, and teachers might be able to live with these laissez-faire arrangements, but teacher unions have had a hard time doing so. Because school boards and administrators have seldom been very good at running their school systems like factories, teacher unions have had difficulty using factory union approaches to maintain their members' unity and commitment. The approaches have provided a source of protection against arbitrary personnel decisions, protection that most teachers recognize is necessary, but they have required union leaders to pretend that decisions critical to their members are none of their concern.

In the private sector, decisions concerning the nature of the product and the design of the work process are defined as management prerogatives and therefore outside the scope of bargaining. Unions, in most cases, have a right to demand bargaining on the impact of such decisions on working conditions but not on the substance of the decisions themselves (Morris, 1971). Those distinctions are relatively easy to draw in manufacturing settings; they are virtually impossible to draw in service settings like public education, where the work of employees *is* the product the organization provides and where the most important working conditions are those that affect a person's ability to do his or her job effectively. Yet, hemmed in by industrial-sector precedent and by court decisions declaring educational policies to be management prerogatives and outside the scope of bargaining, teacher unions have often found themselves unable to affect those school and district decisions that have the greatest impact on their members' work lives (Edwards, 1973; Shedd, 1982).

The artificial distinction between "union issues" and "professional issues" has been a source of tension within teacher unions ever since they won bargaining rights in the 1960s. That tension has sapped the energies of NEA affiliates, in particular, which had to overcome a history of administrative domination before establishing themselves as teacher bargaining agents. Many teachers and staff persons in both the NEA and AFT still recall when boards of education and administrators often defined "a professional" as someone who was cooperative and refrained from challenging the decisions of his or her superiors. For many teachers, the words "professional" and "cooperative" have been associated with servility and antiunionism ever since. For many others—probably the majority—the words "professionalism" and "union" simply had very little to do with one another.

Collective Bargaining Reform

As pressures to restructure collective bargaining take hold, industrial unions throughout the economy are having to reconsider strategies that have served them well for half a century. As Piore points out, the same factors that are forcing a reassessment of traditional approaches to management are also undermining traditional job control unionism, as well. A unionism that is premised on fixed job categories, close links between specific duties and compensation, and detailed rules on how job assignments are made—and on a "common law" that prevents managers from holding workers accountable for mistakes in the organization and planning of work—is bound to be threatened by current economic changes.

If this thesis is right, it is a serious mistake for union leaders to assume, as some do, that the new, more participative (see Chapter Six) management approaches are merely tools for busting or avoiding unions. Some managers certainly find them attractive for that reason, but the main reasons are that first, they provide management with information about production processes that is becoming increasingly vital to their productive efficiency and second, they provide management with needed flexibility in the way work is organized and managed. Union tactics that presume that management expects only blind obedience from employees might well be inappropriate when facing such new management approaches. On the other hand, such approaches also reveal new sources of management dependence on employees that might serve as the bases for new union tactics.

If these arguments are valid in the manufacturing sector

(where machine technologies still afford higher levels of management considerable control over the work process), they are even
more valid in the service sector, in public education, and in teaching
in particular. Few employers are more dependent than school
boards and administrators on their employees' discretion, professional judgment, and willingness to cooperate in translating
general policies into concrete action. Few employees have as much
responsibility as teachers for planning and evaluating the results of
their day-to-day activities, much less for planning, directing, and
evaluating the activities of others. In most settings, these are still
defined as management responsibilities, even if employees are being
invited to share some of them. In public education, they represent
the very core of the work of teachers.

The fact that teachers plan, direct, and evaluate the work of
others—that is, the work of their students—does not make them
supervisors or managers in the traditional labor relations sense.
Their "subordinates" are not employees and the decisions they
make are not, strictly speaking, personnel policies. But teachers are
supervisors and managers in the more generic sense of those terms:
They are responsible for translating general policies into particular
objectives; planning, supervising, and adjusting work activities; securing needed resources; and evaluating both individual performance and the overall success of their work plans.[2]

Teacher unions may be threatened by the demise of top-down
management strategies, but they are also in a good position to take
advantage of that demise. For one thing, they are not threatened by
the declining employment base that is making it difficult for
private-sector industrial unions to convince their members to even
think of cooperating with management. For another, pressing for
collective teacher involvement in school and district decision making offers the possibility of overcoming the split between union and
professional factions within their own organizations by shifting the
focus of thinking about professional issues away from individual
autonomy. Perhaps most important, such a shift might allow
teacher unions to finally take advantage of a source of potential
influence (or, to put the matter more bluntly, a source of power)
that industrial union principles have always required them to over-

look: Their members, as individuals, already manage much of what goes on in most school systems.

The prospect that a reassessment of union strategies might allow them to end the internal bloodletting, secure new monies for education, and build a stronger, more unified organization has provided union leaders with a powerful incentive to try.

Fading Myths and Emerging Principles

Conceptually, the biggest obstacle to negotiating an end to teacher unions' internal friction has always been the myth that teachers' interests as union members and their interests as professionals are inherently incompatible. Like all myths, this one has received constant confirmation because people who believe it to be true have made it come true. But what might we expect if teachers' organizations were premised on the assumption that teachers' interests as union members and their interests as professionals are supportive or even identical?

The basic principles that future teacher unions are likely to follow are easier to discern than the specific arrangements that they and employers will work out. The first principle is that, in a setting like public education, teachers' union and professional interests imply collective responsibility, not individual autonomy. Although teachers can always be expected to be sensitive to their need for discretion (autonomy), the job of protecting that discretion is itself a collective responsibility and not one that entitles the individual to pursue whatever objectives he or she wants to pursue. Whatever more specific vehicles unions and employers choose for promoting closer ties and collective responsibility among teachers, the job of building them is likely to be a central concern of teacher unions in the future.

The second principle is that teachers' working conditions depend largely on whether they are able to be effective teachers. If curriculum or student grouping policies are inconsistent or poorly thought out, if needed time and other resources to plan and carry out one's responsibilities are not available, if opportunities to expand one's subject knowledge and pedagogic skills are not available, or if students enter one's own classroom without the knowledge and skills they need to master the material to be covered, teachers' work lives are rendered more difficult as a consequence. For most teachers, there is nothing more exhilarating than to reach students who were thought to be unreachable; there is nothing more humiliating than to make a fool of oneself in front of trusting children or hypercritical adolescents. Whatever the mechanisms unions and school districts develop in the future for increasing teachers' collective participation in school and district policy and decision making, the notion that a distinction either can or should be drawn between educational policies and working conditions is a patent fiction.[3]

The third principle is that unions are neither inherently conflictual nor necessarily cooperative but are capable of either opposing or accommodating those with whom they deal, depending upon which best serves the interests of their members. As other observers of school labor-management relations have suggested, some conflicts in school bargaining have been provoked by frustration because restrictions on the scope of bargaining or other aspects of the existing system have prevented the parties from addressing serious issues. Other conflicts have been provoked by one or the other party's efforts to change the system of bargaining itself. A system more closely tailored to the public expectations, work processes, and management systems of public education would undoubtedly serve to reduce such conflicts, but that argument would apply in any sector of the economy. To go farther and suggest that labor-management relations in public education will be especially cooperative and nonconfrontational is not only misleading but dangerous.

The strength of any union, as we have argued here, depends as much on its ability to accommodate management's interests as on its ability to threaten it. It is the union's ability to make its willingness to accommodate management interests *contingent* on management's willingness to reciprocate that allows it to play an independent, constructive role in the labor-management relationship. Myths, imposed or self-imposed, that force it to forego one approach and lock it into the other are the greatest threat to its viability.

Teachers will always be more aware of the need for flexibility and individual discretion, and boards and administrators will continue to be more sensitive to the need for coordination of programs and the flow of students through a school system. The parties will continue, in other words, to have different perspectives on what students and other school constituencies need, as well as what school systems can do to meet them. If their representatives are truly representative, these differences will be reflected in the policies and strategies each pursues and in the agreements they work out.

Structures (Likely and Possible)

The basic structure of the agreements that education bargainers will negotiate can be expected to reflect the structure of the overall labor-management relationship in public education, just as the structures of craft and industrial union contracts reflect the relationships that produced them. Teachers will insist on playing a more active role in setting educational policies and programs; boards of education and administrators will almost certainly insist that fixed-term, fixed-length agreements are cumbersome and therefore inappropriate vehicles for addressing the constantly changing situations that such policies and programs address. Teachers and their representatives, in turn, will demand guarantees that their involvement in policymaking is more than token. The result will probably be an increasing reliance on comprehensive negotiations to establish the structure and ground rules for joint decision making that will occur away from the contract bargaining table. They almost certainly will continue to establish district and school committees to address educational issues.[4] They probably also will negotiate provisions that give building principals and their faculties the right to make exceptions to contract provisions that otherwise apply throughout a school district.[5] Both of these arrangements will provide system managers with additional flexibility and teachers with greater voice in the determination of educational policy.

What is more speculative (but also more intriguing) is the possibility that some school districts and teacher unions might go further and eliminate the provision that prevents one party from reopening negotiations before the end of a contract without the other party's consent. That provision is a key element in the industrial-sector deal that protects the employer's reserved right to make management decisions unilaterally.[6] However, in the new framework, it is not clear that school districts either need or necessarily want such protections, since they force unions to file grievances and arbitration appeals (or, in some states, demands for single-issue "impact" negotiations) over issues generated by the changing circumstances of school system management. Giving either party the right to reopen negotiations on any or all provisions of a districtwide agreement would provide managers with increased flexibility and would remove one of the principal objections to expanding the scope of bargaining.[7]

Many observers expect teacher unions and school systems to negotiate changes in the structure of the teaching profession itself, in addition to changes in the scope of bargaining, changes in the structure of agreements, and changes in the bargaining process itself. Indeed, many of the recent debates over education reform have focused on the development of so-called "career ladders" that draw distinctions between the duties of teachers at different "career levels" and that pay teachers according to the level of the ladder that they occupy. We agree that such systems are likely to be discussed and experimented with over the next several years, but the line of argument we have developed here casts a different light on the issue.

Drawing close connections between specific sets of duties and different levels of compensation is a basic feature of the top-down systems in industrial work settings. It is that feature, in fact, that managers in the manufacturing setting are now struggling to overcome and that is forcing unions in that setting to reassess some of the basic tenets of industrial unionism (see Kochan, Katz, and McKersie, 1986). To suggest that public education should move toward more formal differentiation of teaching duties would be to suggest that it should move closer to, not farther from, the industrial model, with its detailed rules on who has a right to bid on what duties, what career level gets what new duties, when the assignment of some higher-level duties requires a temporary promotion, and so forth.

What is most important to note is the willingness of teacher unions and employers in public education to even entertain such radical departures from traditional practices. That willingness probably says more about the pressures that all parties are under than it does about the specific formulas that they will agree to live by in the future. It undoubtedly will take some time for them to work out and finally accept new ground rules, just as it took employers and industrial unions time to work out all the details of what today is recognized as the traditional labor-management formula. But the historical parallel gives confidence in the basic argument outlined here. Economic developments, changes in public expectations, and changes in the ways in which organizations like school systems are being managed are once again undermining the bases of one form of unionism and are creating new forms of power in the employment relationship. Put simply, employers throughout the economy—but above all, in public education—are becoming increasingly dependent on their employees' detailed knowledge of work processes and client needs, on their individual willingness and ability to exercise discretion and judgment, and on their willingness to work cooperatively with one another in the face of constantly changing work situations.

The important question is not whether employers will try to make adjustments to these new forms of dependence—they must do so to survive—but whether unions will be able to develop strategies that allow them to use the power inherent in that dependence. If they do this, they will create a new form of union with the potential of being every bit as vigorous and powerful and as appropriate to their setting as craft unions and industrial unions were to theirs. There are good reasons to believe that that is exactly what is happening today in public education.

It is remarkable but not altogether unprecedented that unions play an active role in shaping the approaches of the managers they deal with. But no other unions have played such an important role in redefining the very concept of management or in claiming for their members such an active role in the process of management itself as today's teacher unions.

Notes

1. The authors are indebted to Professor Thomas Kochan for noting this line of argument.
2. These features probably would make teachers "management officials" under the Supreme Court's recent Yeshiva decision,

which appears to deny bargaining rights to private-sector employees who make or effectively recommend virtually any kind of management decisions or policies and not just ones that pertain to personnel matters. Technically, that decision does not affect teachers and school districts, which bargain under separate public-sector statutes. Unlike private-sector employees who have been denied legal protection because they exercise managerial functions, teachers won bargaining rights from legislators who clearly anticipated that teachers, in particular, would have the right to bargain. But the private-sector logic *does* affect court and board decisions on which subjects are and are not bargainable in public education (Shedd, 1982).

We do not have the need or time to develop this line of reasoning here, but our basic argument is this: The Yeshiva decision is the logical but absurd result of a case law that was originally intended to accommodate employees' bargaining rights to the hierarchical management structures in private industry. The original logic was meant to make bargaining possible. When laws that were passed to facilitate, encourage, and (where necessary) require bargaining become basic obstacles to bargaining, it is time to change the laws themselves, or at least their interpretation.

3. Clearly, this line of reasoning would require changes in the legal definition of what is bargainable in many states.

4. Boards of education may balk at union demands that such committees be given the right to make the final decisions in the policy areas they address, but the reservation of that formal authority may mean less than many assume. If boards and administrators insist on treating these committee arrangements as they sometimes have treated other committees in the past, by manipulating agendas and arbitrarily deciding when they will pay attention to teachers' "advice," they may find that teachers will withdraw their cooperation altogether. Indeed, teachers' willingness to insist on reciprocal cooperation in such settings will probably be the most important test of their union's unity and strength. The assumption that school boards and administrators *need* their cooperation is, of course, fundamental to our entire argument.

5. Johnson's (1983) study of labor-management relations in school systems notes that many principals and school faculties already exercise the informal option of overlooking selected provisions of a contract, just as union stewards, work groups, and supervisors do in other sectors of the economy (Kuhn, 1961). The fact that the formal contract gives employees the right to file grievances and demand adherence to contract terms is a source of power in such "fractional bargaining," for it gives employees the option of falling back on what has already been negotiated if they do not accept the terms of the side agreement being offered. Formally acknowledging the possibility of such side agreements would allow the parties to specify that side agreements do not create "past practices" that undermine the application of contract terms in other parts of the school system.

6. If a union were free to demand that negotiations be reopened at any time, the principle that management retains unilateral discretion over issues not covered by the contract would be meaningless.

7. Neither party would be likely to exercise the right to reopen negotiations cavalierly, because the other might insist on renegotiating provisions that were important to the one initiating negotiations. This would be the crucial difference between these kinds of midcontract negotiations and the single-issue "impact" negotiations used in some states.

 **8**

CONCLUSION: RESTRUCTURING RELATIONSHIPS IN SCHOOLS

This book has focused on the structure of relationships between public school teachers and the organizations in which they work. Its unit of analysis has been neither the individual nor the system but the connections between the two. Rather than characterizing schools as collections of classrooms, or classrooms as mere extensions of schools and districts, we have explored the competing logics and persistent (sometimes institutionalized) patterns that shape relationships between and among the adults who work in public school systems.

At the center of these relationships is a division of labor that assigns to individual teachers responsibility for most of the planning, execution, and assessment of day-to-day activities within their separate classrooms but excludes them from most school and district decisions that set directions and establish parameters for those efforts. As a result, the relationships between and among educators are both loosely coupled and tightly constrained.

These arrangements are natural reflections of the interplay among several basic features of American public school systems: a set of market or environmental relationships that subject educators to a variety of competing demands; a combination of (individually) intensive and (organizationally) extensive work processes that are haphazardly integrated and poorly understood; a group of immediate clients whose needs and abilities vary widely and unpredictably and are constantly changing; and a bizarre combination of ideologies that make it plausible to characterize teachers as laborers, technicians, or autonomous professionals.

The thread that runs through all these features is the *variety* of expectations, demands, needs, activities, and approaches with which educators must deal. Relationships that strike casual observers as haphazard and senseless appear regular and sensible when viewed from the perspective of those who must try to make sense out of all the pieces of variety and variation that each of them faces. Arrangements that serve no particular purpose well probably serve many purposes better than many observers might care to believe.

There are elements of both instability and stability in these relationships. What appears, even to many participants, to be a constant struggle between teachers intent on preserving their autonomy and boards and administrators intent on establishing their control is, in a broader sense, a relatively stable set of arrangements for making ad hoc adjustments to competing pressures. Problem avoidance, insulation from "outsiders," and controlling or pacifying those "beneath" you—whether they are lower-level administrators, teachers, or students—become overriding cultural values that tie practitioners together, even as they contend for each other's attention and resources.

The basic thesis we present here is that these relationships are now beginning to change. What we cannot prove with empirical evidence—for the changes are only now occurring—we have sought to demonstrate by triangulation: Many reasonably independent developments all seem to be pointing toward a renegotiation of the division of labor between and among individual teachers and administrators.

Two developments overshadow (and encompass) all others: the mounting public pressure on school systems to improve in many respects simultaneously, and the adaptation of teacher unions to the institutional setting in which they themselves operate. Public schools have always been able to adapt to new public expectations, whether framed as demands for more rigor, efficiency, equity, warmth, vocational preparation, or responsiveness to individual student needs. In operational terms, each new expectation required adjustments in teachers' level of discretion and administrators' level of control, but the direction of each adjustment was usually clear. What is distinctive about recent efforts to reform American public education is the increasing pressure—backed up with state monies—for school systems to provide more equity and more excellence, more basic skills and more critical thinking skills, more variety and more coherence, *all at once.*

School systems, like private-sector organizations facing analogous pressures, cannot meet these simultaneous demands without giving their principals and teachers more flexibility and discretion over their day-to-day efforts. They cannot meet, much less satisfy, those demands without also achieving higher levels of coordination between programs and among staff members. The traditional division of labor in education would allow educators to accommodate one need or the other, but not both at once. A new definition of roles will have to be negotiated, therefore, or else the system's public masters will have to be told that their demands cannot be met.

As these new external pressures are making themselves felt, another set of pressures is building *within* public school systems. With the advent of collective bargaining and the emergence of teacher unions as powerful actors in district decision making, power gravitated from boards of education, building principals, and favored teachers to superintendents and the teacher officials who deal with them. Tacit bargains that once could have been overlooked or renegotiated whenever they became inconvenient were made explicit and incorporated in fixed-term contracts or in the rulings of grievance arbitrators. The veneer of professionalism and pretense of collegiality that many systems once enjoyed—and that some had honored—was stripped away, exposing the harsh assertions of management authority and teacher self-interest that lay beneath the surface. The tolerance for ambiguity and inconsistency that had sustained traditional teacher-administrator relationships began to erode.

The parties might have been able to digest this dose of industrial discipline if they had still allowed themselves the opportunity to address issues that affected teachers' ability to perform their jobs effectively. But private-sector precedent holds most of those issues to be management prerogatives, and industrial union principles hold that employees should refuse to accept either collective or individual responsibility for product and process decisions over which employers reserve unilateral authority. Both parties have had an interest—or have thought they had an interest—in avoiding the so-called "professional" issues that have the greatest impact on teachers' working lives and teaching conditions.

As time has passed, union leaders' insistence that their members have no responsibility except to follow orders and no interest in overcoming obstacles to their own effectiveness has grown increasingly intolerable to administrators and teachers. Principles that make (or once made) perfect sense in industrial settings, that protect both management and employee interests, have undermined all parties' interests in public education. The parties are thus feeling under increasing pressure to renegotiate the terms of their relationships.

Nothing about any of these developments, external or internal, makes it inevitable that teachers will assume more responsibility for making decisions at the school or school district level. Governors and business leaders can be told that public school systems cannot satisfy all of their demands, and they may eventually accept such an answer. Teacher union leaders may decide that abandoning the traditional formula for union success is too risky and may resign themselves to playing a distinctly passive role in the labor-management relationship. Teachers may conclude that they do not want to accept the responsibility and accountability that come with making decisions in cooperation with others.

But arguments and developments that may not be overwhelmingly persuasive when each stands alone become increasingly powerful as they begin to complement each other. There is a *consistency* to the arguments that are now being raised concerning the nature of teaching, work environment, isolation, pay systems, job hierarchies, career development, collective bargaining, private-sector management practices, and the changing texture of public expectations that makes for an argument that is difficult to resist.

What is most striking—and ultimately, most persuasive—is the consistency of means and ends. The arguments that are being used to describe how schools should be managed are also being used to describe the education that students should receive and the skills they should acquire in the process. These skills include participation, discovery, innovation, creativity, adaptability, continuous self-generated improvement, the capacity to recognize and make choices, cooperation, mutual responsibility, and problem solving. Whether students are thought of as future workers, citizens, scholars, or clients, these factors are assuming growing importance as the goals (ends) of public education (The College Board, 1983; Education Commission of the States, 1983).

This consistency of ends and means has implications that extend far beyond the scope of this book. In a fascinating set of case studies, Linda McNeil (1986) notes the connections among existing school structures, curriculum policies, and the education that children receive: Hierarchical subordination, control, and passivity, she argues, have become values that permeate school systems and that influence decisions at every level. How administrators treat teachers and how teachers treat students become intertwined. What is done becomes what is taught. The implication, then, is obvious: If schools are to *teach* creativity and problem solving and cooperation and involvement, they must *practice* them, not just in the classroom but at all levels of the system.

We should not be surprised that this is so. When discrete decisions become patterns, they begin to convey messages. Something that some persons do becomes "the way things are done," acquiring a symbolic importance and influencing new decisions in ways that the original actors might never have anticipated. Actions can thus become processes, and processes can become systems and structures, without anyone issuing a new policy or rearranging the boxes on an organizational chart.

The relationship between individual and organization is thus circular and interactive, not linear or mechanistic. Or rather, the relationship between individual and organization is *potentially* circular and interactive, if individuals choose to make them so. As Dorothy Emmet (1958) notes, in characterizing the relationship between individual action and the social system:

> [A] social system is . . . a *process* with some systematic
> characteristics, rather than a closely integrated system,
> like an organism or a machine. . . . For its elements
> are mobile individuals with private purpose, conflicts

and allegiances. Their behavior can be canalized to some extent into institutional patterns, . . . [but] the cohesion of the institutionalized activities themselves is made possible by the powers of individuals. Thus the "system" so disclosed is something much less consistent and more flexible than the older functional model suggested. There will be conflicts within the system leading to periodic crises; and few societies nowadays can be insulated from change. There will be critical occasions when adjustments, perhaps major adjustments, are called for, and these may depend largely on the initiative and resourcefulness of individuals. And not only on critical occasions. Along the line, in all sorts of social situations, adaptations, innovations and decisions will be made, with more and less success. The coherence of a society is thus not just an "equilibrium" secured by the automatic coming into opposition of countervailing tendencies; it is something more precarious, always needing to be renewed by efforts of will and imagination (pp. 293–294).

If we are correct in our interpretation of the developments now occurring in American public education, individual efforts "of will and imagination" are beginning to reinforce each other, creating the bases for a new set of relationships. The focus of our attention here has been on the relationships between teachers and administrators and among teachers themselves. But the lessons being learned almost certainly will extend to the relationships between teachers and students and among students, as well. People are learning, we think, that the biggest obstacles to meeting the multiplicity of demands now being imposed upon public school systems are the presumptions that some adults should control other adults, that those other adults should do nothing but teach children, and that children are the passive objects of the educational process. Systems where all adults are encouraged to learn and lead, and where children are allowed to teach, can meet demands that no one has yet imagined.

 APPENDIX

Examples of Job Descriptions
in the 1984 Pima County Employer Wage Survey

Attorney

Under direction, conducts research, prepares briefs, prepares and argues cases in court and may train newer attorneys. *This is intermediate level.* Requires license to practice law, *and 1–3 years experience as a practicing attorney.* EXCLUDE: ENTRY-LEVEL AT-TORNEYS, SUPERVISORS.

Budget Analyst

Under direction, performs budget analyses at the *fully experienced, professional level,* utilizing knowledge of budgetary requirements; analyzes and interprets various financial and related data; evaluates requests and compiles and consolidates budgets; prepares reports showing resources, expenditures and projected balances. *Requires a degree and considerable experience.* EXCLUDE: ENTRY-LEVEL ANALYSTS, SUPERVISORS, ACCOUNTANTS, CONSULTANTS.

Buyer

Under general supervision, performs *experienced professional-level* duties purchasing a variety of materials, supplies, equipment and services; prepares specifications and invitations to bid; conducts bid openings, analyzes bids and selects vendors. Requires *professional buying or purchasing experience.* EXCLUDE: ENTRY-LEVEL BUYERS, SENIOR BUYERS, BUYERS OF SPECIALIZED EQUIPMENT, BUYER SUPERVISORS, BUYERS OF GOODS FOR RESALE OR USED IN REMANUFACTURE, PURCHASING MANAGERS OR OFFICERS.

Personnel Analyst

Under general supervision, performs experienced *professional-level personnel administration* work in such areas as employment, compensation, classification, employee relations. Interprets policies and procedures, prepares reports with findings and recommendations. Requires a college degree and *professional personnel experience.* EXCLUDE: ENTRY ANALYSTS, ADMINISTRATIVE ASSISTANTS, SUPERVISORS, PERSONNEL MANAGERS, PARA-PROFESSIONALS.

Systems Analyst

Under general supervision, performs responsible *experienced professional-level* computer-systems analysis work in determining user data requirements and planning, designing and assisting in the implementation of EDP systems. Requires *experience* in computer applications and systems analysis work. EXCLUDE: SUPERVISORY AND LEAD POSITIONS, PROJECT LEADERS.

Civil Engineer (Registered)

Under general supervision, performs a wide variety of skilled *professional* civil engineering work in the *office and field.* May include supervision. Requires a bachelor's *degree* in engineering and considerable civil engineering or closely related *experience. Requires registration as a professional engineer.* EXCLUDE: ENTRY-LEVEL AND NON-REGISTERED ENGINEERS.

Source: Arizona Department of Economic Security, *1984 Pima County Employer Wage Survey.*

REFERENCES

Adler, M. *The Paideia Proposal: An Educational Manifesto.* New York: Macmillan, 1983.

AFT Task Force on the Future of Education. *The Revolution That Is Overdue: Looking Toward the Future of Teaching and Learning.* Washington, D.C.: American Federation of Teachers, 1986.

Alutto, J. A., and Belasco, J. A. "Patterns of Teacher Participation in School System Decision Making." *Educational Administration Quarterly,* 1973, *9* (1), 117-125.

Anderson, J. G. *Bureaucracy in Education.* Baltimore, Md.: Johns Hopkins Press, 1968.

Anglin, L. W. "Teacher Roles and Alternative School Organizations." *The Educational Forum,* May 1979, pp. 439-452.

Apple, M. W. *Education and Power.* Boston: Routledge and Kegan Paul, 1982.

Applegate, J. H. "Reflective Teaching and Staff Development: A Partnership for Professional Growth." *The Developer,* April 8, 1982, pp. 1-5.

Argyris, C. *Reasoning, Learning, and Action: Individual and Organizational.* San Francisco: Jossey-Bass, 1982.

Ashton, P., Webb, R., and Doda, N. "A Study of Teachers' Source of Efficacy." Final report, Vol. 1. University of Florida, 1982. (ED 231 834)

Ayllon, T., and Azrin, N. H. *The Token Economy.* Englewood Cliffs, N.J.: Prentice-Hall, 1968.

Bacharach, S. B. "Consensus and Power in School Districts." Final report under NIE Grant no. G 78 0080. Ithaca, N.Y.: Cornell University, 1981.

Bacharach, S. B. "Four Themes of Reform: An Editorial Essay." *Educational Administration Quarterly,* 1988, *24* (4), 484–496.

Bacharach, S. B. *Education Reform: Making Sense of It All.* Boston: Allyn and Bacon, 1990.

Bacharach, S. B., and Bamberger, P. "Exit and Voice: Turnover and Militancy Intentions in Elementary and Secondary Schools." *Educational Administration Quarterly,* 1990, *26* (4), 316–344.

Bacharach, S. B., Bamberger, P., and Conley, S. "Between Professionals and Bureaucracies: A Seesaw Approach for the Management of Professionals." In S. Barley and P. Tolbert (eds.), *Professionals in Organizations,* Greenwich, Conn.: JAI Press, 1990.

Bacharach, S. B., Bamberger, P., Conley, S., and Bauer, S. "The Dimensionality of Decision Participation in Educational Organizations: The Value of a Multi-Domain Evaluation Approach." *Educational Administration Quarterly,* 1990, *26* (2), 126–167.

Bacharach, S. B., Bamberger, P., and Mitchell, S. M. "Work Design, Role Conflict and Role Ambiguity: The Case of Elementary and Secondary Schools." *Educational Evaluation and Policy Analysis,* forthcoming.

Bacharach, S. B., Bauer, S. C., and Conley, S. C. "Organizational Analysis of Stress: The Case of Elementary and Secondary Schools." *Journal of Work and Occupations,* 1986, *13* (1), 7–32.

Bacharach, S. B., Bauer, S., and Shedd, J. "The Work Environment and School Reform." *Teachers College Record,* 1986, *88* (2), 241–256.

Bacharach, S. B., and Conley, S. C. "Educational Reform: A Managerial Agenda." *Phi Delta Kappan,* 1986, *67* (9), 641–645.

Bacharach, S. B., and Conley, S. "Uncertainty and Decision-Making in Teaching: Implications for Managing Line Professionals." In T. J. Sergiovanni and J. H. Moore (eds.), *Schooling for Tomorrow: Directing Reforms to Issues That Count.* Boston: Allyn and Bacon, 1988.

Bacharach, S. B., Conley, S., and Shedd, J. "Beyond Career Ladders: Structuring Career Development Systems." *Teachers College Record*, 1986, *87* (4), 563–574.

Bacharach, S. B., Conley, S., and Shedd, J. "A Developmental Framework for Evaluating Teachers as Decision Makers." *Journal of Personnel Evaluation in Education*, Summer 1987, 181–194.

Bacharach, S. B., Conley, S., and Shedd, J. "Evaluating Teachers for Career Awards and Merit Pay." In J. Millman and L. Darling-Hammond (eds.), *The New Handbook of Teacher Evaluation: Assessing Elementary and Secondary School Teachers.* Newbury Park, Calif.: Sage, 1990.

Bacharach, S. B., and Lawler, E. J. *Bargaining: Power, Tactics, and Outcomes.* San Francisco: Jossey-Bass, 1981.

Bacharach, S., Lipsky, D., and Shedd, J. "Teacher Compensation Systems and the Quality of Education." Ithaca, N.Y.: Organizational Analysis and Practice, Inc., 1983. (Mimeographed.)

Bacharach, S. B., Lipsky, D. B., and Shedd, J. B. *Paying for Better Teaching: Merit Pay and Its Alternatives.* Ithaca, N.Y.: Organizational Analysis and Practice, Inc., 1984.

Bacharach, S. B., and Mitchell, S. M. "Critical Variables in the Formation and Maintenance of Consensus in School Districts." *Educational Administration Quarterly*, 1981, *17* (4), 74–97.

Bacharach, S. B., and Mitchell, S. M. "Theory and Practice in Organizations: Schools as Political Systems." In J. Lorsch (ed.), *Handbook of Organizational Behavior.* Englewood Cliffs, N.J.: Prentice-Hall, 1986.

Bacharach, S. B., and Mitchell, S. M. "Teacher Motivation in an Organizational Context." In M. Aikin (ed.), *Encyclopedia of Educational Research.* (6th ed.) New York: Macmillan, forthcoming.

Bacharach, S. B., and Shedd, J. "Power and Empowerment: The Constraining Myths and Emerging Structures of Teacher Unionism in an Age of Reform." In J. Hannaway and R. Crowson (eds.), *The Politics of Reforming School Administration.* London: Falmer Press, 1989.

Bacharach, S. B., Shedd, J., and Schmidle, T. "Teacher Shortages, Professional Standards and Hen-House Logic." Ithaca, N.Y.: Organizational Analysis and Practice, Inc., 1985. (Mimeographed.)

Bailyn, L. "Autonomy in the Industrial R&D Lab." *Human Resource Management,* 1985, *24* (2), 129-146.

Baldridge, J. V., and Deal, T. E. (eds.). *Managing Change in Educational Organizations.* Berkeley, Calif.: McCutchan, 1985.

Barnard, C. *The Functions of the Executive.* Cambridge, Mass.: Harvard University Press, 1938.

Bassin, M., Gross, T., and Jordan, P. "Developing Renewal Processes in Urban High Schools." *Theory into Practice,* 1979, *18* (2), 73-81.

Batt, W. L., Jr., and Weinberg, E. "Labor-Management Cooperation Today." *Harvard Business Review,* Jan./Feb. 1978, 9-17.

Benson, J. K. "The Analysis of Bureaucratic-Professional Conflict: Functional vs. Dialectical Approaches." *The Sociological Quarterly,* 1973, *14,* 378-379.

Berliner, D. "The Executive Functions of Teaching." *Instructor,* 1983, *93* (2), 28-40.

Berman, P., and McLaughlin, M. W. "Factors Affecting the Process of Change." In M. M. Milstein (ed.), *Schools, Conflict and Change.* New York: Teachers College Press, 1980.

Bird, T. "Mutual Adaptation and Mutual Accomplishment: Images of Change in a Field Experiment." *Teachers College Record,* 1984, *86* (1), 68-83.

Bishop, J. "Organizational Influences on the Work Orientations of Elementary Teachers." *Sociology of Work and Occupations,* 1977, *4* (2), 171-208.

Blake, R. R., and Mouton, J. S. *The Managerial Grid.* Houston, Tex.: Gulf, 1964.

Blake, R. R., and Mouton, J. S. *Solving Costly Organizational Conflicts: Achieving Intergroup Trust, Cooperation, and Teamwork.* San Francisco: Jossey-Bass, 1984.

Blase, J. L. "A Qualitative Analysis of Teacher Stress: Consequences for Performance." *American Educational Research Journal,* 1986, *23,* 13-40.

Block, R. N. "The Impact of Seniority Provisions on the Manufacturing Quit Rate." *Industrial and Labor Relations Review,* 1978, *31* (3), 474-481.

Bowers, D. G. "OD Techniques and Theory Results in 23 Organizations: The Michigan ICL Study." *Journal of Applied Behavioral Science,* 1973, *9* (1), 21–43.

Boyd, W. L., and Crowson, R. L. "The Changing Conception and Practice of Public School Administration." In D. C. Berliner (ed.), *Review of Research in Education.* Vol. 9. Washington, D.C.: American Educational Research Association, 1981.

Bredeson, P. V., Fruth, M. J., and Kasten, K. L. "Organizational Incentives and Secondary School Teaching." *Journal of Research and Development in Education,* 1983, *16,* 52–56.

Brookover, W. B., and others. *Creating Effective Schools.* Holmes Beach, Fla.: Learning Publications, 1982.

Brownell, P. "Participative Management." *The Wharton Magazine,* Fall 1982.

Buckley, M. F. "The Relationship of Philosophical Orientation, Participation in Decision Making, and Degree of Fulfillment of Expectations About Participation in Decision Making to Elementary School Teacher Attitudes Toward Leaders, Leader-Teacher Interaction and Membership in the Organization." Unpublished doctoral dissertation, University of Connecticut, 1981. (Cited in J. A. Conway, 1984.)

Burden, P. R. "Teachers' Perceptions of the Characteristics and Influences on Their Personal and Professional Development." 1980. (ED 198 087)

Burden, P. R. "Developmental Supervision: Reducing Teacher Stress at Different Career Stages." 1982. (ED 218 267)

Burello, L. C., and Orbaugh, T. "Reducing the Discrepancy Between the Known and the Unknown in Inservice Education." *Phi Delta Kappan,* 1982, *63* (6), 385–390.

Burke, D. J. "Teacher Involvement in Decision Making and Teacher Satisfaction." Unpublished doctoral dissertation, University of Rochester, 1981. (Cited in J. A. Conway, 1984.)

California Commission on the Teaching Profession. *Who Will Teach Our Children?* Sacramento: California Commission on the Teaching Profession, 1985.

Callahan, R. *Education and the Cult of Efficiency.* Chicago: University of Chicago Press, 1962.

Campbell, R. J. "Career Development: The Young Business Manager." In J. R. Hackman, *Longitudinal Approaches to Career*

Development. Symposium presented at the annual meeting of the American Psychological Association, San Francisco, 1968.

Career Ladder Clearinghouse. "Planning Career Ladders: Lessons from the States." Career Ladder Clearinghouse Newsletter, Mar. 1985.

Career Ladder Clearinghouse. "News from the States." Southern Regional Education Board, Atlanta, July 1987.

"Career Ladder Plan Subject of Controversy." *Alabama School Journal,* Feb. 1, 1985, 6-7.

Carnegie Commission on Teaching as a Profession. *A Nation Prepared: Teachers for the 21st Century.* New York: Carnegie Forum on Education and the Economy, 1986.

Casey, W. F., III. "Would Bear Bryant Teach in the Public Schools? The Need for Teacher Incentives." *Phi Delta Kappan,* 1979, *60* (9), 500-501.

Chamberlain, N. W., and Kuhn, J. W. *Collective Bargaining.* (2nd ed.) New York: McGraw-Hill, 1965.

Chapman, D. W., and Hutcheson, S. M. "Attrition from Teaching Careers: A Discriminant Analysis." *American Educational Research Journal,* Spring 1982, *19,* 93-105.

Christensen, J., Burke, P., Fessler, R., and Hagstrom, D. "Stages of Teachers' Careers: Implications for Professional Development." 1983. (ED SP 021 495)

Chubb, J. E., and Moe, T. M. *Politics, Markets, and the Organization of Schools.* Project Report no. 85-A15, Institute for Research on Educational Finance and Governance, Stanford University, 1985.

Clark, B. "Organizational Adaptation to Professionals." In H. Vollmer and D. Mills (eds.), *Professionalization.* Englewood Cliffs, N.J.: Prentice-Hall, 1966.

Clark, C. M., and Yinger, R. J. "Three Studies of Teacher Planning." Research Series no. 55. East Lansing, Mich.: Michigan State University, Institute for Research on Teaching, 1979.

Cohen, M. "Effective Schools: Accumulating Research Findings." *American Education,* Jan./Feb. 1982, *18,* 13-16.

Cole, S. *The Unionization of Teachers.* New York: Praeger, 1969.

The College Board. *Academic Preparation for College: What Stu-*

dents Need to Know and Be Able to Do. New York: The College Board, 1983.

Commons, J. R., and others (eds.). *A Documentary History of American Industrial Society.* Vol. 3. New York: Russell and Russell, 1958.

Condry, J. "The Role of Initial Interest and Task Performance on Intrinsic Motivation." Paper presented at the annual meeting of the American Psychological Association, Chicago, 1975.

Condry, J., and Chambers, J. "Intrinsic Motivation and the Process of Learning." In M. R. Lepper and D. Greene (eds.), *The Hidden Costs of Reward: New Perspectives on the Psychology of Human Motivation* (Chap. 4). Hillsdale, N.J.: Erlbaum, 1978.

Conley, S. C. "Career Development and Labor-Management Cooperation." Paper presented at the annual meeting of the American Educational Research Association, San Francisco, 1986.

Conley, S. C. "Reforming Paper Pushers and Avoiding Free Agents: The Teacher as a Constrained Decision-Maker." *Educational Administration Quarterly,* 1988, *24* (4), 393-404.

Conley, S. C., and Bacharach, S. B. "'The Holmes Group Report: Standards, Hierarchies, and Management." *Teachers College Record,* 1987, *88* (3), 340-347.

Conway, J. A. "The Myth, Mystery, and Mastery of Participative Decision Making in Education." *Educational Administration Quarterly,* 1984, *20* (3), 11-40.

Cooperman, S., and Klagholz, L. "New Jersey's Route to Certification." *Phi Delta Kappan,* 1985, *66* (10), 691-695.

Corcoran, T. B. "Teacher Participation in Public School Decision-Making: A Discussion Paper." Working paper prepared for The Work in America Institute, Feb. 1987.

Corcoran, T. B., Walker, L. J., and White, J. L. *Working in Urban Schools.* Washington, D.C.: Institute for Educational Leadership, 1988.

Cowden, P., and Cohen, D. "Divergent Worlds of Practice: The Federal Reform of Local Schools in the Experimental Schools Program." Unpublished study sponsored by the National Institute of Education, 1979. (Cited and quoted by D. Ravitch, 1983, pp. 260-261.)

Cuban, L. "Transforming the Frog into a Prince: Effective Schools

Research, Policy, and Practice at the District Level." *Harvard Educational Review*, 1984, *54* (2), 129-151.

Daft, R. L., and Becker, S. W. *The Innovative Organization: Innovation Adoption in School Organizations.* New York: Elsevier, 1978.

Dalton, G. W., Thompson, P. H., and Price, R. L. "The Four Stages of Professional Careers: A New Look at Performance by Professionals." *Organizational Dynamics*, Summer 1977, 19-42.

Davis, L. E., and Cherns, A. B. (eds.). *The Quality of Working Life.* Vol. 1. New York: Free Press, 1975.

Deci, E. L. *Intrinsic Motivation.* New York: Plenum, 1975.

Deci, E. L. "The Hidden Costs of Rewards." *Organizational Dynamics*, Winter 1976, *4*, 61-72.

Dowling, J., and Pfeffer, J. "Organizational Legitimacy." *Pacific Sociological Review*, Jan. 1975, *18*, 122-136.

Doyle, W. "Recent Research on Classroom Management: Implications for Teacher Preparation." *Journal of Teacher Education*, May/June 1985a, *36*, 31-35.

Doyle, W. "Teaching as a Profession: What We Know and What We Need to Know About Teaching." University of Texas at Austin, Research and Development Center for Teacher Education, R&D Report no. 6160, 1985b. (Mimeographed.)

Doyle, W., and Carter, K. "Academic Tasks in Classrooms." *Curriculum Inquiry*, 1984, *14* (2), 129-149.

Duke, D. L., Showers, B. K., and Imber, M. "Teachers and Shared Decision Making: The Costs and Benefits of Involvement." *Educational Administration Quarterly*, 1980, *16* (1), 93-106.

Dulles, F. R. *Labor in American History.* (3rd ed.) New York: Crowell, 1966.

Dunlop, J. T. *Industrial Relations Systems.* New York: Holt, Rinehart & Winston, 1958.

Dyer, L., Schwab, D. P., and Fossum, J. A. "Impacts of Pay on Employee Behaviors and Attitudes: An Update." In H. G. Heneman III and D. P. Schwab (eds.), *Perspectives on Personnel/Human Resource Management* (Chap. 25). Homewood, Ill.: Irwin, 1978.

Edelfelt, R. A. "Critical Issues in Developing Teacher Centers." *Phi Delta Kappan*, 1982, *63* (6), 390-393.

Edelfelt, R. A., and Johnson, M. (eds.). *Rethinking Inservice Education.* Washington, D.C.: National Education Association, 1975.

Edmonds, R. R. "Some Schools Work and More Can." *Social Policy,* 1979, *9,* 28–32.

Education Commission of the States. *Education for a High Technology Economy.* Denver, Colo.: Education Commission of the States, 1983.

Education Commission of the States. *What Next? More Leverage for Teachers?* Denver, Colo.: Education Commission of the States, 1986.

Education Commission of the States. *The Next Wave: A Synopsis of Recent Education Reform Reports.* Denver, Colo.: Education Commission of the States, 1987.

Educational Research Service. *Merit Pay for Teachers.* ERS Report. Arlington, Va.: Educational Research Service, 1979.

Edwards, H. T. "The Emerging Duty to Bargain in the Public Sector." *Michigan Law Review,* 1973, *71,* 885–934.

Elkouri, F., and Elkouri, E. A. *How Arbitration Works.* (3rd ed.) Washington, D.C.: Bureau of National Affairs, 1976.

Emmet, D. *Function, Purpose, and Powers.* New York: Macmillan, 1958.

Empey, D. W. "The Greatest Risk: Who Will Teach?" *Elementary School Journal,* Nov. 1984, *85,* 167–176.

Erickson, D. A. (ed.) *Educational Organization and Administration.* Berkeley, Calif.: McCutchan, 1977.

Fenstermacher, G. "A Philosophical Consideration of Recent Research on Teacher Effectiveness." In L. S. Shulman (ed.), *Review of Research in Education* (Chap. 6). Itasca, Ill.: Peacock, 1978.

Fessler, R., and Burke, P. "Developing a Professional Teacher Growth Program: Teacher Supervision Interaction." *NASSP Bulletin,* 1982. (Cited in Christensen, Burke, Fessler, and Hagstrom, 1983.)

Festinger, L. *A Theory of Cognitive Dissonance.* Evanston, Ill.: Harper & Row, 1957.

Filley, A. C., House, R. J., and Kerr, S. *Managerial Process and Organizational Behavior.* Glenview, Ill.: Scott, Foresman, 1976.

Fisher, K. K. "Management Roles in the Implementation of Participative Management Systems." *Human Resource Management,* 1986, *25* (3), 459-479.

Flannery, D. M. "Teacher Decision Involvement and Job Satisfaction in Wisconsin High Schools." Unpublished doctoral dissertation, University of Wisconsin, Madison, 1980. (Cited in J. A. Conway, 1984.)

Freeman, R. B. "Individual Mobility and Union Voice in the Labor Market." *American Economic Review,* May 1976, *66,* 361-368.

Freeman, R. B., and Medoff, J. L. "The Two Faces of Unionism." *The Public Interest,* Fall 1979, *57,* 69-93.

Freeman, R. B., and Medoff, J. L. "The Impact of Collective Bargaining: Illusion or Reality?" In J. Steiber, R. B. McKersie, and D. Q. Mills (eds.), *U.S. Industrial Relations, 1950-1980: A Critical Assessment.* Madison, Wis.: Industrial Relations Research Association, 1986.

Freidson, E. "Dominant Professions, Bureaucracy and Client Services." In Y. Hasenfeld and R. English (eds.), *Human Service Organizations.* Ann Arbor: University of Michigan Press, 1974.

Fuller, B., Wood, K., Rapoport, T., and Dornbusch, S. "The Organizational Context of Individual Efficacy." *Review of Educational Research,* 1982, *52* (2), 7-30.

Fuller, F. "Personalized Education for Teachers: An Introduction for Teacher Educators." 1970. (ED 048 105)

Fuller, F., and Brown, O. "On Becoming a Teacher." In K. Ryan (ed.), *Teacher Education.* 74th yearbook of the National Society for the Study of Education. Chicago: University of Chicago Press, 1975.

Gage, N. L. "An Analytic Approach to Research on Instructional Methods." In A. Morrison and D. McIntyre (eds.), *The Social Psychology of Teaching.* Hammondsworth, Eng.: Penguin Books, 1972.

Gage, N. L. *The Scientific Basis of the Art of Teaching.* New York: Teachers College Press, 1978.

Garbarino, J. "The Impact of Anticipated Reward Upon Cross-Age Tutoring." *Journal of Personality and Social Psychology,* 1975, *32,* 421-428.

Gelman, D. D. "Working Together: Professional Partners." *Independent School,* Dec. 1977, *37,* 35-37.

Glaser, W. "Comparisons of the Problems of the Hospital Administrator: Some American and Foreign Comparisons." *Hospital Administration*, 1964, *9*, 6–22.

Glassberg, S., and Oja, S. N. "A Developmental Model for Enhancing Teachers' Personal and Professional Growth." *Journal of Research and Development in Education*, Winter 1981, *14*, 59–70.

Glidewell, J. C. "Professional Support Systems: The Teaching Profession." In A. Nadler, J. Fisher, and B. Depaulo (eds.), *New Directions in Helping*. Vol. 3. New York: Academic Press, 1983.

"GM Woos Employees by Listening to Them, Talking of Its 'Team.'" *Wall Street Journal*, Jan. 12, 1989, p. Al.

Goertz, M., Coley, R. E., and Coley, R. *The Impact of State Policy on Entrance into the Teaching Profession*. Princeton, N.J.: Educational Testing Service, 1984.

Goldschmidt, S. M., Bowers, B., and Stuart, L. *The Extent and Nature of Educational Policy Bargaining*. Eugene, Ore.: Center for Educational Policy and Management, University of Oregon, 1984.

Goldschmidt, S. M., and Stuart, L. E. "The Extent and Impact of Educational Policy Bargaining." *Industrial and Labor Relations Review*, 1986, *39*, 350–360.

Good, T. "Research on Classroom Teaching." In L. S. Shulman and G. Sykes (eds.), *Handbook of Teaching and Policy* (Chap. 2). New York: Longman, 1983.

Goodlad, J. I. *A Place Called School*. New York: McGraw-Hill, 1983a.

Goodlad, J. I. "Teaching: An Endangered Profession." *Teachers College Record*, 1983b, *84* (3), 575–578.

Gorton, R. A. *School Administration and Supervision: Leadership Challenges and Opportunities*. Dubuque, Iowa: Brown, 1983.

Gouldner, F. H., and Ritti, R. R. "Professionalization as Career Immobility." *American Journal of Sociology*, 1967, *72*, 491–494.

Graebner, J., and Dobbs, S. "A Team Approach to Problem Solving in the Classroom." *Phi Delta Kappan*, 1984, *65* (2), 138–141.

Gregorc, A. F. "Developing Plans for Professional Growth." *NASSP Bulletin*, Dec. 1973, pp. 1–8.

Grimshaw, W. J. *Union Rule in Schools*. Lexington, Mass.: Heath, 1979.

Gross, E., and Etzioni, A. *Organizations in Society.* Englewood Cliffs, N.J.: Prentice-Hall, 1985.

Guy, M. *Professionals in Organizations: Debunking a Myth.* New York: Praeger, 1985.

Haac, L. "Testing Teachers: What's Wrong with This Picture?" *Leader,* Dec. 15, 1988, pp. 24-31.

Hackman, J. R., and Lawler, E. E., III. "Employee Reactions to Job Characteristics." *Journal of Applied Psychology,* 1971, *55,* 259-286.

Hackman, J. R., and Oldham, G. R. *Work Redesign.* Reading, Mass.: Addison-Wesley, 1980.

Hall, D. T. *Careers in Organizations.* Pacific Palisades, Calif.: Goodyear, 1976.

Hall, R. H. *Occupations and the Social Structure.* Englewood Cliffs, N.J.: Prentice-Hall, 1975.

Hart, A. W. "A Career Ladder's Effect on Teacher Career and Work Attitudes." *American Educational Research Journal,* 1987, *24* (4), 479-503.

Hart, A. W. "Impacts of the School Social Unit on Teacher Authority During Work Redesign." *American Educational Research Journal,* 1990, *27* (3), 503-532.

Hart, A. W., and Murphy, M. J. "New Teachers React to Redesigned Teacher Work." *American Journal of Education,* 1990, *98,* 224-250.

Hawkins, D. "What It Means to Teach." *Teachers College Record,* 1973, *75* (1), 7-16.

Heneman, H. G., Schwab, D. P., Fossum, J. A., and Dyer, L. D. *Personnel/Human Resource Management.* Homewood, Ill.: Irwin, 1980.

Hirschman, A. O. *Exit, Voice and Loyalty.* Cambridge, Mass.: Harvard University Press, 1970.

Hofstadter, D. R. *Godel, Escher, Bach: An Eternal Golden Braid.* New York: Vintage Books, 1979.

Holland, J. J. *Making Vocational Choices: A Theory of Careers.* Englewood Cliffs, N.J.: Prentice-Hall, 1973.

The Holmes Group. *Tomorrow's Teachers.* East Lansing, Mich.: The Holmes Group, Inc., 1986.

Hunter, M. "What's Wrong with Madeline Hunter?" *Educational Leadership*, 1985, *42* (5), 57–60.

Hutson, H. "PAR in Service." *Practical Applications of Research*, 1979, *1* (4). (Cited in Christensen, Burke, Fessler, and Hagstrom, 1983.)

"In North Carolina, Career-Ladder Plan Nears a Crossroads." *Education Week*, Feb. 1, 1989, *8* (19), 1.

Jackson, P. *Life in Classrooms*. New York: Holt, Rinehart & Winston, 1968.

Jain, H. C. *Worker Participation: Success and Problems*. New York: Praeger, 1980.

Jaques, E. *Equitable Payment*. New York: Wiley, 1961.

Jaques, E. *Time Span of Feedback*. London: Heinemann-Educational Books, 1964.

Johnson, S. M. *Teacher Unions in Schools*. Philadelphia: Temple University Press, 1983.

Johnson, S. M. "Can Schools Be Reformed at the Bargaining Table?" *Teachers College Record*, 1987, *89* (2), 269–280.

Kanter, R. M. *The Change Masters: Innovation for Productivity in the American Corporation*. New York: Simon & Schuster, 1983.

Kasten, K. L. "The Efficacy of Institutionally Dispensed Rewards in Elementary School Teaching." *Journal of Research and Development in Education*, 1984, *17*, 1–13.

Katz, F. "Nurses." In Etzioni, A. (ed.), *The Semi-Professions and Their Organization*. New York: Free Press, 1969, 54–81.

Kazdin, A. E. *Behavior Modification in Applied Settings*. Homewood, Ill.: Dorsey Press, 1975.

Kearney, R. C. *Labor Relations in the Public Sector*. New York: Marcel Dekker, 1984.

Kerchner, C. T., and Mitchell, D. "Teaching Reform and Union Reform." *The Elementary School Journal*, 1986, *86* (4), 449–470.

Kerchner, C. T., and Mitchell, D. *The Changing Idea of a Teachers' Union*. London: Falmer Press, 1988.

Kleinman, J. H. "Merit Pay—the Big Question." *NEA Journal*, May 1963, *52*, 42–44.

Kochan, T. A. *Collective Bargaining and Industrial Relations*. Homewood, Ill.: Irwin, 1980.

Kochan, T. A. *Challenges and Choices Facing American Labor.* Cambridge, Mass.: MIT Press, 1985.

Kochan, T. A., Katz, H. C., and McKersie, R. B. *The Transformation of American Industrial Relations.* New York: Basic Books, 1986.

Kochan, T. A., Katz, H. C., and Mower, N. R. "Worker Participation and American Unions." In T. A. Kochan (ed.), *Challenges and Choices Facing American Labor.* Cambridge, Mass.: MIT Press, 1985.

Kornhauser, W. *Scientists in Industry.* Berkeley: University of California Press, 1962.

Kornhauser, W. *Mental Health of the Industrial Worker.* New York: Wiley, 1965.

Kotter, J. P., Faux, V. A., and McAndrew, C. C. *Self-Assessment and Career Development.* Englewood Cliffs, N.J.: Prentice-Hall, 1978.

Kounin, J., and Gump, P. "Signal Systems of Lesson Settings and the Task Related Behavior of Preschool Children." *Journal of Educational Psychology,* 1984, *66,* 554-562.

Kuhn, J. W. *Bargaining in Grievance Settlement.* New York: Columbia University Press, 1961.

Kunz, D. W., and Hoy, W. K. "Leadership Style of Principals and the Professional Zone of Acceptance of Teachers." *Educational Administration Quarterly,* 1976, *12* (3), 49-64.

Lachman, R., and Aranya, N. "Job Attitudes and Turnover Intentions Among Professionals in Different Work Settings." *Organization Studies,* 1986, *7,* 279-293.

Lampert, M. "How Do Teachers Manage to Teach? Perspectives on Problems in Practice." *Harvard Educational Review,* 1985, *55* (2), 178-194.

Lawler, E. E., III *Pay and Organizational Effectiveness: A Psychological View.* New York: McGraw-Hill, 1971.

Lawrence, G. "Patterns of Effective Inservice Education: A State of the Art Summary of Research on Materials and Procedures for Changing Teacher Behaviors in Inservice Education." 1974. (ED 176 424)

Lepper, M. R., and Greene, D. *The Hidden Costs of Reward: New*

Perspectives on the Psychology of Human Motivation. Hillsdale, N.J.: Erlbaum, 1978.

Lieberman, M. C. *Public Sector Bargaining: A Policy Reappraisal.* Lexington, Mass.: Heath, 1980.

Likert, R. *The Human Organization.* New York: McGraw-Hill, 1967.

Lines, P. "Testing the Teacher: Are There Legal Pitfalls?" *Phi Delta Kappan,* 1985, *66* (9), 618–622.

Little, J. W. "Norms of Collegiality and Experimentation: Workplace Conditions of School Success." *American Educational Research Journal,* Fall 1982a, *19,* 325–340.

Little, J. W. "The Effective Principal." *American Education,* Aug./Sept. 1982b, pp. 38–43.

Locke, E. A., and Latham, G. P. *Goal Setting: A Motivational Technique That Works!* Englewood Cliffs, N.J.: Prentice-Hall, 1984.

Locke, E. A., and Schweiger, D. M. "Participation in Decision-Making: One More Look." In B. M. Staw (ed.), *Research in Organizational Behavior.* Vol. 1. Greenwich, Conn.: JAI Press, 1979.

London, M., and Stumpf, S. A. *Managing Careers.* Reading, Mass.: Addison-Wesley, 1982.

Lortie, D. C. "The Balance of Control and Autonomy in Elementary School Teaching." In A. Etzioni (ed.), *The Semi-Professions and Their Organization: Teachers, Nurses, Social Workers.* New York: Free Press, 1969.

Lortie, D. C. *School Teacher: A Sociological Study.* Chicago: University of Chicago Press, 1975.

Lowin, A. "Participative Decision Making: A Model, Literature Critique and Prescriptions for Research." *Organizational and Human Performance,* Feb. 1968, *3,* 68–106.

McClelland, D. C. *Personality.* New York: Sloane, 1951.

McCutcheon, G. "How Do Elementary School Teachers Plan Their Courses?" *Elementary School Journal,* 1980, *81,* 4–23.

McDonald, J. P. "The Emergence of the Teacher's Voice: Implications for the New Reform." *Teachers College Record,* 1988, *89* (4), 471–486.

McDonnell, L. M., and Pascal, A. *Organized Teachers in American Schools.* Santa Monica, Calif.: Rand Corporation, 1979.

McDonnell, L. M., and Pascal, A. *Teacher Unions and Educational Reform.* Santa Monica, Calif.: Rand Corporation, 1988.

McGraw, K. O. "The Detrimental Effects of Reward on Performance: A Literature Review and a Prediction Model." In M. R. Lepper and D. Greene (eds.), *The Hidden Costs of Reward: New Perspectives on the Psychology of Human Motivation* (Chap. 3). Hillsdale, N.J.: Erlbaum, 1978.

McGraw, K. O., and McCullers, J. C. "Monetary Reward and Concept Attainment: Further Research on the Detrimental Effect of Reward." Unpublished manuscript, 1975. (Discussed in K. O. McGraw, 1978.)

McLaughlin, M. W. "Teacher Evaluation and School Improvement." *Teachers College Record,* 1984, *86* (4), 193–207.

McLaughlin, M., and Berman, P. *Federal Programs Supporting Educational Change: Findings in Review.* Santa Monica, Calif.: Rand Corporation, 1975.

McNeil, L. *Contradictions of Control: School Structure and School Knowledge.* New York: Routledge and Kegan Paul, 1986.

McPherson, G. *Small Town Teacher.* Cambridge, Mass.: Harvard University Press, 1972.

Mahoney, T. A. *Compensation and Reward Perspectives.* Homewood, Ill.: Irwin, 1979.

Medoff, J. L. "Layoffs and Alternatives Under Trade Unions in U.S. Manufacturing." *American Economic Review,* June 1979, *69,* 380–395.

Metz, M. H. *Classrooms and Corridors: The Crisis of Authority in Desegregated Secondary Schools.* Berkeley: University of California Press, 1978.

Meyer, J. W., and Rowan, B. "Institutionalized Organizations: Formal Structure as Myth and Ceremony." *American Journal of Sociology,* 1977, *83* (2), 340–363.

Milkovich, G. T., and Newman, J. *Compensation.* Plano, Tex.: Business Publications, 1984.

Miller, D. *Managing Professionals in Research and Development.* San Francisco: Jossey-Bass, 1986.

Miller, R. *What's a Plan Without a Process? A Training Handbook for Staff Workgroups.* Philadelphia, Research for Better Schools, 1984.

Mintz, A. L. "Teacher Planning: A Simulation Study." Unpublished doctoral dissertation, Syracuse University, Syracuse, N.Y., 1979.

Mitchell, S. M. "Negotiating the Design of Professional Jobs." Working paper presented at the annual meeting of the American Educational Research Association. Ithaca, N.Y.: Organizational Analysis and Practice, Apr. 1986.

Mohrman, A. M., Jr., Cooke, R. A., and Mohrman, S. A. "Participation in Decision-Making: A Multidimensional Perspective." *Educational Administration Quarterly,* 1978, *14* (1), 13–29.

Morris, C. J. *The Developing Labor Law.* Washington, D.C.: Bureau of National Affairs, 1971.

Mosston, M. *Teaching: From Command to Discovery.* Belmont, Calif.: Wadsworth, 1972.

Nadler, D. A. "The Effective Management of Organizational Change." In J. W. Lorsch (ed.), *Handbook of Organizational Behavior.* Englewood Cliffs, N.J.: Prentice-Hall, 1986.

Nadworny, M. J. *Scientific Management and the Unions.* Cambridge, Mass.: Harvard University Press, 1955.

National Commission on Excellence in Education. *A Nation at Risk.* Washington, D.C.: U.S. Government Printing Office, 1983.

National Education Association. *The Conditions and Resources of Teaching.* Washington, D.C.: NEA Reseach Division, 1988.

National Education Association/National Association of Secondary School Principals. *Ventures in Good Schooling: A Cooperative Model for a Successful Secondary School.* Washington, D.C.: National Education Association, 1986.

National Governors' Association. *Time for Results: The Governors' 1991 Report on Education.* Washington, D.C.: National Governors' Association Center for Policy and Research, 1986.

Nemser, S. F. "Learning to Teach." In L. S. Shulman and G. Sykes (eds.), *Handbook of Teaching and Policy* (Chap. 6). New York: Longman, 1983.

"The New Industrial Relations." *Business Week,* May 11, 1981.

Newman, K. K. "Middle-Aged Experienced Teachers' Perceptions of Their Career Development." Unpublished doctoral dissertation, The Ohio State University, 1978.

New York Stock Exchange. *People and Productivity: A Challenge to Corporate America.* New York: New York Stock Exchange, Office of Economic Research, 1982.

Nightingale, D. V. *Workplace Democracy: An Inquiry into Employee Participation in Canadian Work Organizations.* Toronto: University of Toronto Press, 1982.

Nurick, A. J. "The Paradox of Participation: Lessons from the Tennessee Valley Authority." *Human Resource Management,* 1985, *24* (3), 341–356.

O'Leary, K. D., and Drabman, R. "Token Reinforcement Programs in the Classroom: A Review." *Psychological Bulletin,* 1971, *75,* 379–398.

Organ, D. W., and Greene, C. N. "The Effects of Formalization on Professional Involvement: A Compensatory Process Approach." *Administrative Science Quarterly,* 1981, *26,* 237–252.

Organizational Analysis and Practice. *The Principal in a Participative Environment.* Ithaca, N.Y.: Organizational Analysis and Practice, Inc., 1989.

Osborne, D. *Laboratories of Democracy: A New Breed of Governor Creates Models for National Economic Growth.* Cambridge, Mass.: Harvard Business School, 1988.

Ouchi, W. G. *Theory Z.* Reading, Mass.: Addison-Wesley, 1981.

Packard, R. D., and Bierlein, L. "Arizona Career Ladder Research and Evaluation Project: Research and Development for Effective Educational Change and Reform." Baseline data report for the Joint Legislative Committee on Career Ladders, Dec. 17, 1986.

Peres, S. H. *Factors Which Influence Careers in General Electric.* Crotonville, N.Y.: Management Development and Employee Relations Service, General Electric Company, 1966.

Perrow, C. *Complex Organizations: A Critical Essay.* Glenview, Ill.: Scott, Foresman, 1972.

Peters, T. J., and Waterman, R. H., Jr. *In Search of Excellence.* New York: Warner Books, 1982.

Peterson, A. R. "Career Patterns of Secondary School Teachers: An Exploratory Interview Study of Retired Teachers." Unpublished doctoral dissertation, The Ohio State University, 1978.

Peterson, K., and Kauchak, D. *Teacher Evaluation: Perspectives, Practices, and Promises.* Salt Lake City: Center for Educational Practice, Utah University, 1982. (ED 233 996)

Pikulski, J. "Effects of Reinforcement on Word Recognition." *The Reading Teacher,* 1970, *23,* 518-522.

Piore, M. J. "American Labor and the Industrial Crisis." *Challenge,* Mar./Apr. 1982, pp. 5-11.

Piore, M. J. "Computer Technologies, Market Structure, and Strategic Union Choices." In T. A. Kochan (ed.), *Challenges and Choices Facing American Labor.* Cambridge, Mass.: MIT Press, 1985.

Price, J. L. *Organizational Effectiveness.* Homewood, Ill.: Irwin, 1968.

Purkey, S. C., and Smith, M. S. "Effective Schools—a Review." *Elementary School Journal,* 1983, *83* (4), 427-452.

Raelin, J. A. "The Basis for the Professional's Resistance to Managerial Control." *Human Resource Management,* 1985, *24,* 129-146.

Ravitch, D. *The Troubled Crusade.* New York: Basic Books, 1983.

Rosenfeld, S. A. "Commentary: Educating for the Factories of the Future." *Education Week,* June 22, 1988, p. 48.

Rosenholtz, S. J. "Effective Schools: Interpreting the Evidence." *American Journal of Education,* May 1985, pp. 352-388.

Rosenholtz, S. J. "Understanding the Learning Workplace: The NEA Conditions and Resources of Teaching Survey and the Research on Effective Teaching." In National Education Association, *Conditions and Resources of Teaching,* 1988.

Rosenholtz, S. J., and Smylie, M. A. "Teacher Compensation and Career Ladders." *The Elementary School Journal,* Nov. 1984, *85,* 149-166.

Ross, A. M. "Do We Have a New Industrial Feudalism?" *American Economic Review,* Dec. 1958, *48,* 903-920.

Runkel, P. J., and Harris, P. *Bibliography on Organizational Change in Schools: Selected, Annotated and Indexed.* Eugene: Division of Educational Policy and Management, University of Oregon, 1983.

Salancik, G. R., and Pfeffer, J. "An Examination of Need-

Satisfaction Models of Job Attitudes." *Administrative Science Quarterly*, 1977, *22* (3), 427-456.

Salancik, G. R., and Pfeffer, J. "A Social Information Processing Approach to Job Attitudes and Task Design." *Administrative Science Quarterly*, 1978, *23* (2), 224-253.

Sarason, S. *The Culture of the School and the Problem of Change.* (2nd ed.) Boston: Allyn and Bacon, 1982.

Sashkin, M. "Participative Management Is an Ethical Imperative." *Organizational Dynamics*, Spring 1984, pp. 14-22.

Schein, E. H. *Process Consultation: Its Role in Organizational Development.* Reading, Mass.: Addison-Wesley, 1969.

Schlechty, P. C., and Joslin, A. W. "Images of Schools." *Teachers College Record*, 1984, *86* (1), 156-170.

Schon, D. A. *The Reflective Practitioner.* New York: Basic Books, 1983.

Schonberger, R. J. *World Class Manufacturing: The Lessons of Simplicity Applied.* New York: Free Press, 1986.

Scott, W. R. "Professionals in Bureaucracies: Areas of Conflict." In H. Vollmer and D. Mills (eds.), *Professionalization.* Englewood Cliffs, N.J.: Prentice-Hall, 1966, 265-275.

Sergiovanni, T. J. "Factors Which Affect Satisfaction and Dissatisfaction of Teachers." *Journal of Educational Administration*, 1967, *5*, 66-82.

Sergiovanni, T. J. "Landscapes, Mindscapes and Reflective Practice in Supervision." *Journal of Curriculum and Supervision*, 1985, *1* (1), 5-17.

Shanker, A. "The Making of a Profession." Speech delivered to the representative assembly of the New York State United Teachers, Niagara Falls, N.Y., Apr. 27, 1985. (Mimeographed.)

Shedd, J. B. "An Assessment of the Duty to Bargain in the Public and Private Sectors." Working paper. Ithaca, N.Y.: Cornell University, 1982.

Shedd, J. B. "Involving Teachers in School and District Decision-Making." Ithaca, N.Y.: Organizational Analysis and Practice, 1987.

Shedd, J. B. "Collective Bargaining, School Reform, and the Management of School Systems." In S. B. Bacharach (ed.), *Educa-*

tional Reform: Making Sense of It All. Boston: Allyn and Bacon, 1990.

Shedd, J. B., and Malanowski, R. M. *From the Front of the Classroom: A Study of the Work of Teachers.* Ithaca, N.Y.: Organizational Analysis and Practice, 1985.

Shedd, J., Malanowski, R., and Conley, S. "Foundations for a System of Career Development for Teachers: Criteria and Standards for Advancement." A research report prepared for the National Education Association Research Division. Ithaca, N.Y.: Organizational Analysis and Practice, 1985.

Shedd, J. B., Malanowski, R. M., and Conley, S. C. "Teachers as Decision-Makers." Paper presented at the annual meeting of the American Educational Research Association, San Francisco, 1986.

Shepherd, C. "Orientations of Scientists and Engineers." *Pacific Sociological Review,* 1961, 79–83.

Shulman, L. S., and Carey, N. B. "Psychology and the Limitations of Individual Rationality: Implications for the Study of Reasoning and Civility." *Review of Educational Research,* Winter 1984, *54,* 501–524.

Sizer, T. R. *Horace's Compromise: The Dilemma of the American High School.* Boston: Houghton Mifflin, 1984.

Sizer, T. R., and Koermer, T. F. *Perspectives: A Review and Comment on National Studies.* Reston, Va.: National Association of Secondary School Principals, 1983.

Skinner, B. F. *Contingencies of Reinforcement.* New York: Appleton-Century-Crofts, 1969.

Slavin, R. E. "Component Building: A Strategy for Research Based Instructional Improvement." *Elementary School Journal,* 1984, *84,* 255–269.

Sonnenfeld, J. A. *Managing Career Systems: Channeling the Flow of Executive Careers.* Homewood, Ill.: Irwin, 1984.

Sonnenstuhl, W., and Trice, H. "Linking Organizational and Occupational Theory Through the Concept of Culture." In S. Bacharach (ed.), *Research in the Sociology of Organizations.* Vol. 6. Greenwich, Conn.: JAI Press, 1988.

Sorensen, J., and Sorensen, T. "The Conflict of Professionals in

Bureaucratic Organizations." *Administrative Science Quarterly*, 1974, *19* (1), 98–106.

Southern Regional Education Board Career Ladder Clearinghouse. *More Pay for Teachers and Administrators Who Do More: Incentive Pay Programs. 1987.* Atlanta, Ga.: Southern Regional Education Board, December 1987.

Stogdill, R. M. *Handbook of Leadership: A Survey of Theory and Research.* New York: Free Press, 1974.

Susman, G. I. *Autonomy at Work: A Socio-Technical Analysis of Participative Management.* New York: Praeger, 1979.

Taft, P. *Organized Labor in American History.* New York: Harper & Row, 1964.

Taylor, F. W. *The Principles of Scientific Management.* New York: Norton, 1967. (Originally published 1911.)

Thierbach, G. L. "Decision Involvement and Job Satisfaction in Middle and Junior High Schools." Unpublished doctoral dissertation, University of Wisconsin-Madison, 1980. (Cited in J. A. Conway, 1984.)

Thomas. W. I., and Thomas, D. S. *The Child in America.* New York: Knopf, 1928.

Thompson, P. C. *Quality Circles: How to Make Them Work in America.* New York: AMACOM, 1982.

Thompson, P. H., and Dalton, G. W. "Are R&D Organizations Obsolete?" *Harvard Business Review*, Nov./Dec. 1976, pp. 105–116.

Thurow, L. *Generating Inequality: Mechanisms of Distribution in the U.S. Economy.* New York: Basic Books, 1975.

Trist, E. "The Evolution of Socio-Technical Systems—a Conceptual Framework and an Action Research Program." Occasional paper no. 2. Ontario Ministry of Labour, Ontario Quality of Working Life Centre, Toronto, 1981.

Turner, A. N., and Lawrence, P. R. *Industrial Jobs and the Worker.* Boston: Harvard Graduate School of Business Administration, 1965.

Tyack, D., and Hansot, E. *Managers of Virtue: Public School Leadership in America, 1820–1980.* New York: Basic Books, 1982.

United States Department of Labor, Bureau of Labor-Management Relations and Cooperative Programs. "U.S. Labor Law and the

Future of Labor-Management Cooperation." BLMR 104. Washington, D.C.: U.S. Government Printing Office, 1986.

Unruh, A., and Turner, H. E. *Supervision for Change and Innovation*. Boston: Houghton Mifflin, 1970.

Vance, V. S., and Schlechty, P. C. "The Distribution of Academic Ability in the Teaching Force: Policy Implications." *Phi Delta Kappan*, 1982, *64* (1), 22-27.

Vroom, V. *Motivation and Work*. New York: Wiley, 1964.

Waller, W. *The Sociology of Teaching*. New York: Wiley, 1932.

Walton, R. E. "From Control to Commitment in the Workplace." *Harvard Business Review*, 1985, *85* (2), 77-84.

Warner, W. M. "Decision Involvement and Job Satisfaction in Wisconsin Elementary Schools." Unpublished doctoral dissertation, University of Wisconsin-Madison, 1981. (Cited in J. A. Conway, 1984.)

Weatherley, R., and Lipsky, M. "Street-Level Bureaucrats and Institutional Innovation: Implementing Special-Education Reform." *Harvard Educational Review*, 1977, *47*, 171-197.

Weber, A. R. (ed.). *The Structure of Collective Bargaining: Problems and Perspectives*. New York: Free Press, 1964.

Weber, M. *Max Weber: The Theory of Social and Economic Organization*. (T. Parsons, ed. and trans.) New York: Free Press, 1947.

Weick, K. E. "Educational Organizations as Loosely Coupled Systems." *Administrative Science Quarterly*, 1976, *21* (1), 1-19.

Weick, K. E. "The Management of Organizational Change Among Loosely Coupled Elements." In P. Goodman (ed.), *Change in Organizations: New Perspectives on Theory, Research, and Practice*. San Francisco: Jossey-Bass, 1982.

Weisbord, M. R. "Participative Work Design: A Personnel Odyssey." *Organizational Dynamics*, Spring 1985, pp. 4-20.

Weissman, R. "Merit Pay—What Merit?" *Education Digest*, May 1969, *34*, 16-19.

Wilensky, H. "The Professionalization of Everyone?" *American Journal of Sociology*, 1964, *25* (2).

Williamson, J. *Emergency Teacher Certification*. Task Force on Teacher Certification, American Association of Colleges for Teacher Education, 1984.

Wise, A. E. *Legislated Learning: The Bureaucratization of the*

American Classroom. Berkeley: University of California Press, 1979.

Wise, A. E., Darling-Hammond, L., McLaughlin, M. W., and Bernstein, H. T. *Teacher Evaluation: A Study of Effective Practices.* Santa Monica, Calif.: Rand Corporation, 1984.

Wolcott, H. F. *Teachers vs. Technocrats: An Educational Innovation in Anthropological Perspective.* Eugene, Ore.: Center for Educational Policy and Management, 1977.

Wynne, E. A. "Looking at Good Schools." *Phi Delta Kappan,* 1981, *62* (5), 377-381.

Zeichner, K. M. "Alternative Paradigms of Teacher Education." *Journal of Teacher Education,* 1983, *34* (3), 3-9.

Zumwalt, K. K. "Research on Teaching: Policy Implications for Teacher Education." In A. Lieberman and M. W. McLaughlin (eds.), *Policy Making in Education.* First yearbook of the National Society for the Study of Education, Part 1. Chicago, Ill.: University of Chicago Press, 1982.

INDEX

A

Accountability: and goal clarity, 43–44; for growth, 94–101, 102
Adler, M., 68
Administrators: control viewed by, 49–50; in Cooperative Relationships Project, 151–164; teachers in relationships with, 7, 60–61, 68–69, 83–85; unions beneficial for, 178
Alabama: job ladders in, 118; tenure standards in, 83
Alutto, J. A., 131
American Federation of Teachers (AFT), 129, 181
Anderson, J. G., 65
Anglin, L. W., 68
Aranya, N., 50
Argyris, C., 134, 140
Arizona: Department of Economic Security (DES) in, 24, 25, 27, 28n, 199; job ladders in, 118
Ashton, P., 137
AT&T, career development at, 82
Authority: and influence, in participation, 142–143; and unions, 175–176

Autonomous work groups, 144
Autonomy: control and, 42–69; and identity, for motivation, 88–94, 102; need for, 43–46, 67; operational, 57, 68; policy constraints on, 89–91, 102; resource constraints on, 91–93; time constraints on, 93–94
Ayllon, T., 107
Azrin, N. H., 107

B

Bacharach, S. B., 1, 4, 5, 18, 32, 35, 39, 42, 44, 45, 48, 49, 56, 58, 59–60, 64, 71, 84, 90, 101, 104, 105, 110, 113, 114, 118, 120, 130, 131, 132, 136, 140, 142, 165, 168, 169, 170, 178
Bailyn, L., 68
Bamberger, P., 18, 45, 49, 131, 132
Barnard, C., 176
Bauer, S. C., 39, 60, 84, 90, 131, 132
Becker, S. W., 131
Belasco, J. A., 131
Benson, J. K., 50
Berliner, D., 140
Berman, P., 131, 132

Bishop, J., 105, 137-138
Blake, R. R., 144
Block, R. N., 173
Boards of education: in Cooperative
  Relationships Project, 151-164;
  and unions, 188
Bowers, B., 166
Bridgeport, evaluation system in,
  96-100, 102
Brown, O., 79
Burden, P. R., 78-79
Bureaucracies: concept of, 5; as
  management approach, 54-57,
  64-66; professionals in, 1-12
Burke, P., 78, 81

C

California, job ladders in, 118, 119
California Commission on the
  Teaching Profession, 129
Callahan, R., 53, 59, 133, 177
Campbell, R. J., 82
Caplow, T., 2
Career ladders. See Job ladders
Carey, N. B., 76
Carnegie Commission on Teaching
  as a Profession, 129
Carnegie Corporation, 129
CART survey, 68-69, 138
Carter, K., 75
Casey, W. F., III, 106
Chamberlain, N. W., 167
Chambers, J., 109
Chapman, D. W., 71, 118, 125, 131
Christensen, J., 78, 81
Chubb, J. E., 44
Civil engineers, as comparable to
  teachers, 26, 27, 29
Clark, B., 50
Clark, C. M., 76
Cohen, D., 68
Cohen, M., 116, 122
Cole, S., 176, 177
Collective bargaining. See Unions
College Board, 194
Colorado, job ladders in, 118
Commons, J. R., 170
Communication, importance of, 84

Compensation: by ad hoc pay and
  work assignments, 126-127;
  analysis of systems of, 103-128;
  assumptions about, 124-125;
  background on, 103-104; comparisons of systems for, 103-104;
  and competition, 115-116, 122;
  ends and means confused in,
  124-128; by job ladders, 117-124;
  by merit pay, 104-117, 128; nonmonetary forms of, 105-106; as
  tool, 127; by unified salary
  schedules, 125-126; and unions,
  178-179
Competition, and compensation
  systems, 115-116, 122
Condry, J., 107, 109
Conley, S. C., 4, 32, 35, 39, 44, 49,
  58, 64, 67, 90, 104, 113, 114, 118,
  120, 130, 131, 136, 140
Control: administrative solution to,
  49-50; and autonomy, 42-69;
  background on 42-43; case for,
  46-49, 67; and compensation systems, 116, 123-124; conflicts and
  compromises in, 49-59, 67-68;
  equilibrium perspective on, 50-
  51; and need for discretion, 43-
  46, 67; professional solution to,
  49-50; tacit deals and tangled
  hierarchies for, 59-67, 68-69
Conway, J. A., 131
Cooke, R. A., 132, 138
Cooperation: and conflict, with
  unions, 169-171, 184; and participation, 9
Cooperative Relationships Project
  (CRP): aspects of, 151-164; process of, 157-160; progress of,
  154-156, 161; purposes of, 151-
  152; scope of, 153-157; structure
  of, 152-153; support for, 160-164
Coordination: case for, 46-49, 67; of
  management, participation in,
  138-141; and unions, 179-180
Corcoran, T. B., 65, 69, 132, 147
Counseling, teacher responsibility
  for, 17, 31, 39
Cowden, P., 68

Craft workshop approach: to management, 57–59, 64, 68; to unions, 172, 175

D

Daft, R. L., 131
Dalton, G. W., 79, 123
Deci, E. L., 107, 109
Decision making: accountability for, 95–100; better, 136–137; cycle of, 157–158; participation in, 129–164; roles in, 159–160; skill development in, 74–75, 78; by teachers, 29–32, 40
Discretion: internal and external, 45–46; need for, 43–46, 67; time-span of, 67
Doda, N., 137
Dowling, J., 169
Doyle, W., 32, 75, 76
Drabman, R., 107
Duke, D. L., 11, 132
Dulles, F. R., 171
Dunlop, J. T., 167, 176
Dyer, L. D., 71

E

Edmonds, R. R., 131
Education Commission of the States, 129, 130, 194
Educational Research Service, 113, 128
Edwards, H. T., 180
Effectiveness, organizational, and job ladders, 121–123
Efficiency, concepts of, 53–54, 55
Elkouri, E. A., 175
Elkouri, F., 175
Emmet, D., 194–195
Erickson, D. A., 44
Etzioni, A., 50
Europe, works councils in, 145
Evaluation: and accountability, 94–101, 102; criteria for, 97; and merit pay issues, 113–114
Expectancy Theory, and merit pay, 106–107, 110

F

Factory approach, to management, 52–54, 64, 69, 174, 177
Feedback: and challenge, 82–83; and motivation, 73–88, 102
Fessler, R., 78, 81
Filley, A. C., 10
Flannery, D. M., 131
Florida, job ladders in, 118, 119
Ford Motor Company, participatory management at, 133
Fossum, J. A., 71
Freeman, R. B., 173
Freidson, E., 50
Fuller, F., 79

G

Gage, N. L., 37, 74
Garbarino, J., 108, 109–110
General Electric, career development at, 82
General Motors, participatory management at, 133
Glaser, W., 49, 50
Glassberg, S., 79
Glidewell, J. C., 138
Goal clarity, and autonomy and control, 43–44, 47–48, 52, 55, 58–59
Goldschmidt, S. M., 166
Goldsen, R. K., 12
Goodlad, J. I., 65, 120
Gouldner, F. H., 50
Greene, C. N., 50
Greene, D., 107
Gregorc, A. F., 79
Grimshaw, W. J., 166
Gross, E., 50
Gump, P., 75
Guy, M., 50

H

Haac, L., 118
Hackman, J. R., 9, 46, 72–73, 83, 88, 89, 101–102, 106, 122, 144
Hagstrom, D., 78, 81

Hall, D. T., 78, 82
Hall, R. H., 2
Hansot, E., 4, 55, 59, 133, 177
Harris, P., 131
Hart, A. W., 118, 119, 132
Hawkins, D., 80
Heneman, H. G., 71
Hierarchies: professionals in, 3; re-
    structuring, 190-195; tangled,
    59-67, 68-69
Hirschman, A. O., 9
Holland, J. J., 71
Holmes Group, 129
House, R. J., 10
Hoy, W. K., 59, 62
Hunter, M., 32, 76, 77
Hutcheson, S. M., 71, 118, 125, 131

I

Identity and autonomy, for motiva-
    tion, 88-94, 102
Imber, M., 11, 132
Indiana, job ladders in, 118
Influence, and authority, in partici-
    pation, 142-143
Innovation, participation for, 131-
    132
Integration, by teachers, 34-40, 140
Involvement. See Participation
Isolation of teachers, overcoming,
    137-138

J

Jackson, P., 30, 32, 44, 59, 88
Jain, H. C., 145
Japan, management techniques in,
    133
Jaques, E., 67
Job enrichment, 144
Job ladders: aspects of, 117-124; and
    differential duties, 119-120; and
    organizational effectiveness, 121-
    123; problems of, 118-119; quo-
    tas in, 119-120; reasons for, 117-
    118; technical, 123; and unions,
    186
Johnson, S. M., 166, 167, 189

Joslin, A. W., 68

K

Kanter, R. M., 134, 136, 140
Katz, F., 50
Katz, H. C., 9, 135, 144, 186
Kazdin, A. E., 107
Kean, T., 151
Kearney, R. C., 166
Kerchner, C. T., 165, 166, 167
Kerr, S., 10
Kleinman, J. H., 105
Knowledge, prescriptive or pro-
    scriptive, 76-77
Kochan, T. A., 9, 135, 144, 167, 186,
    187
Koermer, T. F., 68
Kornhauser, W., 49, 50, 71
Kounin, J., 75
Kuhn, J. W., 167, 189
Kunz, D. W., 59, 62

L

Labor-management committees,
    144
Lachman, R., 50
Lampert, M., 30, 38, 77
Latham, G. P., 9
Lawler, E. E., III, 9, 72-73, 83, 89,
    101-102, 106, 110, 116
Lawler, E. J., 142, 170
Lawrence, P. R., 72
Leadership and learning, ethic of,
    6, 195
Lepper, M. R., 107
Lieberman, M. C., 166
Likert, R., 9
Lipsky, D. B., 101, 104, 105, 110,
    113, 114, 178
Lipsky, M., 132
Little, J. W., 59, 87, 115, 118, 122,
    132, 137
Locke, E. A., 9, 10, 142
Lortie, D. C., 30, 32, 44, 59, 60, 62,
    67, 78, 79, 87, 101, 105, 111, 112,
    115, 118, 137, 138, 140
Lowin, A., 9, 10

M

McClelland, D. C., 71
McCullers, J. C., 107
McCutcheon, G., 76
McDonald, J. P., 132
McDonnell, L. M., 166
McGraw, K. O., 107-108, 109
McKersie, R. B., 186
McLaughlin, M. W., 131, 132, 137
McNeil, L., 65, 194
McPherson, G., 30, 38, 44
Mahoney, T. A., 110
Malanowski, R. M., 13, 59, 67
Management: bureaucratic approach to, 54-57, 64-66; conflicts and compromise in, 49-59, 67-68; continuum in, 50-51; coordination of, participation in, 138-141; craft workshop approach to, 57-59, 64, 68; factory system of, 52-54, 64, 69, 174, 177; of human resources, 135; by objectives, 144; and participation, 133-136; professional approach to, 64, 66-67; scientific, 53, 54, 64, 69, 134, 171, 174, 177; and unions, 172-175, 184
Managers, teachers as, 32-34, 139-140, 182, 187-188
Masters, F., 68
Medoff, J. L., 173
Merit pay: aspects of, 104-117, 128; evaluation issues in, 113-114; and motivation, 104-111; and nature of teaching, 111-117, 128; quotas for, 115; teacher opposition to, 113, 114-115
Metz, M. H., 30, 38, 44
Meyer, J. W., 169
Milkovich, G. T., 110
Miller, D., 49
Miller, R., 159
Mills, C. W., 2
Mintz, A. L., 76
Missouri, job ladders in, 118
Mitchell, D., 165, 166, 167
Mitchell, S. M., 45, 48, 56, 59-60, 71, 91, 105, 131, 132, 149

Moe, T. M., 44
Mohrman, A. M., Jr., 132, 138
Mohrman, S. A., 132, 138
Morris, C. J., 180
Mosston, M., 32
Motivation: autonomy and identity for, 88-94, 102; factors in 72-73; intrinsic and extrinsic, 105-107; and job characteristics, 70-73, 101-102; and merit pay, 104-111; and participation, 8-9; skill variety and feedback in, 73-88, 102
Mouton, J. S., 144
Mower, N. R., 9, 135, 144
Murphy, M. J., 118

N

Nadler, D. A., 9
Nadworny, M. J., 174
National Association of Secondary School Principals, 129
National Commission on Excellence in Education, 103
National Education Association (NEA), 129; CART survey by, 68, 138, 139; and motivation, 84, 85, 86n, 88, 89, 90, 91, 93; and unions, 180-181
National Governors' Association, 129
Needs, and job characteristics, 70-73
Nemser, S. F., 75, 76, 78, 80-81, 87
New Jersey, State Department of Education in, 151, 153
New York Stock Exchange, 133
Newman, J., 110
Newman, K. K., 79
Nightingale, D. V., 8, 142
North Carolina, job ladders in, 118
Nurick, A. J., 144

O

Oja, S. N., 79
Oldham, G. R., 46, 72-73, 83, 88, 122, 144
O'Leary, K. D., 107
Organ, D. W., 50

Organizational Analysis and Practice (OAP), 141, 149, 151, 153, 154, 160, 161
Ouchi, W. G., 45, 134, 136

P

Participation: aspects of, 129-164; background on, 129-130; case for, 130-141; and cooperation, 9; Cooperative Relationships Project for, 151-164; in coordination of management, 138-141; for decision making, 136-137; ethical right to, 8, 9; and external congruence, 163-164; forms of, 141-150; and internal consistency, 161-163; and management, 133-136; for morale and job satisfaction, 8, 10; and motivation, 8-9; for overcoming isolation, 137-138; processes of, 147-149, 157-160; recommendations on, 164; and reform movement, 11-12; research on, 130-133; scope of, 145-146, 153-157; strategies for, 143-145; structure of, 146-147, 152-153; support for, 149-150, 160-164; traditional arguments for, 8-12; and unions, 181-182
Pascal, A., 166
Peres, S. H., 82
Perrow, C., 45, 46
Peters, T. J., 45, 79, 122, 134, 136
Peterson, A. R., 79
Peterson, D., 133
Pfeffer, J., 71, 169
Pikulski, J., 107
Pima County Employer Wage Survey, 24, 28n, 197-199
Piore, M. J., 134, 135, 136, 181
Policy constraints, on autonomy, 89-91, 102
Price, J. L., 45
Price, R. L., 79, 123
Professionalism: in bureaucracies, 1-12; and control, 49-50; criteria for, 2-3; in hierarchies, 3; and management, 64, 66-67; and par-

ticipation, 11-12; and student differences, 44; by teachers, 2-5; and unions, 183-185
Purkey, S. C., 65, 131

Q

Quality circles, 144
Quotas: in job ladders, 119-120; in merit pay, 115

R

Raelin, J. A., 49
Ravitch, D., 68
Reform: and participation, 11-12; propositions in second wave of, 1; of schools, 5-8, 191-192; of unions, 181-183, 187-188
Reinforcement theory, and merit pay, 107-110
Resources: and autonomy and control, 44, 47, 48, 52-54, 55, 58-59, 67, 91-93; for participation, 150
Responsibilities: defining and communicating, 60-64; variety of, 14-17, 35, 39, 40-41
Responsibility Matrix, 35, 39
Rewards: extrinsic, in social setting, 108-109, 110; intrinsic, and merit pay, 105-106; negative impact of extrinsic, 107-109
Ritti, R. R., 50
Rosenholtz, S. J., 65, 89, 101, 102, 116, 119, 131, 137, 140
Ross, A. M., 173
Rowan, B., 169
Runkel, P. J., 131

S

Salancik, G. R., 71
Sashkin, M., 8, 9
Schlechty, P. C., 68, 131
Schon, D. A., 12, 74, 78, 82
Schools: autonomy and control in, 42-69; consistency of means and ends in, 193-194; cultural values of, 191, 194; goal-oriented, 66-67;

models of, 64–66, 68; organization of, 3–5; reform pressures in, 5–8, 191–192; restructuring, 190–195

Schwab, D. P., 71

Schweiger, D. M., 9, 10, 142

Scott, W. R., 49, 50

Segall, R., 128

Sergiovanni, T. J., 32, 105

Shanker, A., 120

Shedd, J. B., 13, 59, 67, 84, 101, 104, 105, 110, 113, 114, 120, 131, 132, 140, 145, 165, 168, 169, 178, 180, 188

Shepherd, C., 49, 50

Showers, B. K., 11, 132

Shulman, L. S., 76

Sizer, T. R., 65, 68, 126

Skills: development of, 78–83; sources of, 85–86; variety of, and motivation, 73–88, 102

Skinner, B. F., 107

Slavin, R. E., 37

Smith, M. S., 65, 131

Smylie, M. A., 119

Sonnenfeld, J. A., 122

Sonnenstuhl, W., 49

Sorensen, J., 50

Sorensen, T., 50

Southern Regional Education Board Career Ladder Clearinghouse, 118

Staff development, for motivation, 80–88

Standards, in evaluation system, 96–110

Stogdill, R. M., 8

Stuart, L. E., 166

Students: differences among, and autonomy and control, 44, 47, 52, 54–57, 58; role models for, 6–7

Susman, G. I., 9, 45, 142

T

Taft, P., 171

Task Force on Teaching as a Profession, 129

Taylor, F. W., 69, 134, 174

Taylor, G., 176

Teachers: administrators in relationships with, 7, 60–61, 68–69, 83–85; analysis of work of, 13–41; autonomy and control for, 42–69; background on, 13–14; beginning, 81–83; comments by, 13, 20–21, 31, 36, 38, 63–64, 77–78, 84–85, 87–88, 92–93, 95; compensating, 103–128; in Cooperative Relationships Project, 151–164; decision making by, 29–32, 40; differences among, by level, 18–22, 41; division of labor for, 7–8, 190–192; in elementary school, 18–19; growth of, 94–101, 102; integration by, 34–40, 140; interactions among, 86–88, 92–93; isolation of, 137–138; as managers, 32–34, 139–140, 182, 187–188; participation by, 129–164; as professionals, 2–5; responsibilities of, 14–17, 35, 39, 40–41, 60–64; in secondary schools, 19; staff development for, 80–88

Teaching: aspects of restructuring, 70–102; autonomy and identity for, 88–94, 102; body of knowledge for, 44; descriptors of, 24–25; effective practices in, 75–77; evaluation of, 94–101, 102; jobs comparable to, 22–29, 41; managerial/supervisory features of, 26–28; merit pay and nature of, 111–117, 128; and motivation, 70–73, 101–102; process of, and autonomy and control, 44, 47, 52, 55, 57–59, 67, 68; process dimension of, 29–30, 37; professional/technical features of, 27–28; purposes, dimension of, 30, 37; skill variety and feedback in, 73–88, 102; unpredictability of, 44

Television news directors, as comparable to teachers, 23–24, 29

Tennessee, job ladders in, 118, 119

Tenure, standards for, 83

Texas, job ladders in, 118
Thierbach, G. L., 131
Thomas, D. S., 3
Thomas, W. I., 3
Thompson, P. C., 144
Thompson, P. H., 79, 123
Thurow, L., 173
Time constraints: on autonomy, 93-94; on discretion, 67
Trice, H., 49
Trist, E., 144
Tuition tax credits, impact of, 67
Tucson, work of teachers in, 13-41, 63-64, 68, 77-78, 83, 84-85, 86-87, 92, 95
Tucson Education Association, 13
Turner, A. N., 72
Turner, H. E., 79
Tyack, D., 4, 55, 59, 133, 177

U

Unions: aspects of changing role of, 165-189; background on, 165-166; changes by, 192-193; conflict and cooperation in, 169-171, 184; craft, 172, 175; future forms of, 168-169, 185-187, 188-189; half-logic of industrial, 176-181, 187; history of industrial, 171-176; impact of, 166-169; industrial model of, 3-4, 167, 171-181, 186, 187; and management, 172-175, 184; and negotiated contracts, 174-175, 185-186; principles emerging for, 183-185, 188; and professionalism, 183-185; reform of, 181-183, 187-188; and scope of bargaining, 180-181
U.S. Department of Labor, 133
U.S. Supreme Court, and Yeshiva decision, 187-188
Unruh, A., 79
Utah, job ladders in, 118

W

Walker, L. J., 69
Waller, W., 78
Walton, R. E., 133
Warner, W. M., 131
Waterman, R. H., Jr., 45, 79, 122, 134, 136
Weatherley, R., 132
Webb, R., 137
Weber, A. R., 167
Weber, M., 64
Weick, K. E., 59, 139
Weisbord, M. R., 144
Weissman, R., 105
White, J. L., 69
Wilensky, H., 2, 49, 50
Wisconsin, job ladders in, 118
Wolcott, H. F., 132
Works councils, 144-145
Wynne, E. A., 65, 87, 122, 140

Y

Yeshiva decision, 187-188
Yinger, R. J., 76